Empowering Educators

A Comprehensive Guide to Teaching Grades K, 1, 2

Kirsten Lee Howard ● Amy Wade ● Becky Wanless ● Lisa Dewey Wells

Center for Responsive Schools, Inc.

ISBN: 978-1-950317-18-9
Library of Congress Control Number: 2021944428

Photographs by Jeff Woodward
Additional photographs by Oliver Scott Photography, Cory Ryan, Kirsten Lee Howard, Amy Wade, Becky Wanless, and © Alice Proujansky

Center for Responsive Schools, Inc.
85 Avenue A, P.O. Box 718
Turners Falls, MA 01376-0718

800-360-6332
www.crslearn.org

Contents

Publisher's Acknowledgments

Center for Responsive Schools is deeply grateful for the combined talents and expertise of Linda Berger, Kirsten Lee Howard, Julie Kelly, Andy Moral, Emily Parrelli, Jenni Lee Groegler Pierson, Brian Smith, Amanda Stessen-Blevins, Amy Wade, Becky Wanless, Lisa Dewey Wells, and Heather Young. Their hard work, collective wisdom, and collaboration made this series of books valuable resources for other educators.

Center for Responsive Schools would also like to express appreciation to the following people for their involvement in the creation of this book: Michelle Benson, Kevin Bradley, Barbara Findlen, Michelle Gill, Elizabeth Greene, Emily Hemingway, Allison Henry, Cathy Hess, Dr. Lora Hodges, Lindsey Lynch, Jeff Miller, Noelle Serafino, and Anne Sussman.

● ● ● ● ● ● ● ● ●

Introduction

• •

At Center for Responsive Schools, we believe that educating all children is the most important work in the world. But it's no easy task.

Teachers of early elementary grades have the honor and responsibility of championing their young students in the first stage of their educational journey—and witnessing the curiosity, wonder, enthusiasm, and imagination that children demonstrate along the way. Students in kindergarten, first grade, and second grade are like sponges. They absorb skills and knowledge so quickly that learning gains in these grade levels typically occur at a much higher rate than in later years. Studies show that the academic, social, and emotional outcomes of early elementary grades are predictors of future success, both in school and outside of it. It takes a special kind of adult guidance to help early elementary students attain the kind of growth they are capable of. Educators need to bring to their teaching the right combination of skill and playfulness, empathy and creativity, and calm and organization. Developing this balance is just one of the early elementary teacher's many talents.

Who Should Read This Book?

The goal of this book is to help early elementary educators do their essential work. Each chapter offers tools, tips, and strategies for building classrooms where all students feel safe, seen, and significant and where educators are empowered to respond to all students' academic, social, emotional, and developmental needs.

To create positive and healthy school and classroom communities, diversity, inclusion, and equity must be at the center of one's pedagogy. Woven throughout these chapters, you will find relevant, impactful practices that can reach every child in every school, every day. All of these practices are based on the *Responsive Classroom* approach, whose six guiding principles form the core of this book. Those principles are:

1. Teaching social and emotional skills is as important as teaching academic content.

2. How we teach is as important as what we teach.

3. Great cognitive growth occurs through social interaction.

4. How we work together as adults to create a safe, joyful, and inclusive school environment is as important as our individual contribution or competence.

5. What we know and believe about our students—individually, culturally, developmentally—informs our expectations, reactions, and attitudes about those students.

6. Partnering with families—knowing them and valuing their contributions—is as important as knowing the children we teach.

Especially in difficult times, these guiding principles remind us of what is most important and motivate us to create classrooms that are inspiring, student centered, and rigorous. All educators, new and veteran ones alike, will find ideas, insights, and innovative approaches in the pages that follow.

How to Use This Book

This book encompasses three different grade levels. We encourage you to read each grade-level section. Equipped with this range of information, educators who teach a single grade level will understand more deeply where their students have come from developmentally, where they are, and where they're going. Educators who teach multiple grade levels, perhaps in multiage classrooms or as special area teachers, will find valuable information on kindergarten, first grade, and second grade in this book. For ease of use, the book is color coded so you can quickly find the grade you are looking for: yellow for all grades, orange for kindergarten, pink for first grade, and purple for second grade.

You can use this book in many ways. You might want to read the book in order, from cover to cover. You might choose to focus on certain chapters or sections based on your needs and interests, or you might refer to different sections throughout the school year. The chapters are organized in the approximate order in which you might approach your school year planning and are filled with information and ideas that are appropriate at any time.

What You'll Find Inside

Most chapters begin with an overview offering background information and general guidance. Following that, you will typically find sections specific to each grade level. Each section contains useful information that is easily applicable to other grade levels with some minor adaptation.

In **Chapter 1**, "Developmentally Responsive Teaching," you will explore your students' developmental ages and stages to understand more about their developmental journey in your year together.

Chapter 2, "Effective Management," leads you through setting up your physical classroom space and considering the consistent schedule, routines, and procedures you will use throughout the year, while **Chapter 3**, "Positive Community," offers tips, strategies, and approaches for building and maintaining positive community in your classroom.

By **Chapter 4**, "Engaging Academics," it's time to delve into academics, with a focus on engaging all learners, setting high expectations, and guiding instruction based on insights from your knowledge and observations of your students.

The final two chapters focus on the adults in your classroom community. **Chapter 5**, "Connecting With Parents," is a guide to partnering with parents to better support your students and their families. (In this book, for ease of reading, we use the term "parent" to represent all the caregivers involved in a child's life.) **Chapter 6**, "Social and Emotional Learning for Teachers," focuses on you and what you need to be effective, fulfilled, and flourishing as an educator—all year long, not just after a restful school break!

At the end of this book, you will also find a robust appendix with ready-to-use resources you can incorporate into your instruction right away. You can also scan this QR code for access to numerous additional downloadable resources.

Voices in This Book

This book was written collaboratively by four experienced educators. They blended their combined decades of teaching experience to offer advice, strategies, and tips that all educators can learn from. The advice and approaches they describe are backed by evidence and research, but just as important, they are also tried and tested by the authors themselves in real classrooms with real students.

Kirsten Lee Howard

Kirsten Lee Howard was born and raised in New England and currently lives in Northern Virginia. She is an avid reader, houseplant collector, and baker. She has taught special education, kindergarten, and first grade during twenty years of teaching and currently teaches preschool at Annandale Cooperative Preschool in Annandale, Virginia. She is a certified *Responsive Classroom* teacher and trainer. Her favorite thing about teaching young children is the daily reminder that the ordinary can be extraordinary. She wrote the kindergarten sections in this book.

Amy Wade

Amy Wade is a school counselor for prekindergarten through second grade at Canandaigua Primary School in Canandaigua, New York, where she has been an integral part of the school community for the past twenty-eight years. She also serves as her district's *Responsive Classroom* trainer as well as a consulting teacher with Center for Responsive Schools and has trained countless educators over the past twenty years in the *Responsive Classroom* approach. Her favorite thing about working with young children is the joy they find in the simple things—puppets, play, stories, and songs. Amy has thoroughly enjoyed writing the chapter overviews to set the stage for the wisdom shared in each grade-level section of this book.

Becky Wanless

Becky Wanless is a *Responsive Classroom* consulting teacher and educator from Columbus, Ohio. Throughout her fifteen-plus years in education, Becky has taught first and second grade and has worked with preschool through sixth grade educators, support staff, and special area teachers in implementing *Responsive Classroom* practices in their classrooms. Becky has two master's degrees from The Ohio State University, one focused on language, literacy, and culture and the other in education administration. A few of her favorite things about working with students in kindergarten through second grade are their newfound independence, their love of learning, and the curiosity they hold for the world around them. Becky wrote the sections about second grade.

Lisa Dewey Wells

Lisa Dewey Wells is a native of central New York but has called Annapolis, Maryland, home for more than twenty years. She has taught nearly every elementary grade over her almost thirty-year teaching career and is currently a consulting teacher for Center for Responsive Schools and a parenting and education coach. Lisa was lucky enough to teach primarily in a small school that used *Responsive Classroom* schoolwide and where her now adult children attended. She witnessed the tremendous impact these practices have, not just as a teacher, but also as a parent. Writing the first grade sections of this book brought back vivid memories of learning and laughing with former students, several of whom have shared the thoughts and memories woven into this book.

We hope this book will be a helpful resource for you, one that reminds you of the deep value of your work, imparts practical tips and perennial wisdom, and empowers you to teach with hope and joy.

Chapter 1

Developmentally Responsive Teaching

● ●

Overview

I've learned a lot about being a teacher from my mom. Early on in my teaching career, my mom and I would take long walks after dinner and talk about our school day—our high points, our low points, our funny stories. I had just taken a job as a primary school counselor, and my mom was a veteran elementary school teacher.

I'll never forget the story my mom told me about the time she switched grade levels for a day with a teaching colleague. Her school offered teachers this "switch for a day" opportunity as a chance for professional growth. My mom, a fifth grade teacher who never taught anything lower than third, decided to be adventurous and switch with a first grade colleague.

I chuckled to myself when my mom told me that she thought she was getting the easier end of the deal. She was feeling guilty leaving her first grade colleague to review long division, introduce the new social studies unit, and manage three classes of fifth grade boys watching a health class video. I told my mom not to feel guilty and that I bet she'd face some challenges of her own—and boy, did she!

The evening after the big switch, we took our usual nightly stroll. We laughed so hard we could barely walk as she told me how the day went. This class of first graders had an early morning special and needed to be at the gymnasium first thing. So after she took attendance and did the lunch count, she said, just as she would to her fifth graders, "Okay, gang, let's head down to the gym," and she headed out the door. When she looked back from the doorway, she saw that complete mayhem had broken loose!

You see, by this time of the year in her fifth grade class, my mom could simply say, "Let's head to the gym," and her students would know the routine of walking with a friend or two, talking quietly along the way, as she supervised them in the hall. This was a routine she established in order to prepare her students for the independence of middle school, but it was a routine these first graders didn't know and certainly couldn't handle. My mom quickly realized her error and began what she described as "herding cats into a line to head to the gym." My mom went on to tell me the comical errors she made throughout the day as she was discovering how best to teach and manage six-year-olds.

What Is Developmentally Responsive Teaching?

Developmentally responsive teaching is taking our best knowledge about how children learn and grow and using that information to inform our teaching practices—from how we set up our physical classroom space, to what choices we offer for practicing a skill, to how we give directions. In other words, our knowledge of child development should drive everything we do.

What Do Developmentally Responsive Teachers Do?

The first and perhaps most important step in being a developmentally responsive teacher is getting to know your students. Chip Wood, the author of *Yardsticks*, says, "Students go to school in many different types of communities, learn in a wide variety of classroom settings, and are taught by teachers using a broad and ever-changing array of curricula and methods. Yet one condition holds constant: To reach their fullest potential, students need teachers who know and understand them" (2017, 5). In getting to know your students, consider them in three specific ways:

- **Individually.** To get to know each of our students personally, we must take time to observe them and to listen to them: What are their likes and dislikes? What are their strengths and growth areas? What learning strategies and partnerships work best for them? When we know our students like this, we are better equipped to teach them and better equipped to help them navigate through their individual developmental journey.

- **Culturally.** In a sense, everything is cultural. To be successful in today's diverse classrooms, we not only have to be aware of cultural differences and our own implicit cultural biases, but we have to be able to flex or adapt our teaching practices to best support the individual and collective needs of our students. The more we know about our students' cultures, the better equipped we will be to make these kinds of intentional decisions.

- **Developmentally.** While knowing children as individuals is important, there are also common characteristics at each developmental stage that are equally as beneficial to know. A common trait for kindergartners is the need to ask for and receive permission for things. First graders tend to be noisy, while second graders crave security. To be developmentally responsive in our teaching, we need to know what is considered developmentally typical social-emotionally physically, cognitively, and linguistically so we can use that information to inform our decisions and practices.

C.A.R.E.S. and Social-Emotional Learning

Social and emotional learning is a process through which children learn, develop, and demonstrate key skills that lead to success in the school community and in life. One of the most basic ways we can help all students develop social-emotional competence is to emphasize skill development in five social-emotional competencies known as C.A.R.E.S.: cooperation, assertiveness, responsibility, empathy, and self-control. The skills that make up these competencies can and should be taught in the same way that any academic or life skill is taught.

- **Emotional competence** refers to one's ability to identify, understand, and regulate their emotions.

- **Social competence** is one's ability to cooperate, get along with others, and be a positive member of their class community.

Beyond taking this important step of getting to know their students personally, developmentally responsive teachers work to establish a supportive framework for learning. The following practices forward this approach:

- **Developmentally responsive teachers create classroom environments that represent and consider the developmental needs of all students.** We need to look at our classroom space through the eyes of our students: the furniture we choose and how we arrange it, how we make class materials accessible to promote independence, and what teaching displays we choose to support learning. And we should adjust these plans throughout the year as our children grow and change. Matching the physical space with the developmental needs of the students we teach is critical in creating an optimal learning environment.

- **Developmentally responsive teachers recognize that learning should be active and interactive.** We consider where students are developmentally when making student groupings and by using interactive learning structures, a fun way to make learning more engaging by bringing together social interaction, movement, and content. To use interactive learning structures successfully, we must consider the developmental stage of our students. I learned the importance of taking developmental stages into account the hard way when I attempted to use an interactive learning structure, Inside-Outside Circles, with a group of first graders. I envisioned the students standing in two concentric circles talking briefly with a partner and then singing a song as they moved around the circle to find a new partner. Instead, the result resembled a five-car pileup on the highway as these six-year-olds trampled over each other around the circle, pushing, shoving, and falling to the ground. I should have considered what I know about first graders—they can be enthusiastic, energetic, and competitive—and used that knowledge in my decision-making. I should have approached this by simplifying Inside-Outside Circles and having fewer working parts, which would have made this activity more successful with first graders. Doing a simple partner chat would have given more time for them to talk and honored the fact that first graders enjoy sharing their ideas, thoughts, and explanations.

- **Developmentally responsive teachers know their words are powerful.** Our words have the ability to shape, guide, build up, or tear down. We should choose our words carefully, then, to meet the individual and collective developmental needs of our students. Kindergartners are very literal and will not always be ready to understand abstract concepts such as responsibility. I use my words to attach concrete behaviors to these abstract ideas. For example, I might say to my kindergartners, "I noticed you put the blocks neatly back on the shelf; that's being responsible during cleanup time."

- **Developmentally responsive teachers know that a just-right picture is worth a thousand words.** Using nonlinguistic models such as visual schedules, graphic organizers, and role-plays can be just as powerful—and sometimes more powerful—than words. Taking what we know about a particular developmental stage and pairing it with the just-right picture can be very helpful in supporting our young learners. For seven-year-olds who are "moving forward cautiously, craving security and structure" (Wood 2017, 70), a visual schedule or directions posted with graphics can provide a much-needed source of comfort in their school day.

What Do We Know About Child Development?

Child development is a wondrous thing. There is so much mystery in how children grow and change. I once had a kindergarten girl, Kristen, in one of my social skills groups. She was referred to me because she didn't speak. I wasn't sure if she was painfully shy, was a select mute, or didn't speak because, as the youngest of four girls, all of her sisters spoke for her. Each week, as we sat around the table ready to greet one another, a little boy in the group would always say, "She don't talk!" I would reply with a warm smile in her direction, "Not yet, but she will when she's ready." One day, as I was scurrying to set up the materials for our group, I heard a voice I didn't recognize say, "Hi, Mrs. Wade." I turned to see who it was, and to my surprise, it was Kristen. "Kristen! You're talking!" I said excitedly. She replied, "I know. I'm six now!" That day was her birthday, and in Kristen's world, when you're six, you speak. Who knew?

But for all the mysteries of child development, there is a lot we do know. From years of observation and research in the fields of psychology and education, common patterns of development have emerged and have stood the test of time. Along with these developmental patterns, there are four key principles (Wood 2017) to keep in mind when it comes to child development:

1. **Stages of growth and development follow a reasonably predictable pattern.** As a young mom taking my firstborn to her first doctor appointments, I recall the doctor asking me questions such as "Is she recognizing you?" "Does she reach and grab for things?" "Is she rolling over?" And each time I would say, "No, not yet," and then the next day or two it seemed as if she would start doing that very thing. These kinds of predictable patterns don't stop after that first year when rapid change is so evident. While these changes may be subtler as children grow, these predictable patterns will continue throughout childhood. Consider, for example, how handwriting develops. When students are five years old, letters tend to be large and uppercase; by comparison, when students are seven, letters are often nearly microscopic in size.

2. **Children and adolescents do not proceed through each stage at the same pace.** I love reviewing the draw-a-person pictures when we screen our incoming kindergartners. I'll have two drawings, both by five-year-olds. One drawing has the arms coming straight out of the head, while the other drawing has a head, a neck, a body, and even eyelashes. While these predictable patterns follow the same order, they may not happen at the same rate. Any chronological age may be bubbled within a three-year developmental span. A chronologically aged five-year-old may present more like a developmental four-year-old or a developmental six-year-old.

3. **Children and adolescents progress through the various aspects of development at their own rate.** My younger daughter was an early talker. In fact, she skipped her first word and went right to a first sentence: "I want that!" was the first recognizable thing she said. She was also a thumb-sucker. When she was about three years old, she came to me with dirty hands from playing outside. She said, "Mommy, I want to suck my thumb but it's dirty . . . Do you think I should wash it first because it's pretty dirty?" I remember thinking, if you can say all that, maybe you don't need your thumb anymore! But her language

development was ahead of her emotional development. Each aspect of development progresses in its own time. This is particularly evident in primary age students when we look at physical development. A line of second graders can have a student who looks to be the size of a preschooler, while standing next to that child is a student whose size is that of a fifth grader.

4. **Growth is uneven.** There is an ebb and flow to development with periods of rapid growth similar to the first year of life, and there are quieter periods when growth is hardly noticed. There are even those times when development seems to be going backward. For example, you might find six-year-olds chewing on everything, as if they were teething again. That's due to those incoming six-year molars. Instead of using teething rings, six-year-olds chew up all of the pencils!

The Power of Play

Every year I host a school event called The Power of Play. K–2 classes come down to my ready-made play area where I have set up a play station for each grade. The post office setup is always a big hit. Kindergartners get to practice their fine motor skills as they adhere postal stamps to envelopes, some of which end up with so many stamps you can no longer see the address! First graders problem-solve as they try to decide who will get to wear the postal worker's shirt and carry the bag with deliveries. Second graders beam with confidence and pride as they watch their peers read the letters they wrote, addressed, and sent through the mail to them all by themselves.

Play is the language of learning for young children. Play shows children how to interact with and make sense of their world and the world around them. Through play, children develop creativity and imagination. They develop language and communication skills. Play gives children the opportunity to build self-esteem, self-confidence, and self-control. Children learn to understand and express their feelings, to work cooperatively, and to problem-solve.

Play is naturally motivating for children and can be a powerful opportunity for learning. Play is not frivolous, nor should it be thought of as an extra or what to do when the "real" work is done. Play allows children to explore, discover, and create, so we should make learning a playful adventure.

The more we know about how children grow and develop, and the implications for our classrooms and our teaching, the better educators we can be. This chapter offers guidance about developmentally responsive teaching of students from kindergarten through second grade, each of which is discussed in a separate section. But because development is fluid and grade levels have age ranges, you will likely find valuable information in each section regardless of the grade level you teach. In the grade-level sections of this chapter that follow, you will find the following:

- Specific information on the developmental ages ranging from five to eight years old

- Practical classroom tips that honor child development

- Explicit teaching ideas for social and emotional learning

Grade Ⓚ

One day my son, then a kindergartner, described a time when he felt frustrated because he had to stop playing with his building blocks to get ready for school. He told me that he was angry that he had to stop because he was having so much fun. But then he remembered something we had practiced for those times when he felt angry or frustrated, and he went to his bedroom and took some deep breaths to calm himself down. I said to him, "It sounds like you used a really helpful strategy. Could you tell me about what you did after you were frustrated?"

He replied, "I just . . . enjoyed the rest of my day!"

That sums up a five-year-old in one statement: strong, sudden feelings followed by contented periods of calm. He had been frustrated, and then he got over it. To a five-year-old, life is good. They love their parents, their teachers, and their friends. Five is an age when the rapid cognitive, physical, and vocabulary growth of the four-year-old starts to consolidate.

Five-Year-Olds

Five-year-olds provide a unique set of eyes on the world. They are simultaneously enthusiastic, exhausting, and very literal. They derive much of their self-esteem from feeling capable, exceptionally so. They seek opportunities to show what they can do. For example, putting a book up on a higher shelf and saying to a group of young children, "The book is up here—now nobody can reach it" will bring the group over to the shelf immediately. Older children can intuit that you are telling them the book is off-limits. Fives, on the other hand, may jump, stretch, or climb to reach that book. They are not disobeying, not in the least. On the contrary: they are showing you how supremely capable they are. They can reach that book on the high shelf because they are big, helpful five-year-olds!

Five-year-olds are also very literal. Bennett, a kindergartner, was listening to his STEAM teacher describe a program that was designed to get students to focus on directional words: forward, backward, up, down, left, right. The teacher posed this question: "All right. I am stuck in this land. I'm blindfolded and can't see where I'm going. I call you on my phone and say, 'Can you please help me get to the cabin with the monkey?' What would you tell me to do first?"

Bennett whispered to himself, "Take off your blindfold."

The teacher called on another child, Channelle, who answered, "Take off your blindfold!"

As teachers of these literal-minded five-year-olds, we need to recognize how they understand our questions—and their response to something that is obvious to them can bring humor and a helpful reminder that through a five-year-old's eyes the most obvious answer might sometimes be the best one.

Tips to Support Five-Year-Olds in the Classroom

- Be consistent in your language and expectations.

- Allow for regular modeling and practice (five-year-olds need lots of practice).

- Introduce new materials with plenty of open-ended time for exploration. Five-year-olds need to explore first on their own terms.

- Provide plenty of time for talking and sharing with other students.

- Spend time talking to each child regularly. Five-year-olds thrive when they feel a sense of connection with their teacher.

Six-Year-Olds

One year during the second week of kindergarten, my class was about to take a movement break and dance to a version of "The Chicken Dance." The class was excited. I had modeled the movements and told them it was going to get faster and faster. They were ready. One of my older students, Breyanna, eyed me with some suspicion. As the music started, she watched me closely for a moment, and then looked around the circle and saw every one of her classmates participating. She was quiet for a moment, taking it all in, and then had a moment where she was clearly thinking, *Okay, well, if this is what we're doing*, and joined in eagerly with everyone else.

Six-year-olds can be like that: because they are maturing, they start to notice more of the reality in their world and what people are doing. While five-year-olds don't always connect cause and effect, six-year-olds are deepening their empathy and can consider other points of view. Like five-year-olds, six-year-olds will also revel in your encouragement. Even with all of this internal development going on, six-year-olds are still tiny humans who love the magic of the universe. They sometimes need the freedom to know that everyone else is doing it, too, before participating, which frees them up to let go and be their true, full selves and feel that magic, through and through.

As five-year-olds are consolidating a lot of their development from age four, six-year-olds are eager to jump into everything. They are experiencing rapid cognitive and physical growth at this age, and it shows: they are noisy, movement-based learners. Classrooms that allow for regular movement and conversation are places where six-year-olds excel. When they feel comfortable, six-year-olds are your wingmen. They are excited to start every project, and they shout your praise to the rooftops (sometimes quite literally). For six-year-olds, the process is far more important than the product. The sky's the limit, and they are in a hurry to explore every part of it.

Tips to Support Six-Year-Olds in the Classroom

- Use reinforcing language consistently to help build their positive self-image.

- Keep routines and expectations consistent, but think novelty: Can you hide the new learning material under a piece of fabric and remove it dramatically to build excitement? Do you have a set of different counters that will energize a favorite math game?

- Allow them to talk during learning times—they need to talk—and deliberately teach them what that "talk" sounds like. Before a writing workshop, ask: "What might writing talk sound like today?" Model how you might talk to your math partner about the math game.

- Be flexible within your expectations. If it's writing time and one of your students is having a rough day, ask them if today is a "writing day" or a "drawing day." The knowledge that their teacher has their back in hard times makes a world of difference.

Redshirting

Kindergarten expectations in many schools have changed over the years. Not all of these changes, though, are developmentally appropriate for five-year-olds. In many communities, parents have held their children out of school for a year so they are more mature and ready for some of the more rigorous expectations. This is commonly known as redshirting, a term that derives from college athletics where athletes are allowed to participate in practice and work on their skills without the pressure to compete and without affecting their eligibility. It essentially gives the student an additional year to acquire some of the skills that will make them better at the game.

For teachers, this provides a unique challenge: How do we meet the needs of students who are chronologically more than a year apart? In teaching, there is never an easy, single answer to anything, because we're dealing with complex people. One way to meet these needs is to make sure that you also know the typical development of six-year-olds. In this book, read the sections that focus on first grade as well as kindergarten. Provide learning opportunities that allow for children to progress at their own level. Offer opportunities for children to work together and harness their natural desire to help each other by providing turns for each person to be in charge. A helpful hint: remember that even though the children in your class may be a year apart, they're still kids. Do what you do naturally to engage young children: be animated, be silly, be fun. The development patterns of five-year-olds and six-year-olds are not so different and can be very complementary. You've got this.

Going to kindergarten brings together children with a wide variety of experiences. Some children have been in childcare settings for years and bring with them that knowledge and experience. Other children have been in school part-time and might be challenged by a longer day. For many, though, this is their first school experience.

Regardless of their experience, kindergartners need to feel a sense of joy and ownership and a sense of connection and significance to their community. They need teachers who will listen with empathy because a kindergartner's behavior doesn't always match what adults perceive as the intent. When we notice the positives in their behavior and reinforce those positives specifically, children feel safe knowing what to do. All kindergartners learn best through play, though their play can look wildly different at different stages of development.

Development fluctuates, and children don't all go neatly through developmental stages at the same time. Kindergarten teachers have a very real challenge of meeting the needs of both older and younger students in the classroom. A basic formula? Create play and learning sessions that offer freedom of choice within clear expectations. These sessions involve deliberate selection of content and materials on the teacher's part, and thoughtful choice on the part of the student. Through choice, children build a sense of independence and autonomy and are allowed to approach the learning from their own best developmental level. They are able to move forward, fueled by their natural curiosity and enthusiasm.

Developmental Characteristics in the Classroom

Consistency is key for kindergartners. When the schedule is predictable, when teachers are explicit with expectations, children feel safe to try new things and work within their competency level and interests.

In kindergarten, workshop learning times offer a powerful strategy for creating opportunities to maximize student learning. Workshops can include familiar structures such as a regular writing workshop. A workshop model can be used in all subject areas. It usually includes a mini-lesson with a goal, children making decisions that allow them to practice this learning goal, and then regrouping to share and reflect on their learning. This model allows teachers to strategically choose what options are available and differentiate for children's unique learning needs.

If you're feeling concerned about creating these choices, start with materials. If children are practicing counting by grabbing handfuls of manipulatives, then offer both small counters and large ones. Discuss why you might choose larger or smaller materials and allow children to make that choice. If children are tasked with sharing their understanding of a story or concept, then materials might include modeling clay and other building or art materials. Just as a kindergarten writing workshop will include children at various levels—those who are only drawing to those who are writing and sounding out words—understand that your students will be at various levels, and a workshop format will allow you to create a space that allows everyone to participate.

Cognitively, five- and six-year-olds are noticing differences, and they are starting to generalize about what they see, hear, and watch. Their curiosity drives them to want to talk about it or explore it through their play.

See the appendix, p. 349, for resources for a diverse classroom library.

With this in mind, talk frankly about melanin and why people's skin colors look different. Be deliberate in curating a classroom library and read-aloud repertoire of books that feature characters of all races and nationalities. Choose books that feature both children and grown-ups making mistakes and persevering through hard challenges and that have characters showing typical gender norms as well as characters that challenge those gender norms. Allow for the children's noticing and questions. Kindergartners are going to wonder why, and they are going to ask uncomfortable questions. Being allowed to wonder and question in a safe environment helps them build a growth mindset. Plots and characters in books allow for a jumping-off point for almost any discussion that teachers may want to dig into.

Kindergartners are capable of sustained attention for fifteen to twenty minutes when they are interested in what they're doing. It's also not hard to find ways to pique this interest! Provide ample opportunities for them to be active with small and large muscles. Young children need plenty of time to build, draw, play, and explore. Learning should include a balance of structured and exploratory activity. Five-year-olds thrive when they know what the expectations are, but they should be allowed to be free and curious within those boundaries.

Fairy tales and folktales are of great interest to five-year-olds because they will often have a literal message of right and wrong. Six-year-olds love novelty and a new take on something familiar. Read multiple versions of these tales, and be sure to seek out books that feature Black people, Indigenous people, and people of color, and include folk tales from other countries.

The verbal and cognitive explosion from age four generates a wide variety of thoughts and questions in the five-year-old's mind. Children this age want—and need—multiple opportunities to share. For different reasons, six-year-olds need plenty of opportunities to talk. They learn by talking! Weave multiple sharing opportunities throughout the day. Create a news board where children can add drawings and photos about events in their lives. Partner children regularly to share a drawing, an idea, a way of sorting, or something they created in the block corner.

Social and Emotional Learning

Kindergarten is a time when children are ripe and ready to learn from what their teacher models. Because children this age are so open, it is a perfect time to show and practice important social and emotional skills. Children are eager to learn new skills and please others. They do well with teachers who are patient and who understand that this practice will last a while. Five-year-olds excel in expressing sympathy and six-year-olds are deepening their empathy, offering many rich opportunities for social and emotional learning.

Cooperation

Because children in this age group are curious and interested in working and playing with other children, kindergarten is a natural time to build the skills of cooperation. Opportunities to practice these skills include free play and cooperative games on the playground, math games, and other academic content (for example, planting seeds, caring for the plants as they grow, and creating drawings to mark their growth).

The peer group becomes more important as five-year-olds age toward six. While they still adore and want to please teachers and other important adults in their lives, they also start paying a lot of attention to peers. They gravitate toward those with similar interests and may show a preference toward same-gender playmates.

Their conflicts and squabbles become less about toys, as when they were younger, and are related more to social issues that arise through their play. Pay attention to these disagreements: they can show us what the children need us to teach and model next.

To support the development of cooperation in your kindergartners, focus on teaching these skills:

- Inviting someone to play

- Asking others if you can play with them

- Working out a problem with a classmate when you disagree

- How to ask a question

- Taking turns in a game

- Deciding who will go first

- Knowing what to do when you notice someone is upset

Assertiveness

In a classroom that understands and prioritizes both academic and social-emotional learning, five- and six-year-olds flourish. Regular instruction and modeling about how to express their own ideas, feelings, and rationales help kindergartners develop the independence and confidence to feel and express emotions without hurting others. They also build an understanding that others can do the same. This allows them to bolster their patience with themselves and with others and frees up their energy so they are comfortable taking risks to learn new things.

To support the development of assertiveness in your kindergartners, focus on teaching these skills:

- Expressing strong emotions without hurting others

- Accepting help when something is especially challenging

- Sharing an idea with others

- Being patient when something proves difficult

- Asking to join in

- Offering help

Responsibility

In kindergarten, children start to recognize the difference between fair and unfair and the importance of making intentional choices.

Many five-year-olds will start to accept responsibility for wrongdoing, but they may need time. They may also need time and space to process and accept their wrongdoing. Allowing them to fix a mistake may come later. As they grow—and with patient adult guidance—kindergartners start to understand that a mistake does not show their character: it does not mean they are "bad." As teachers, it's important that we regularly model making mistakes and fixing them, and that we read literature that shows a growth mindset and accepts that all people are learning: you mess up, you fix it, you move on.

To support the development of responsibility in your kindergartners, focus on teaching these skills:

- Admitting mistakes and trying to fix them

- Knowing how to apologize

- Making sure everyone is included

- Taking care of materials and putting them away properly

- Managing classroom jobs

- Managing one's own supplies

Empathy

There's a common experience I've heard in a few circles of kindergarten teachers that always brings the laughter of recognition: when a child is hurt on the playground, all of the five-year-olds cluster around to help, including the child that just pushed the hurt child down.

Five-year-olds are developing their empathy skills, but those skills are still maturing. Some five-year-olds often see the results of an action but don't see the antecedent as connected. However, older five- and six-year-olds can become uncomfortable as that empathy develops: they connect the unfortunate result to an impulsive action they just did that they shouldn't have done, and this is troublesome for them because it doesn't fit with their self-image as a person who helps. Some children will lie about an impulsive action they took, not because they didn't do it, but because they don't want to believe they did it or want to save face. Kindergartners need teachers who understand this and react without judgment: "You crumpled his paper because he took the blue crayon you wanted to use. Let's go find a new paper that you can give him instead. When someone takes something you were using, say these words: 'I'm using that blue crayon. Would you like me to give it to you when I'm done?'" When kindergarten teachers lead with and react with empathy, children more eagerly learn that behavior, and choices, are fixable.

To support the development of empathy in your kindergartners, focus on teaching these skills:

- Accepting others that are different from oneself
- Showing kindness to those who are different
- Using polite words with others
- Welcoming someone in
- Inviting someone else to play
- Knowing how to talk to someone who seems sad or upset

Self-Control

As adults, we have a fully developed prefrontal cortex (the area of the brain that moderates social behavior, among other functions), but we can still struggle with our own willpower or impulse control. (I know that I often find it hard to resist leftover chocolate cake!) At ages five and six, children have nowhere near a fully developed brain, so it's no surprise that managing their own behavior can be difficult. When kindergartners are allowed to practice and reflect regularly, they start to see it as a learning process, not as an achievement. There's no self-control medal out there that you can receive that signifies you're done.

Building self-control and the executive function to manage their body as well as their emotions is still developing in all young children. When we give them regular chances to practice stopping, shifting, and transitioning in fun ways, it allows children to build that emotional and muscle memory and deepen their own capacity for both.

Try freeze games where everyone moves their body and stops when the music stops. Play Walk and Stop when walking in the hallway. For emotional practice, get everyone laughing at the same time until a teacher shows a stop signal. Other options include transitioning between emotions: everyone practices an angry face and says, "I'm angry," and then immediately shifts to a new emotion. Call out emotions and let kids show it on their faces for a count of three, and then call out another one.

To support the development of self-control in your kindergartners, focus on teaching these skills:

- Using strategies to calm down when feeling upset

- Asking for help when feeling overwhelmed

- Waiting patiently in a game or other situation

- Sticking with something, even if it's difficult

Years ago, I had a small group of five- and six-year-olds for a short week of learning. Our content focus was the neighborhood around us. As we took a walk outside to make lists and take photographs of everything we could see, every five-year-old was quiet, and every six-year-old pointed out multiple things. Over the next two days, we created a large floor map of the neighborhood, with children choosing what they were going to make and add to our map from what we'd seen on our walk. After the map was completed, we took our final walk, and all of the children—five- and six-year-olds alike—were abuzz with excitement. By representing all of the children, and giving them time to process, they were ready to talk about everything they saw and incorporated into the map.

Kindergartners are a bundle of energy, wonder, and authenticity. As they grow and learn, they need a chance to make sense of new information. Representation is key to building and showing this understanding. Offer as many opportunities as you can for five-year-olds to draw, create, or play out the learning they are doing. You'll find it pays off in numerous ways!

Kindergartners

Common Characteristics	School Implications

Social-Emotional

• Need a great deal of adult approval—like to know exactly what's expected and that they're meeting those expectations.	• Give frequent positive and specific reinforcement to all children, including when they accomplish tasks independently.
• Enjoy helping and following the rules.	• Check in with children frequently to make sure they understand directions.
• Like to ask for and receive permission.	• Try to have predictable schedules and routines.
• Often have difficulty seeing things from another person's point of view; tend to think there's only one "right way."	• Use children's literature, drama, role-play, and other strategies to help kindergartners develop a repertoire of social skills (for example, what to do when they're upset, how to put themselves in someone else's shoes, how to explore alternative ways of doing something, and how to monitor their own work).
• Enjoy routines and structure.	
• Often cry when upset, embarrassed, angry, or confused.	
• Older five-year-olds may challenge adult authority and seem oppositional at times.	

Physical

• Focus best visually on objects or writing that is close to them.	• Avoid having children copy from the board or from a chart placed far away from them.
• Are better at gross motor tasks (such as running and jumping) than at earlier ages, but still can be awkward with small motor movements.	• Provide frequent movement breaks and include movement in daily lessons and routines.
• May find printing challenging—for instance, they may reverse certain letters or numbers.	• Give children regular opportunities for recess and physical play.
• Are very active and energetic.	• Provide scaffolding for fine motor tasks, especially printing. Place dots on the paper to show where to start writing or give children a craft stick (or remind them to use their finger) to help them space between words.
• Are prone to falling out of chairs, often sideways; may prefer to work standing up.	
• Still developing left-to-right visual tracking essential for reading fluency.	• Observe students to determine the best working arrangement and adjust as needed. Offer standing desks if available.
• Usually pace themselves well; will generally rest before they're exhausted.	

Kindergartners

Common Characteristics	School Implications

Cognitive

• Like to repeat experiences and copy previous products.	• Provide learning experiences that are mostly active and interactive, and include repetition.
• Often have difficulty seeing more than one way to do something.	• Reinforce their efforts, but gently nudge them into trying new things and reassure them that mistakes are okay.
• Can pace themselves and work quietly for longer periods of time (eventually up to fifteen or twenty minutes), but will generally need teacher approval and support to change activities.	• Provide a few models for how to do assignments beforehand, and allow for frequent sharing of their work.
• Like to learn through direct experience or hands-on learning.	• Check in with children briefly before expecting them to change activities.
• Have a developing sense of time; don't clearly know what "five minutes" or "in a little while" means.	• Respond well to use of a sand timer where they can see time passing.
• Are not ready to understand abstract concepts such as fairness	• Provide examples of abstract concepts (for example, "Each one of you gets the help you need to learn new things—this is how I will be fair to everyone in our classroom').
• Have vivid imaginations and complex imaginative expression.	• Offer opportunities for students to express themselves through words, drawing, and drama.

Language

• Are often very literal and basic in their understanding of language.	• Think through (and sometimes even write out for yourself) your directions and explanations in advance. Display class rules, key routines, and schedules, and choral-read them.
• Express themselves briefly—sometimes in just a few words.	• Break assignments and tasks into easily understood and manageable parts. Expect and allow quiet talking during work time.
• Often think out loud (for example, saying, "I'm going to choose the black crayon" before taking the black crayon) and read out loud even when asked to read silently.	• Check in frequently and assess children's understanding.
• Older five-year-olds like to explain things and have things explained to them; will often give elaborate answers to questions.	• Avoid overreacting to impulsive statements. Instead, guide children to think before speaking (for example, teach them to wait a few seconds before responding).

The information in this chart is based on *Yardsticks: Child and Adolescent Development Ages 4–14*, 4th ed., by Chip Wood (Center for Responsive Schools 2017) and Child Development Guide by Center for Development of Human Services at SUNY Buffalo State (New York State Office of Children and Family Services 2015).

Grade ①

Imagine you are not an outdoors person, but you are a curious problem-solver. You accept a challenge to be left in the woods with a few resources to help you navigate a path through the woods, along a stream, and eventually to a place where all your needs are met. Barring any tumultuous weather or hungry predators, most of us could probably find our way using our experience and resilience, as well as the tools and tactics we might pick up along the way. But wouldn't this task be more manageable—as well as fun and engaging—if we had some background knowledge about the terrain, if we knew what to expect and which tools would genuinely be of service? Would that help us feel more confident in our ability to tackle challenges and enjoy the present moment, knowing we were armed with what we needed? And while a hike in the woods is rarely the same hike twice, some parts are predictable and navigable when we are prepared and understand the general path, both behind us and ahead of us.

Teaching first graders can be akin to an outdoor adventure—exciting, exhausting, compelling, and predictable when we truly take the time to understand just who the first graders are at the moment. When we dedicate time to understanding child development and developmentally responsive teaching, we can see children for who they are and better understand the path that brought them to this moment. This approach, combined with our knowledge of solid pedagogical practices and content knowledge, allows us to respond to students' individual, cultural, and developmental needs and strengths. These are useful tools that will enable us to navigate the predictable paths as well as the hills and valleys of teaching first graders. Add a healthy dose of adventure and humor, and your experience in the often wild and exhilarating land of first grade will be paved with greater clarity and purpose. You'll also have confidence knowing you're helping these eager learners maximize their first grade year.

I've taught long enough that I have classes of former first graders who are in college and beyond. Because we live in a small town, and since social media makes it easy to connect, I often hear from these first graders. I spoke with one who remembers the expansiveness of first grade—including having the space to work on the carpet for math and reading, a busy classroom with art, items to tinker with and build, plenty of books, and an ever-present sense of order amid the industriousness of their learning. This particular student had been a struggling reader with a creative imagination. Dictating his stories rather than writing them himself bolstered his confidence to tell an intricate fantasy piece about a blue alien who ate doughnuts. This was also a child with a sensitive heart and love of animals, so he was our bug collector, tasked with catching and releasing any arachnid who joined our space.

In first grade, no task is too big or impossible, especially when teachers step in with questions such as "What materials might you need?" or "How will you know whose job that is?" Often the first graders' big ideas need subtle tethering or a brief pause to see how the classroom rules apply or how to envision working step-by-step. The sense of discovery is buoyed by their deepening friendships and blossoming ability to understand another perspective.

The physical growth in first grade is evident—loose teeth can mean chewing on sleeves, collars, or pencils. The children tire easily and can be prone to frequent colds. They are busy and often in such a hurry that they appear clumsy or sloppy. Chairs can feel rigid or constraining, and it's not uncommon for six-year-olds to fall off sideways (floor seating or standing to work may be good alternatives). Overall, the dynamic nature of this age makes six-year-olds engage in a flurry of activity. Carefully planned energizers and interactive learning structures help them maximize, without comprising learning, their propensity to move and socialize. Frequent breaks for outdoor activities or free play help balance their fluctuations of energy.

First graders want to do it all and not miss a beat, but they are often moving too fast to take it all in. Consequently, first grade classrooms often bubble over with excitement and energy, with ideas and images, energy and exhaustion. This is a year marked by growth in cognitive skills, friendships, and broad interests. Children at this age are steady and feel much trusted, and lighthearted adults help them explore their world and manage what can become an overwhelming sense of self and what they can do.

Active Learning

For first graders, novelty and excitement always lead to deep engagement. One year, my teaching partner and I developed a unit on communication for our first graders. Our search was focused on finding something innovative, provocative, and hands-on so that our first graders could be immersed in active learning about this topic. We had just wrapped up learning American Sign Language, and we now wanted to cover a communication mode that opened our students up to something new.

We also kept in mind that first graders love sharing what they know or think they know. They like trying things for themselves, especially grown-up things—pens instead of pencils, clipboards for writing, or anything they perceive as grown-up.

The children's handwriting and spelling spanned the expected range from semiphonetic stage to phonetic stage to even transitional stage. Some of our first graders struggled with the physical process of writing, so it wasn't unusual to see writers standing with their paper taped to an easel or to the wall or to see the children laid out prone on the floor to write.

New tools and ways to work were always greeted with enthusiasm and a sense of purpose by first graders. These observations and awareness of what it means to be six years old were central to our consideration as we constructed this new unit of study.

Putting the Plan in Place

We decided to create a unit on photojournalism as a way to combine the content we needed to cover for communication with what we knew about our students. We happened to have two parents who were professional photographers and another one who was passionate about photography as a hobby. In addition, we received a grant for two digital cameras that we used to document our learning.

We examined the tools of a photographer's trade—from old-school Polaroid cameras, to 35-mm ones, to digital devices. We then looked at some of the images that the parents had captured, places many of us might never see in person. We considered how these images told a story—the details, the landscapes, the portraits. Our first graders were confident they *knew* the stories in these images as they made personal connections. Later, our parent photographers came in to share the oral histories of these photos. Many times these histories jibed with our classes' hypotheses, and when they didn't, it led to new learning about what life is like in different cultures or at different times.

The parents brought in the cameras that they used in their work, and each child learned how to safely hold the cameras and how to shoot pictures. We then made a map of our school and divided up the space, and each child was given the assignment to photograph a "day in the life" at our school, using the real-life skills of portrait, landscape, or close-up. In the end, one of our parents curated a slide deck with the children's images. We worked with small groups to add narration to their pictures, knowing that the children's oral language would add details in a way far more accessible than their writing could.

Indeed, we were lucky to have these parents to help us with the materials and hands-on assistance with this research. But it would not have been possible without careful consideration of where our students were at the time. We had built a strong community that recognized each student. The children were accustomed to making choices in what and how they learned, and they knew they'd have to explain why they made choices in their learning.

See the appendix, p. 333, for more on Interactive Modeling.

Over the course of the year, we used Interactive Modeling to practice routines and use tools for our learning. When we brought the cameras into our lessons, we leaned on the past successes of sharing and taking turns with materials and taking care of materials so that everyone would have them to use. As older six-year-olds, the children enjoyed working in small groups and delegating jobs and, as such, basked in pride as they held real cameras and navigated all corners of our school building. Their tendency to work and move quickly was carefully monitored, with proactive reminders about travel in the hallways and reinforcing language when they returned cameras to their cases correctly.

Rethinking Unit Design

Think about a unit you designed. How might you adjust it with the knowledge you have now? Is there a unit you're now inspired to try after reading the example here?

Social and Emotional Learning

Keeping in mind the hallmarks of ages six and seven, first grade teachers can set students up for success as they work independently and participate in group activities.

Cooperation

Six-year-olds can make and keep friends, and most desire to have dear friends. Read-alouds, role-play, and imaginary play offer excellent opportunities to model and discuss what friendship looks like, feels like, and sounds like. Again, reinforcing prosocial behaviors goes a long way in helping first graders feel secure in their budding friendships.

First graders are brimming with excitement and energy. They can be competitive or bossy, slow or speedy. Use modeling and practice to teach your students when to take turns and how to control their bodies and impulses, and savor those moments of spontaneity that are invaluable in the first grade classroom.

Here are cooperation skills first graders should learn:

- How and when to take turns
- Controlling their impulses
- Working in a positive, constructive way with others in a group or one-on-one

- Inviting someone to play

- Working through disagreements

- Taking turns in a game

Assertiveness

The skill of assertiveness refers to the ability of students to stand up for themselves and others by asking for help, as well as doing the right thing for the greater good of the group. One of the most important social skills for children to build on in first grade is identifying emotions. We can support the development of this skill by helping students to expand the language of feelings and emotions beyond "happy, sad, and mad" and deliberately teaching them how to name a wide range of feelings. Having a visual reference for children to consider as they work to name emotions, especially those tricky or uncomfortable ones, can empower first graders to access suitable language to express themselves. If children are practicing and learning to name these emotions on their own, it can be helpful for first grade teachers to expose them to language with observations such as, "It looks like you might be feeling frustrated that you have to wait for a turn with the building blocks. What could you do while you wait that feels okay?"

Here are emotional skills that first graders should begin to develop:

- Identifying their emotions

- Expanding the language to best identify what they are feeling

- Learning how to ask for help

- Understanding what's best for the group

Responsibility

Six-year-olds also love asking questions and doing projects, which they can do with increasing autonomy. They often thrive in jobs that allow them to be the caretaker of class supplies or their own property. While their efforts at projects or cleanup tasks may not always be perfect, they benefit from encouragement and reinforcement when they find ways to solve problems, help others, or contribute to the classroom environment's care.

Although first graders love jobs, they tend to be speedy. Assigning jobs for the week provides multiple opportunities to practice each position and a significant role for each student to play in taking care of the class community.

The following are responsibility skills first graders should practice:

- Learning how to care for their own materials and class supplies
- Carrying out classroom jobs and assignments
- Assisting others

Empathy

First graders love to hear language and stories, which makes literature the ideal vehicle for discussing a wide range of social and emotional skills, feelings, and strategies. Children in this age group are beginning to understand the point of view of others, and often this is easier to do in a fictional context rather than in real time. Proactively reading stories that address possible hot spots (listening to others, taking turns) can help first graders think ahead to possible conflicts and options for resolutions. As you observe interactions and individuals, you may also choose read-alouds that allow you to address any issues you see. Follow up read-alouds with props in dramatic play or materials in your art area for children to explore what they absorbed from their reading, or send a list of related books to your students' families. (See the appendix, page 350, for recommended books for grades K–2.)

First graders should learn the following empathy skills:

- Listening to the point of view of others
- Becoming more sensitive to how others may be feeling
- Understand others' point of view

Self-Control

The teacher's skillful use of reinforcing language helps first graders recognize when they are on the right path or making responsible choices: "I notice that you remembered to do all of your settling in jobs this morning, James, and now you're ready for the day!"

Proactive reminders allow first graders to pause and remember what comes next. These reminders leverage their need for encouragement and support so they will not become overwhelmed with big tasks. The alternating rhythm of Morning Meeting—from a cheerful greeting to taking turns sharing, to a lively activity and then closing with a calm choral reading of the message—allows first graders to experience the ebb and flow of energy. Interactive Modeling provides a clear process for how to take turns talking rather than blurting out answers and interrupting others. Active learning allows for group work and partner chats, providing first graders with more opportunity to speak and listen to others.

First graders should begin to learn these self-control skills:

- Patience while awaiting their turn
- Asking for help
- Persevering through a challenging situation

When setting up the classroom or designing lessons, bear in mind the vibrancy of children this age and their abiding desire to do well. This will help you to set up these learners for success and to give them plenty of opportunity to practice the social and emotional skills needed to be positive community members.

First Graders

Common Characteristics	School Implications

Social-Emotional

Common Characteristics	School Implications
• Are enthusiastic, ambitious, energetic, and competitive.	• Provide lots of noncompetitive, cooperative games and activities.
• Are very social and enjoy working and playing in groups; may start having a best friend.	• Require students to be quiet only when it's absolutely necessary, and then keep the duration short.
• Thrive on encouragement and are often crushed by even small criticisms.	• Reinforce students' positive attributes or behaviors rather than focus on mistakes.
• Can be bossy.	• Be understanding of their testing behaviors and bossiness with friends, while providing direct guidance and firm limits.
• May begin to test the limits of authority.	
• Like doing things for themselves; ready to try taking on individual and group responsibility.	

Physical

Common Characteristics	School Implications
• Are very noisy and active; often fall out of chairs and may need to work standing.	• Give frequent movement breaks; incorporate movement into the daily curriculum (movement helps students stay focused).
• Can tire easily and get sick frequently.	• Give students space to spread out their work if possible. Let them work standing up or on the floor.
• Enjoy being active, both inside and outdoors.	• Use Interactive Modeling to show students what to do if they fall out of a chair.
• Are better at tracking from left to right than younger children; this is an ideal age for learning to read.	• Vary the pace of instruction (quick opening lesson in a circle, back to desks for a focused assignment, return to circle for a discussion), and keep assignments short (five to ten minutes at the beginning of the year).
• May like to chew on pencils and other objects because new teeth are coming in.	
• More aware of their fingers as tools; can use their fingers to count on, trace a maze, maneuver electronic devices, balance a scale, pour exact amounts.	• Consider having frequent healthy snacks that satisfy students' hunger and chewing urge.

First Graders

Common Characteristics	School Implications

Cognitive

• Are more engaged in process than product.	• Break activities, assignments, and projects into small, doable chunks.
• Are very interested in learning and doing work, but sometimes take on projects that are too big for them.	• Weave art into as many aspects of the curriculum as possible; provide a wide variety of art materials for exploration.
• Experience an explosion in artistic interest and expression; love to color and paint.	• Provide lots of opportunities for imaginative and dramatic play both in the classroom and at recess.
• Are beginning to be able to conceptualize past and present and cause and effect.	
• Engage in more elaborate dramatic play.	
• Are very curious; love discovery, new ideas, and asking questions.	

Language

• Love poems, riddles, and songs.	• Weave poems, riddles, and songs into many parts of the day.
• Enjoy explaining their thoughts, how something happened, how things work.	• Provide many opportunities for students to talk and explain their thinking.
• Ask many questions.	

The information in this chart is based on *Yardsticks: Child and Adolescent Development Ages 4–14*, 4th ed., by Chip Wood (Center for Responsive Schools 2017) and Child Development Guide by Center for Development of Human Services at SUNY Buffalo State (New York State Office of Children and Family Services 2015).

Grade ②

Second grade students are full of energy and imagination and appreciate the world around them. They enjoy discovering new things in their environments and unearthing different ways to go about solving perceived problems.

This was evident to me on a warm fall day during recess when a group of second grade students playing a fast-paced game of hide-and-seek came across an active beehive high in a tree on the playground. Driven by curiosity, it did not take long for the entire second grade class to gather around the tree where the beehive was located and begin squealing, "*Look!* It's a beehive!" with pure elation and amazement.

The curious nature of these seven- and eight-year-olds brought on a slew of questions indicative of their appreciation of the beauty of nature and their ultimate concern for safety. What was the beehive doing on the playground? Have other students noticed this new addition? They toyed around with helping to make a plan to move the hive to a safer place, and they had many conversations with each other about bee stings and the likelihood of bees stinging us and others while we played in that area. Soon our time outside came to an end, but their curiosity and questions about the playground bees followed us back to the classroom.

Needless to say, we ended up spending the rest of the afternoon reading books and researching online to find the answers to our questions. The classroom was abuzz as our initial wonderings were answered and more information about our playground visitors was learned. We wrapped up our learning with a few important action steps, which included notifying the adults in the building about our discovery so they could help the bees and alerting the rest of the school community to our discovery so we could spend time sharing what we had learned.

This experience of working together to learn more about a common interest so early in the year helped solidify us as a community of learners and reinforced our larger role within the school community. In the coming days, our curiosity around the playground beehive soon subsided, and in true second grader fashion, the class moved on to another area of interest that they were eager to explore.

Seven-Year-Olds

Seven-year-olds are creatures of habit who thrive in stable and predictable learning environments. They like to know the day's schedule and will often question any modifications of the typical schedule that they are used to following. Due to their developing sense of time, you might hear seven-year-olds asking about lunchtime, snack time, or math stations and commenting to their peers about what is coming next in the day. A daily schedule is an important classroom tool for seven-year-olds in that such a schedule provides them with comfort in knowing the plan for the school day. Having consistent and predictable routines and procedures also helps seven-year-old students feel safe at school and cared for by their teachers. For seven-year-olds, the more explicitly the teacher can model classroom expectations along with the many important routines and procedures needed during the school day, the better students will feel about their time in the classroom.

Tips to Support Seven-Year-Olds in the Classroom

- Post a daily classroom schedule.
- Discuss changes in the daily schedule as a group during Morning Meeting.
- Use Interactive Modeling to teach routines and procedures.
- Use reinforcing language to help seven-year-olds build their confidence in classroom routines and procedures.

Second graders find it helpful when their classroom teacher spends time to prepare them for upcoming changes in routine. For example, a seven-year-old's need for stability is often tested when the main classroom teacher is absent. Guest teachers might find it particularly challenging to convince the class that the routines and procedures remain the same even when their classroom teacher is absent, and they may find it frustrating to continually hear, "That's not the way our teacher does it," while trying to stick to the lesson plans for the day. Whether the change facing your class is a guest teacher or, for example, an assembly that will happen during your normal Morning Meeting time, preparing students for variations in the class's day-to-day routine can make the day go smoothly.

See the appendix, p. 344, for more on preparing for a guest teacher.

Seven-year-olds are active in their friendship making and frequently bounce from friend to friend. Children this age are notorious for moving from friendship to friendship, often having many "best friends" throughout the school year, or even a few in one week! Expect seven-year-olds to hop in and out of friend groups while they navigate the dynamics of many groups and try out different friendship styles.

Eight-Year-Olds

Eight-year-olds wake up each morning ready to take on the world. They are known for their imaginative nature and "I can" attitude. This confidence is driven by their growing competence in their environment and continued mastery of a number of classroom tools including technology devices, writing utensils, and math manipulatives. The world is their oyster, and they now have the skills and confidence to go forth and explore. They often move from one interest to another with such speed that it can sometimes be hard to keep up. One day they are interested in reading graphic novels, and the next day they have moved on to a nonfiction book series about outer space. It is up to us, their teachers, to help eight-year-olds harness all of that energy and give it focus and direction.

For all of their excitement for school, friends, learning, and their teachers, eight-year-olds can also be impatient and easily frustrated. This is particularly true when faced with a challenging task in which the answer does not come easily or quickly. When this happens, you might hear these children say, "I'm bored," which is really code for "This is too hard." It's important to remember that although eight-year-olds are growing in confidence, they still need support from their teachers to continue to grow, especially during challenging tasks. Eight-year-olds benefit from teachers modeling a growth mindset and showing them how to work through strategies to use when faced with a challenge, both social and academic. You might consider using role-play to help eight-year-olds think through a

See the appendix, p. 337, for more on role-play.

challenging task prior to their participation in order to inspire perseverance and an "I can" attitude.

At eight years old, students benefit from the occasional change in routine, a departure from their more structured seven-year-old selves. This is the perfect age for an occasional schedule change or surprise during the school day, such as a few minutes of extra recess, a special guest reader, or the addition of a new quiet time choice. Such surprises and changes in routine have the ability to lighten the mood for the sometimes moody eight-year-old and can be beneficial in helping them re-engage in their learning.

Another key feature of eight-year-olds is that they are more interested in socializing in larger groups than they were at age seven. Eight-year-olds are beginning to solidify friendships with classmates and can often be found in the same small group with the same peers day after day. It's important to recognize this trait in eight-year-olds and sprinkle in teacher-created groups throughout the day to help these children socialize with a number of different classmates. Within their friendship groups, eight-year-olds can often be heard telling jokes. It's at this age that their ability to recognize and understand humor develops. Eight-year-olds gravitate toward joke telling and can often be found creating their own jokes to share with others (whether the jokes make sense or not!). Be prepared for several knock-knock jokes that will leave you scratching your head.

Tips to Support Eight-Year-Olds in the Classroom

- Break up schoolwork and home assignments into smaller chunks to help eight-year-olds experience incremental success in their academic work.

- Use interactive learning structures and small-group activities to provide eight-year-olds with opportunities to socialize and work with others.

- Use redirecting language to help eight-year-olds harness and focus their energy on necessary tasks and persevere through challenging tasks.

- Considers ways to occasionally surprise eight-year-olds with a slight change in routine or special guest.

Social and Emotional Learning

It was the beginning of a new school year, and I had done all of the necessary preparations for my new group of second graders. My classroom was all set up, I had thought through my lesson plans for the first few days, and I had planned what I considered fun and joyful classroom activities. On the second day of school, I decided that it would be fun to have the class participate in a design challenge where they would be tasked to work together to create a paper chain from one piece of construction paper. I explained the directions, laid out the supplies, and put them into groups of three to four before setting them loose. In my head, I envisioned smiles, laughter, and conversations based around problem-solving. Instead, I heard loud arguments just seconds before the tears started. It took about five minutes before chaos ensued. It seemed like *everyone* was crying or yelling at each other, and the majority of the class was coming up to me begging for help. It was obvious that they were not ready for an activity that relied so heavily on a slew of social and emotional competencies. I was so focused on planning an activity that I thought would meet students' need for fun that I missed the mark on making sure they had the skills to enjoy such activities. Immediately, I stopped the activity and brought the students back together just to say to them, "I notice this isn't going the way we want it to go. Why don't we stop for now and come back to this activity tomorrow?" Through the frustration, many nodded their heads in agreement. We left the materials where they were so everyone could calm down, and we moved on to a read-aloud.

That night I went back to the drawing board and thought through how to make this design challenge work best for this group of students. I relied on where they were developmentally and what I knew about them after a few days of being together. I recalled that many students were young seven-year-olds and probably worked best in partnerships rather than in the groups of three to four I had originally planned. I also thought about the fact that we had only been together for a couple of days and our developing social-emotional learning community (based on cooperation, assertiveness, responsibility, empathy, and self-control) had just begun. Taking all of this into consideration, I was able to modify the original design challenge and create a lesson that worked for the whole class.

Our second attempt at this design challenge resulted in smiles and laughter. As a teacher, this was the moment in my career that highlighted, underlined, and bolded the need for students to learn and practice a set of social and emotional competencies in order to be successful in and outside of school.

The following outlines the social and emotional competencies that are beneficial to teach and reinforce with second grade students along with specific skills for each competency.

Cooperation

Second graders' ability to successfully cooperate with one another depends on the amount of modeling and practice given to this social and emotional competency. At seven, students are most interested in working in pairs and, with practice, are successful working in partnerships. As second graders turn eight, they begin to gravitate toward larger groups and prefer group activities.

Second grade is the perfect time to plan lessons on how to work together and to focus on the following cooperation skills:

- Working toward a common goal

- Resolving conflicts with peers

- Being a productive member of a group

- Helping with tasks when asked

Assertiveness

For second graders, the skill of assertiveness refers to the ability of students to stand up for themselves and others by asking for help, as well as doing the right thing for the greater good of the group. Second grade is the time when students begin to work things out among themselves rather than needing help from the teacher. You will notice fewer tattling behaviors than in first grade as students have developed stronger problem-solving and communication skills.

The following are additional assertiveness skills to teach in second grade:

- Knowing different ways to ask for help
- Agreeing and respectfully disagreeing with others
- Making appropriate choices for the good of the group
- Taking initiative
- Working through challenging tasks

Responsibility

Taking ownership for one's choices and materials is a key skill for second graders. They are better aware of how their choices affect others along with the consequences of misplacing materials. This is often why you might notice heightened emotions from a second grade student who left school materials at home and vice versa.

Second grade is also a period in which students are developing their sense of social, civic, and digital responsibility. This is the perfect time to introduce students to lessons around digital citizenship as they begin to become more familiar with digital resources at home and at school. The following are responsibility skills to focus on in second grade:

- Taking ownership over choices and property
- Holding oneself accountable for actions—doing the right thing even if nobody is watching
- Identifying how one's actions affect others
- Demonstrating inclusivity

Empathy

Second graders are focused more on others and the larger community around them than they were in first grade. With this developing awareness of others in their community, second grade lends itself to opportunities for learning about and celebrating diversity and varying cultural norms. Students at this age can benefit from opportunities to learn from others who have different views and cultural backgrounds as a way to add to their current knowledge base.

Following are some skills to build empathy:

- Respecting and valuing diversity
- Respecting differing cultural norms
- Recognizing and managing one's own emotions
- Recognizing others' emotions

Self-Control

In second grade, students are moving from developing self-control over their bodies to developing self-control based on classroom rules and common guidelines. They are making decisions based on what is socially acceptable for the group around them and what is in the best interest of the group's guidelines. This makes the explicit teaching of classroom rules very important for second graders. They need to know what is socially appropriate and what that looks like in the classroom and in the school community.

Some skills to build self-control include:

- Aligning choices to classroom or school guidelines
- Making connections between individual actions and socially unacceptable behaviors
- Showing hope and perseverance
- Managing one's emotions

Ways to Support Social-Emotional Learning in Second Grade

- Use Morning Meeting to practice the five social-emotional competencies (cooperation, assertiveness, responsibility, empathy, and self-control).

- Plan short activities based around each skill, which allows students to demonstrate success with a skill and you to reflect on students' abilities and needs in order to plan future learning.

- Use role-play and Interactive Modeling to help students learn and practice all of the competencies.

- As a class, create anchor charts to reference throughout the school year. A popular format is a chart that indicates, with appropriate headings, what each skill "Looks Like," "Sounds Like," and "Feels Like."

- Provide consistent opportunities for practicing skills throughout the school year.

Range of Needs

Getting your class list can be one of the most exciting parts of preparing for a new school year. Before long, the names on your class list will come to life as bright-eyed, eager learners who are full of hope and excitement for the year ahead, and you get to be a significant part of the journey. In order to create the optimal learning space for students, it is important to consider the wide developmental ranges of the students in the classroom. The Birthday Cluster exercise, developed by Chip Wood, is one way to get a sense of the overall developmental abilities and behaviors that you are likely to see in class. Once you've completed this exercise, you can use it to gain a deeper understanding of the developmental needs of the learners in your classroom at any time throughout the school year. Your class's birthday cluster will show you whether the students you will be teaching are overall "young" (mostly seven) or "old" (mostly eight) or somewhere in between. Once you have this information, you will be able to create a learning environment, develop lesson plans, and craft expectations that align with the developmental expectations of students in a second grade class.

See the appendix, p. 339, for more on the Birthday Cluster exercise.

Younger and Older Second Graders

In any second grade classroom, you'll find a wide range of chronological and developmental ages. Some students will begin the year having just turned seven, while others might turn eight at the beginning of the school year. Both types of students may require additional research and special considerations. The following explores characteristics specific to second grade students who are chronologically younger or older than their peers.

Younger Seven-Year-Olds

Younger sevens might appear more like six-year-olds. They may be more talkative than the average seven-year-old and will be highly energetic. In addition, here is a sampling of a few key developmental characteristics to consider with young seven-year-olds:

- **They are highly social and energetic.** Use learning structures that allow conversations and provide opportunities for cooperative activities.

- **They tend to be physically active.** Provide a lot of energizers and short movement breaks throughout the course of the day.

- **These students are in a hurry and excited to learn but are not concerned with creating a perfect product.** Recognize their efforts and focus on their work process and learning rather than on the product. They'll grow into caring more about their finished products as they turn eight.

Older Eight-Year-Olds

Students entering second grade having already turned eight years old might demonstrate characteristics similar to nine-year-olds as they grow throughout the school year. They might gravitate toward larger groups of friends and enjoy working in teams rather than working alone or with a partner. The following are examples of points to consider when working with older eights:

- **They enjoy working in groups.** Give these students a choice to work in larger groups. Expect a mix of work and socializing.

- **They are interested in logic, classification, and how things work.** Provide hands-on experiences in math, science, and social studies that involve the use of concrete tools to explore abstract concepts.

- **They love to explain their ideas.** Provide different outlets for older eight-year-olds to explain their ideas, including poems, stories, recordings, or slide presentations.

The combination of second graders' eagerness to learn and dedication to their teachers makes this grade especially rewarding to teach. These children look to their teachers for guidance and rely on us for encouragement as they begin to take more risks in their environments. With an understanding of what to expect from second grade students in the classroom, you will be best able to meet the needs of the students you work with each day.

Second Graders

Common Characteristics	School Implications
Social-Emotional	

Common Characteristics	School Implications
• Are self-focused, with distinct likes and dislikes.	• Show appreciation and understanding of students. Private conversations and notes mean a great deal.
• Are inward-looking, sensitive to others' feelings, and empathetic.	• Use playfulness and humor to lighten their tension.
• Can be serious, moody, or shy.	• Stick to predictable schedules and routines. Provide coaching if these must change (assembly, special event, guest teacher, etc.)
• Dislike taking risks and making mistakes.	
• Need security and structure.	
• Like working and playing alone or with one friend; often find group work overwhelming.	• Give mostly individual or one-partner assignments.
• May change friendships quickly.	• Provide private, quiet spaces (reading corners, desks with privacy dividers).
	• Assign seats, but rotate them frequently to encourage working with a variety of classmates.

Physical

Common Characteristics	School Implications
• Are more coordinated physically (better at sports, for example); get confidence boost from newfound success in physical activities.	• Provide plenty of opportunities for outdoor games.
• Can focus on small, close-up things and prefer confined spaces; have difficulty seeing things far away, such as the board.	• Minimize tasks involving copying from the board.
• Often write and draw compact, small letters and figures; find it difficult to write big.	• Accept small handwriting (expecting big writing may be counterproductive). May be best to wait until they're older to teach cursive.
• Have many aches, pains, and injuries (real and imagined).	• Show understanding and reassurance about aches and pains.

Second Graders

Common Characteristics	School Implications

Cognitive

• Try hard to make their work perfect.	• Expect high-quality finished products. Let students see classmates' works in progress (to realize the importance of process as well as end product).
• Enjoy repeating tasks and reviewing learning.	
• Enjoy inquiry and hands-on tasks; often wilt under time pressure.	• Give open-ended assignments (write about a topic in their own words, investigate a phenomenon in science, etc.), but spell out clear steps to follow.
• Need frequent check-ins with the teacher.	
• Like to classify and sort.	• Eliminate or greatly limit timed assignments.
• Enjoy board and computer games.	• Give a heads-up that a work period is about to end.
	• Teach students ways to check in with you while you're working with others.
	• Provide a range of board games, puzzles, manipulatives, blocks, and craft materials.

Language

• Show significant growth in listening skills.	• Make use of students' growing listening skills. Gradually lengthen instruction and discussion periods (five to ten minutes at start of the year, fifteen to twenty minutes by end of the year).
• Speak with precision.	
• Enjoy one-on-one conversations, especially with adults.	• Provide listening centers and audio-books.
• Show great interest in words and have rapidly developing vocabularies.	• Weave wordplay, word games, and vocabulary activities into many parts of the day.

The information in this chart is based on *Yardsticks: Child and Adolescent Development Ages 4–14*, 4th ed., by Chip Wood (Center for Responsive Schools 2017) and Child Development Guide by Center for Development of Human Services at SUNY Buffalo State (New York State Office of Children and Family Services 2015).

Chapter 2
Effective Management

• •

Overview

During my college years, when I was home for winter break, I would substitute teach at the elementary school I had attended as a child. One year, there was a particular first grade classroom that had a reputation of being "challenging," and no one wanted to serve as a substitute for it when the teacher was out. When my mom heard the secretaries in the office talking about the dilemma, she volunteered me. As a substitute teacher, one of things I dreaded most was walking the class to places. I didn't always know where I was going, and I didn't want to look like I didn't know what I was doing if the class got out of control. So when it was time to walk this rowdy bunch of first graders to lunch, I told them we were going to play a game as we walked in the hall. I grabbed a timer and explained that as we walked to the cafeteria, I was going to time them and see how long they could walk silently. As we walked, I used every nonverbal reinforcer I could think of—smiles, thumbs-up, shocked faces, dance moves— to keep the momentum going. The class walked quietly down to the cafeteria, and seeing their joyful cooperation felt great.

Effective classroom management is more about what we, the teachers, do than what the kids do. Effective management starts with teacher leadership. At the helm of any well-run classroom is a good leader. At the heart of a teacher's leadership style is what that teacher believes about children and about the teacher's role in the classroom.

A leadership style that emphasizes establishing clear expectations and actively teaching students how to live up to those expectations helps students develop self-control and empathy for others. Effective teacher-leaders teach students how to behave responsibly, how to think ethically, and how to be positive members of the class community, both by example and through explicit instruction. A teacher's leadership style is reflected in their classroom management skills and their behavior management strategies. There are key practices that help create a calm, orderly classroom environment, the kind of classroom that promotes autonomy and allows students to focus on learning.

Teacher Language

Teacher language is one of the most powerful tools we have. What we say and how we say it matters. The way I talk to children today is different from the way I did five years ago, ten years ago, and certainly twenty years ago. Our teacher language grows and changes with time, experience, and reflection, just like any other of our teaching practices. When we use genuine words that are clear, simple, and direct, our teacher language is encouraging, empowering, and effective. Here are the key types of teacher language:

- **Reinforcing language.** This is our "go" language, used when we want students to keep doing what we see. Go beyond the general praise of "Good job!" and name the concrete, specific behavior you see.

- **Reminding language.** This is our "slow down" language. It helps keep students on track before problems arise or when they are just beginning to get off track by prompting them to remember for themselves what they have been taught to do.

- **Redirecting language.** This is our "stop" language. We use it when students are clearly off track, unsafe, have lost control of their emotions, or are unlikely to be able to fix things on their own at that moment.

Effective Management Begins With Being Proactive

I like to think of effective management as a pie, the biggest piece of which must be our proactive strategies. By taking the following preemptive actions, we set our students up for success.

Know your students. We have to be deliberate and purposeful in taking time to get to know our students. We have to know them individually, culturally, and developmentally, and we have to use that knowledge to guide our classroom management.

Set up your classroom space effectively. One year, our school made it a rule that when teachers move classrooms or change grade levels, they did not take their furniture with them. Instead, in an effort to make each classroom more equitable in terms of furniture and supplies, the teacher inherited whatever furniture was in the room when they moved in. Ready to teach my opening guidance lesson to a new class of kindergartners, I went into a room that had been occupied by a second grade class the year before. As I stood in front of the class, I saw a group of five- and six-year-olds sitting at desks so tall their chins were resting on the desktops and on chairs so high their feet were dangling inches above the floor. I looked over at their teacher, and she just smiled and said, "My old furniture is being moved in tomorrow."

The physical space needs to be organized in a way that fosters student safety and autonomy and that creates a classroom that says, "This space was designed with you in mind so that you can do your best learning every day." The physical space, furniture and all, must be suited to the students.

Teach and model classroom rules, and build in opportunities for students to practice following them. Routines and procedures are essential for any classroom and must be explicitly taught. *Responsive Classroom* techniques can be seamlessly integrated into the school day to teach students these routines and procedures. For instance, use Interactive Modeling to show students how to line up in a way that is safe and respectful. Guided Discovery can be used not only to excite students about watercolor paints, but to show them how to use these responsibly.

See the appendix, p. 332, for more on Guided Discovery.

See the appendix, p. 337, for more on role-play.

You can use role-play to show students how to decide who is going to go first when playing a game in a way that is fair and takes care of others.

Utilize simple strategies. A universal quiet signal, such as the calming sound of a chime or the soothing sound of a rain stick, can bring children's eyes, ears, and minds to focus without you needing to say a word.

Purposefully structure your day. Start the day on a positive note with Morning Meeting. Offer a midday booster shot with quiet time to allow students to rest, relax, and recharge for the afternoon's learning. Bring a peaceful close to the day with a closing circle, reflecting on the day's learning—both academic and social. Sprinkle energizers throughout the day—helping students to transition, get a pick-me-up during a long lesson, or learn how to be playful in a prosocial way.

The Reactive Piece of the Pie

Even when we take all of those good proactive steps, students will still misbehave, not follow the rules, and test the limits. They will still do these things to see what happens when they do them. Even in our well-run classrooms, students will break rules. It's part of how children learn and grow. The problem isn't so much that students misbehave but rather that if left unchecked or mishandled, this misbehavior can get out of control or disrupt learning. How we respond to misbehavior is important, and the way in which we respond to misbehavior can either preserve the dignity of the child and class community or tear it down.

When dealing with students who misbehave, keep these guidelines in mind:

- **Have empathy for the rule breaker.** Remembering why we break rules can help. And remembering that your students are not adults in little bodies will help too. They are still learning, still developing. Keep in mind also that they may come from home environments with cultural norms and attitudes that are different from those in the schools they attend. It can be hard for these students to figure out what rules apply under different circumstances, and when and how to follow them.

- **Approach discipline in a way that respects the child and preserves the dignity of the group.** Use strategies such as proximity and nonverbal cues. Use redirecting teacher language that is clear, simple, and direct: tell students what to do rather than what not to do.

- **Teach children to fix their mistakes and learn from them.** Use the *Responsive Classroom* technique of logical consequences to stop the behavior in the moment, to keep it from escalating, and to restore positive behavior quickly. I like to call this approach the trifecta because each of these three goals should be at the forefront of responding to misbehavior. When positive behavior is restored, circling back around with reinforcing language such as "Now you're doing it" or "Now you're waiting nicely" is key to sustaining the positive momentum. Make students a part of the conversation when misbehaviors persist, and have a wheel of options to help them work toward a solution.

Many teachers, both new and experienced, struggle with bouncing back and forth between autocratic and permissive extremes. They flip-flop: "No! Well, maybe one more chance. Now, that's it. I mean no." Sometimes teachers move back and forth this way because of a lack of support regarding classroom management. Sometimes it is because of increasing demands and students who are less equipped with school-readiness skills.

It's Not About Managing Children

Effective management is teaching children to manage themselves and creating the kind of classroom environment that allows them to do just that. When students can self-regulate in this way, they feel as if they have just the right amount of autonomy, responsibility, and support to meet the expectations of the teacher, the classroom, and the learning. Teachers will feel empowered to teach, with more attentive and engaged students to teach. And teachers will have more time and energy to address the social, emotional, and behavioral needs of the class. All of this will lead to a more positive learning community, which we'll talk more about in Chapter 3.

In the grade-level sections of this chapter, you will find wonderful stories, examples, and ideas to support you in creating an effective learning environment:

- Classroom organization, including spaces, supplies and materials, displays, classroom libraries, and technology
- Schedules, routines, and procedures
- Classroom management, including responding to misbehavior

Grade

Classroom Arrangement and Organization

In Chapter 1, we talked about the importance of knowing children: developmentally, individually, and culturally. When we know our students, we are better able to set them up for success. Imagine a group of kindergartners trying to learn in a sixth grade classroom: individual desks and chairs that are too high, no easel to allow for large-arm movement, and books that are too hard (and probably none of them are about dinosaurs!). It's not a good classroom space for five- and six-year-olds.

We know that developmentally, five- and six-year-olds are active learners. They need the opportunity to explore, play, and talk. This is how they learn. Kindergartners are successful with learning opportunities that allow them to make active choices about what they're doing. They want a sense of ownership and connection, and they want to feel significant. When we approach teaching with these key points in mind, we set kindergartners up for success.

Setting Up the Space

There is something satisfying about taking a pile of boxes and a stack of furniture and transforming it into a space for children's investigation and learning. The classroom should be an extension of who we are as a community, and therefore an arrangement should not be permanent. It can (and should!) shift and change as we live and learn in the space together. Watch the children: they will let you know what is and isn't working.

In a perfect world, every kindergarten classroom would have a large open space with built-in shelving, a double sink, a water fountain, and all the supplies needed to support the creation of such a space. In reality, though, we are often provided with imperfect spaces. Treat it as a challenge: spaces can do double (and triple) duty if we consider in a thoughtful and consistent manner how we will teach the children to use the area. Also keep in mind that for some children this might be their first classroom and for

See the appendix, p. 345, for more on classroom organization.

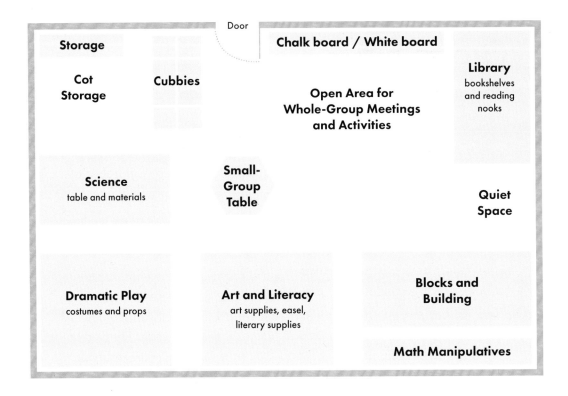

others their fifth classroom. No matter what your students' experience, the classroom should be warm and welcoming, with spaces for large-group gatherings, small-group work, and play.

Even the most beautiful classroom can quickly turn into chaos if we don't plan ahead and teach our students how to use it. One year, my teaching partner and I worked together to set up each other's classrooms. She had set a beautiful molded foam-letter puzzle rug as the base in the block area. Within fifteen minutes of arrival on the first day of school, the children had disassembled it. We hadn't considered the invitation that this lovely puzzle rug offered the children. Our mistake taught us three things:

1. **We were thinking like adults.** We saw the puzzle and thought, "This is something that seems pretty and appropriate for a kindergarten floor."

2. **Our students think like children.** They saw it and thought, "Ooh, what can I do with this?" They saw it as a toy for their use, as they should have done.

3. **We needed to teach the children the expectations and how to use different materials.** We should have anticipated the children's curiosity and that they would "explore" the rug, and explain that it was a rug to walk on and not one to pull apart. Or, we should have not used it as a rug at all.

We disassembled that puzzle rug and put it in a bin on the shelf so the children could build with it, trace the letters, or do any other number of things with it. A donated five-by-seven rug replaced the puzzle in the block area.

When you walk into a kindergarten classroom, you will find the children in many different positions: lying down, sitting at tables, or standing at easels or tables. Furniture should allow for this. You should have enough seating for every child in your class, but remember that some children may do their best drawing standing up. Easels and tall tables will allow for that. When I had enough space in my classroom for a teacher's desk, I kept everything in the drawers so the desktop could serve as a play and learning space for students. At the end of the day, I could simply pull out any work I needed to do.

Try to make sure as many areas as possible are doing double duty. Two shelves pushed together back-to-back might store art supplies on one side and book baskets on the other side. Pushed together, they are a perfect height for children to stand at and work on.

Classroom Spaces in a Kindergarten Classroom

Classroom spaces can be adapted as your class requires. Many of the spaces in this list could be combined or used differently at different times.

- Meeting area
- Tables for work
- Quiet area
- Science and observation area
- Dramatic play area
- Block area (can be combined with dramatic play area)
- Art area
- Classroom library (might be part of the meeting area)
- Computers and tablets
- Listening station
- Sensory bin or table

Meeting Area

Plan your meeting area carefully: you will be spending much of your time there. The meeting area is where your community comes together—it is the heart of the classroom. It's a place to laugh, sing, read, share, learn, and cry. It's a safe space where your class can do salsa dances and learn to count past one hundred. If your meeting area is also the block and dramatic play area, think of how you can keep those supplies from distracting the children. One colleague used a large sheet to cover the block shelf during meeting times. When it was time to use the blocks, the sheet was easily pulled away.

Consider ways to draw children into the meeting area as well. One year I was trying to teach myself to take better care of my plants, so I kept a plant on top of a shelf in the meeting area next to my chime and a book display holder where I'd put two of the day's read-alouds. This allowed me a central home for the chime, drew the children in every day to see some of the books we'd be reading, and helped me to remember to water my plant!

Supplies and Materials

Five- and six-year-olds are developmentally in a place where they are ready to learn and practice cooperation. Supplies offer a natural way for you to build this practice into the school day. Many classroom supplies, such as manipulatives and blocks, are ones that children naturally have to share, but consumables such as crayons and markers provide another opportunity.

Supplies should be well organized, labeled, and accessible for the children to retrieve and then put away. Your classroom space and setup will dictate how and where you store supplies, but you also have a lot of flexibility. For example, if your classroom has large tables, you can keep a materials caddy filled with supplies in the center of each of them, so that you will not need to clear and set them on a shelf after each use. As you think about where to place supplies, consider which materials children will use regularly at the same time so that there will be enough for everyone, and which materials will be used only in a particular station or in small groups.

Classroom Supplies

Community

- Class library
- Supply caddies (pencils, markers, crayons, glue sticks, scissors, and pencils)
- Dry-erase lapboards
- Dry-erase markers and erasers (socks or rags)
- Writing paper
- Plain paper
- Construction paper
- Pencil sharpeners (one for pencils and one that can also sharpen colored pencils)
- Math manipulatives (Unifix cubes, counting bears, loose parts, etc.)
- Science materials
- Glue

Individual

- Press-and-seal bag for individual reading materials
- Work folders to store work
- Cubby or hook area for backpack and coat

A kid-ready caddy can hold pencils, glue sticks, scissors, markers, and crayons—materials that children will use multiple times per day and need access to regularly. Before purchasing new caddies, use what you have. There may be unused caddies from an old classroom, or maybe a friend or relative has a stash of baskets or bins that they might happily donate to your class. You can also visit thrift stores to find baskets and bins made of natural materials.

When organizing a supply basket for kindergartners, use cups to organize within the caddy. Cups contain and hold the materials upright so children can easily find the color they need. Other materials such as glue, water colors, and collage materials can be stored in an accessible art area where children can retrieve them as needed.

Be sure that any supplies you don't wish students to work with yet are stored out of view, but still accessible for future use. At the beginning of the school year, I'd use curtains or butcher paper to cover shelves holding materials that the class wouldn't need until later in the year. In another classroom, I had a standing worktable with fabric attached around the bottom. Children could stand to work and play using the tabletop, and the space underneath behind the fabric was used to keep things we weren't using.

Classroom Displays

I once set up a display in the hallway outside our classroom with clothes-pins, each of which had a student's name on it. There was a sign above the display proclaiming: "We are proud of our work!" Every month my students would examine the work they had created and choose pieces to save for our end-of-the-year celebration, those to take home, and one they wanted to hang in our display. I'll never forget listening to one student take his mom by the hand at Back to School Night, bring her over to his displayed work, and proudly proclaim: "Look, Mama, I *made* this."

It was early in my teaching career, and it made me want to take down everything hanging on the walls and replace it with student work. Since then, though, I have learned the power of stopping and reflecting before making sweeping changes. Be sure to give some thought to what you choose to display in your classroom. Here are some key points to keep in mind:

- When children see their own work, it tells them that their work matters. It has value.

- When children see work done by other children—both in anchor charts and in displays—it represents something attainable. If another kindergartner can do it, so can they. (Note that exhibiting student work does not replace using anchor texts and displays for learning; rather, children should see a mix of anchors made by adults and anchors made by children.

- There is beauty in the evidence of learning. We've all seen beautifully curated spaces, but consider this: How beautiful is children's hand-writing as they are learning to print? How much do we delight in kindergartners' drawings of people and their favorite characters?

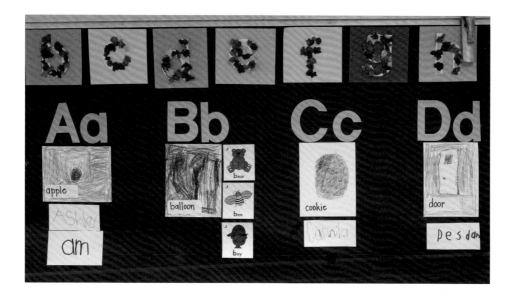

Kindergarten and preschool teachers have always understood the power of photographs and pictures to support student learning. For our earliest readers, the pictures can be their way in. For our youngest students, seeing children represented—seeing *themselves* represented—involves them and draws them in as almost no other way can.

Here are some things you can do to help children feel ownership:

- Include photographs of the children on your daily schedule.

- Create books together and put them in the classroom library.

- Incorporate photographs into displays as often as possible. If your class has collaborated on a mural, print out a few images of the children who worked on that mural and display them alongside the mural. Not only will they see the product they worked on, but they will also get the message that the process is valuable.

- Involve the children in preparing bulleting boards. When you are introducing crayons or markers early in the year, have the children practice by drawing on rolls of adding machine tape. You can then use these creations to swap out a premade border on one of your bulletin boards with child-made borders.

See the appendix, p. 350, for a list of recommended K–2 books.

Classroom Library

The library area has always been a favorite space for me and for my students. I've had many class libraries over the years, but the essence of them has always been the same: a welcoming space for children, filled with familiar books that the class had read and reread together, as well as with books the children had written themselves. The books were visible and accessible to the children, and they saw themselves represented in the books.

In a child-centered classroom, the meeting area is the heart of the classroom, and the class library is the soul. It's a space where children go to relax and calm down; to be challenged, soothed, and inspired; and to come together. They peruse the pictures in favorite books to look at photographs of interesting places and animals (sea creatures are a favorite) and to learn about ordinary people and change makers from the past and the present. Whereas a good book can transport you, a library of them can be transformative.

In simplest terms, a classroom library for kindergartners should have books they can reach, find, and put away independently. Kindergartners need to see the covers of books. A waterfall bookcase can help you to set books up for easy access by children and allow you to place favorite books on display. Baskets and low bins help corral books and keep them organized by topic, author, and idea, and have the added benefit of allowing children to see the covers as they flip through them. If your space has only tall shelf units, leave the bottom two to three shelves for your classroom library and the top shelves for your own storage. Distinguish student shelves from teacher shelves by covering the ones you wish to keep for your own materials with fabric or using baskets, and

Book Ideas the Class Can Create Together at the Beginning of the Year

- Our favorite colors
- My name is . . .
- I like to eat . . .
- Outside, I like to play . . .
- The people in my family
- My favorite fruit is . . .
- Today at school I played with . . .

make this distinction clear to students so you don't find an enterprising five-year-old climbing up to grab something they spy on the top shelf (this may or may not have happened to me).

The books you read should represent people of all races—this should be the norm, not the exception. Children need to see themselves represented. When your class is creating books together, the content—pictures and stories—should come from sharing what the children do throughout the day. For example, when children share about a favorite color during Morning Meeting, their writing that day can include drawing a picture in that color. The teacher can collect the pages and then type up descriptive sentences such as "Melinda likes the color blue," "Mariana likes the color red," and "Jovani likes the color purple," and glue these to each student's page. Students will feel a sense of belonging, and a classroom library that includes these books made by the class (and individuals) will not only showcase the importance of books as an important tool, but will also highlight that this is a class of writers!

A listening center might fit easily into your classroom library, or you can create one that moves. One year I was in a very small classroom. I asked friends for old MP3 players and then created four small listening center boxes that included a physical book, an MP3 player with one or two audio files, and a set of headphones. Your mobile listening station might include tablets or laptops that have your school system's digital reader bookmarked. Children can take the listening station anywhere in the classroom to read, and then return it to its home when they're done.

Technology

Technology can be so useful to incorporate into the classroom. The world is ever changing, and new tools and applications can be outdated within six months. It can be daunting to keep up.

I give myself permission to use, learn about, and try new tools with my students that will help support their learning, but I try to frame the experience by asking myself, "How can I help children build independence with this material?" A rule of thumb I arrived at with kindergartners was that I needed to model something at least three times before about 75 percent of my class would be ready to navigate it independently. For example, if I were scheduled to use the laptop cart on a Thursday morning, I would start modeling on Monday. I'd spend two to three minutes each on Monday, Tuesday, and Wednesday modeling how to open the laptop, how to click and type my username, and then how to click and type my password. Each day, more students would understand and know the steps. By Thursday, three-quarters of my class would be ready to attempt logging in on their own and one-quarter would still need my help.

Solving Problems

I taught my students to try to solve a problem three ways by themselves, and if they were unable to find a solution, they should find something to do in the basket I kept by each work station and talk to me at the end of the work period. The basket would have paper, crayons, and other activities that children could do so they could continue to be independently productive at the station.

Schools and districts will have different requirements for technology, so I encourage you to ask these questions when incorporating it into your classroom:

- How does this technology support my students' learning?
- How can I help them become independent with this technology?
- What skills is this technology supporting?
- How will I teach them to troubleshoot?
- What will they do if they can't solve the problem without me?

Schedules, Routines, and Procedures

The flow of the day is important for kindergartners. They are capable of sustained work, but they also need plenty of time for movement and laughter. Keep this balance in mind as you establish schedules, routines, and procedures.

Schedules

In many schools, teachers have little control over the master schedule. If that describes your school, think about where you do have control within the schedule assigned to you. One year, our master schedule had language arts in the afternoon. I had never taught language arts in the afternoon. How could I possibly meet the needs of my students with language arts in the afternoon? Kindergartners are tired in the afternoon—some of them have only recently given up an afternoon nap! But I was able to reframe it and think about this problem as a puzzle: What are the goals for my students? What do I know about five- and six-year-olds and how they learn best? How can I use that information to best structure this time? After giving it some thought, I was able to start the school year with the confidence that my students would thrive.

The result: I ended up loving language arts in the afternoon. We bridged the short rest time into a read-aloud time and that led into our reading workshop. Then we had specialist time. After specialist time, we finished the day with a writing workshop and had our closing circle.

Regardless of what your master schedule looks like, ask yourself these questions:

- What are the needs of my students at the beginning of the year? (Know that the schedule can grow and adapt as your students grow.)

- How can I structure the school day so that it incorporates an ebb and flow of calm work times balanced with active times?

- How will I include student choice throughout the day—and multiple times per day?

See the appendix, p. 341, for sample schedules.

Routines and Procedures

The first rule of teaching routines and procedures to kindergartners: teach everything! Young children have a natural curiosity and exuberance. Not only do they appreciate participating in discussions of how to use and put away materials, but they have so many ideas too. Taking the time so that you can model these procedures, and students can practice them, accomplishes many things: it establishes clear expectations so children don't have to *guess* what you want them to do, it allows for a collaborative conversation that lets children feel ownership, and it provides everyone with a baseline starting point and shared vernacular so it becomes a common experience to link back to.

See the appendix, p. 333, for more on Interactive Modeling.

During the school year (and especially the first six weeks of school), I use the *Responsive Classroom* strategy of Interactive Modeling to teach most of the routines and procedures we use. It becomes a familiar structure, and the children easily adapt to noticing and practicing. At the beginning of the year, I use the full seven steps of Interactive Modeling, and as students get comfortable with routines, I may shorten it or do a modified version, based on what my students need. As the children learn and practice, you'll see where the tricky areas are. A note of caution: when you notice children have difficulty with something, don't assume right away that it means it's not developmentally appropriate or that the children aren't ready for it. As much as you can, lean into observing and trying to understand what may feel like chaos. The observation might reveal the need for a simple change that can make all the difference.

One year I was teaching in a small classroom, and nearly all of my spaces had to serve double duty. There was a small shelf behind a workspace close to our interactive whiteboard where we kept our classroom supply of dry-erase lapboards and dry-erase markers. I modeled how to get the supplies and then how to sit down on one of the tape lines to get ready for a lesson. I noticed, though, that despite my modeling, children were having difficulty getting the materials, and I soon realized that having a table in front of the shelf was causing some of the chaos: children were going in on one side of the table and others were going in on the other side, creating a mess.

By taking the time to observe, I learned that the furniture was the problem, not that the students were not ready for boards and markers. I couldn't move the table, but I could be more specific in my directions. The next day I modeled going in on one side of the table, getting the materials, and then coming out on the other side. The one-way flow of traffic was exactly what my students needed.

A key lesson I learned early on in teaching kindergarten was that no matter how much I might enjoy talking and giving lots of exposition about things, kindergartners can only hold a few directions in their head at a time. When you're giving directions, keep it to a few brief steps—two to three steps at a time is best.

There are so many things we want to help our students do successfully, both in the classroom and at other times: when they're with a specialist, during field trips, and even in emergencies. To set children up for success, model emergency procedures well before your first fire drill. That first time the alarm sounds will be startling and might be scary for your students, so having a calm teacher and the knowledge that they already know what to do will help those first emergency practices go well.

Important Routines to Teach Early in the Year

- Unpacking and getting ready for the day
- Responding to the attention signal
- Coming to the meeting area
- Handling, reading, and putting away books
- Using materials (crayons, markers, scissors, glue sticks, and manipulatives)
- Having snacks
- Washing hands
- Following the classroom guidelines for bathroom use
- Leaving the classroom and taking attendance during fire drills
- Lining up to leave the classroom
- Walking in the hallway

When we take the time to teach routines and procedures to students, we are not only setting them up for success, we are also adding to their own sense of safety and predictability. When we teach in this way, children learn that we will show them what the expectations are, we will invite their ideas, and we will be there as they attempt and practice the routines. They learn to trust that school is a place where you can do hard things, because the teachers show you how to do them and support you as you are learning.

One year, we had an intern from a local college working with us. In early June, she was absent for a week to get ready for finals and graduation. I hatched a plan for our class to surprise her outside the college auditorium when graduation was over. Her college was only a mile away, and I knew my class could make the walk. I enlisted the help of a parent and set to work preparing my class to surprise our intern at her graduation.

Simple Ways to Fill Five Minutes During Transitions

- Bring a ring of alphabet cards and have students "whisper call out" whatever you show: name the letter, say a word that starts with the letter, say the sound, name an animal that starts with that letter, and so on.

- Play Copy Me and swap it up: have students copy you in reverse, in slow motion, in fast motion.

- Play a version of I Spy. Provide three clues for something you see around you, have the children whisper their guess to a partner, and then as the children offer their guesses, use the three clues to check to see if their guess meets all the clues.

Even now, when I tell that story, people look at me strangely. I've had many people come out and say, "You took a group of twenty kindergartners for a walk through the busy streets of Boston with only one other adult? *How?*"

My answer: I taught them how. My students were used to learning routines and procedures. They were used to reflecting on things that worked well and thinking about strategies for things that might be new or difficult. Our class regularly walked to the library, to local businesses for field trips, and to the public transportation station. They were comfortable waiting to cross streets and staying together. We talked about what we knew about being safe when taking walks together as a class, and we talked about some of the new things that we had to see and do. I even walked the route ahead of time and took pictures of a few things we would see along the way and showed them the photographs.

I share this story not to show how capable students are or how what we do with our students changes over the school year. This particular experience was one that we built up to over the course of kindergarten. In the early weeks and months, we modeled, practiced, and walked to places nearby. Then we went farther—crossed streets and took public transportation—as the children became more comfortable.

Children do best when we set them up for success by thinking through what might be difficult and helping to break it down for them. Remember, too, that transitions can be some of the trickiest times of the day—cleaning up from a learning block, getting ready to leave the classroom, or arriving at a specialist and having to wait a few minutes. Thinking through and modeling those transitions ahead of time can make all the difference.

Classroom Management and Responding to Misbehavior

Effective management is, at its heart, not about *managing students*. It's about teaching children to *manage themselves*, with guided, kind, and firm support from their teachers. As you read in the overview for this chapter, much of your management energy should be spent proactively setting up children for success. All of the strategies we talk about in this chapter fall within the realm of proactive management.

When I think back to my own experience of kindergarten when I was a child, I don't have a lot of specific memories of what we did. Most of my memories are feelings: the excitement of going to school, the warmth my teacher showed us. I remember the joy of singing, playing, and learning, and of feeling safe and loved.

A few years ago, I watched a video of Zaretta Hammond (author of *Culturally Responsive Teaching and the Brain*) giving a talk to a group of educators. She spoke about being a "warm demander of cognitive development." That phrase stuck with me because it is exactly who we need to be as teachers: we should be supportive cheerleaders who expect our students to do their best learning, with us reassuring, guiding, and facilitating that learning. We start at the beginning of the year with the high priority of building and maintaining a relationship with all of our students, and then, once we know them individually, culturally, and developmentally, we are able to anticipate what they will need and what will be hard for them, and adjust our teaching accordingly.

As kindergarten teachers, we have the opportunity to set the tone for our students' future years of schooling. When we start with an assumption of positive intent and notice the positives out loud to students, they know specifically what they are doing well: "I see kindergartners with their eyes on Marianna as she is sharing. You're really showing Marianna that you are listening." When we use the positive to bridge and support behavior we want our students to change, we're showing them that we have faith that they *can* change: "I see kindergartners with their eyes on Marianna as she is sharing. What can we do with our mouths to make sure everyone can hear her?"

When children make mistakes, the language we use when we respond can become their inner voice. As teachers, we must realize that we have an incredible opportunity to help shape the self-talk children will develop as they get older. We can make sure they understand that mistakes are part of learning and growing, and we can do this by cultivating a community where students talk about their mistakes, acknowledge their own mistakes, and show how they learned from them. We want to help children restore positive behavior quickly and safely, and we can do so by using a matter-of-fact voice: "Jeremy: pause. Use walking feet inside the classroom. Try again." We also want children to learn they can fix mistakes: "Oops, the water spilled! Here's a sponge. Let me know if you need any help."

When we respond quickly, calmly, and without judgment to a child who has made a mistake, we maintain their dignity and send a message to the rest of the students that mistakes happen, and we are there to provide support when they do.

Grade ❶

Classroom Arrangement and Organization

The physical classroom environment is the third teacher. Adults learn from students, students learn from adults, and we all learn from what the space offers. The space must be inviting, functional, user-friendly, and aesthetically pleasing. It's also a map that allows us to visualize learning and periodically revisit our journey to ensure that we understand the landscape and terrain. It's the canvas on which we explore, create, and reflect.

Setting Up the Space

I need a lot of time to get my space set up before school starts. I'll often set it up once, and then I'll revise and reconfigure the space a few more times before students arrive. More than once I've had a colleague stop by and say, "Okay, time's up!"—my cue to stop puttering, nesting, and procrastinating.

See the appendix, p. 345, for more on classroom organization.

Staying mindful about the space involves an ongoing process that keeps the focus on student growth and learning evolution, and it should be a space that communicates curiosity and joy. It's important to keep in mind, too, that the classroom space is not just mine. It's a communal space that teacher and student will inhabit together, and it will evolve as we evolve through the year. Somewhere along the way, I modified a familiar refrain to remind me: "This space was made for you and me."

Making sure each piece of furniture has at least two purposes is a benchmark I use in each classroom I set up or have been asked to provide advice about. Here are some ways classroom furniture can serve a dual purpose:

- A bookcase on wheels can also serve as a divider between the block area and the art studio.

- A five-foot-tall metal shelf can house art supplies *and* have a wire that extends from the top of the unit to the wall for displaying student work.

- Low benches placed against the wall can provide a safe place for students to stand on when using the whiteboard, and they can also serve as seats for students when they are reading or working. In addition, the benches can be relocated around the room.

- Plexiglas pieces hung from the ceiling can provide a place for displaying student work and at the same time form a visual boundary between workspaces.

- If instead of a large desk chair the teacher uses an office chair or a therapy-ball chair on wheels, it can be easily relocated for use at read-alouds and assessments, or it can even be used as alternative seating for students. (In general, minimize teacher-only spaces such as desks, file cabinets, or large desk chairs.)

Ideas for the Start of the Year

- A "Coming Soon" sign on bulletin boards covered with brown craft paper or neutral fabric

- A bulletin board border, created with white card stock, that students can decorate after introducing markers

- White index cards, written on in black marker pens, that label areas of the classroom—to which students can add background color after they've been introduced to watercolors

- Wall space dedicated to each student where they can add family photos or work samples of their choice

Of course, as teachers, we all wish to set up our classrooms from scratch, using furniture and supplies that are new or just gently used. In practice, most of us have to work with the materials presented to us. Here are the guideposts I've kept in mind when setting up classroom spaces.

- **Make the most of what you've got.** We inherit furniture or space and have to make the best of it and keep the status quo. The classroom layout may feel immutable—or is it? Often, small changes to simplify our space make it far more conducive to active and interactive learning than we might at first have expected. When setting up classroom spaces, I ask myself, "Does it communicate curiosity and joy?" The furniture and equipment, as well as the arrangement of the room, should kindle curiosity, engagement, and independence.

- **Think outside the box of your four walls.** Check with other teachers to see if they have furniture to swap with you. Scour online yard sales or swap sites for bargains. My children once had a talented and resourceful teacher with one of the most visually appealing and well-organized classrooms I've seen. Their teacher had a treasure chest she bought from the Goodwill store. She would place books from the classroom library in the chest, and then, when getting ready for a new book for read-aloud, she would look at the chest and give the children clues. When the children guessed correctly, she would unlock the chest, take out the appropriate book, and start to read. This inexpensive purchase not only brought something unique, exciting, and functional to the reading area, but it also leveraged six-year-olds' love of novelty and surprise.

> **Ideas for Midyear**
>
> - Anchor charts with reminders for routines, including photos of students performing the steps
> - Charts with lists such as "Books We've Read," "Greetings We've Used," and "Energizers We Love"
> - A "Wow!" board that displays student-selected work that highlights something from the week they are proud of, worked hard on, or learned from
> - A gallery of photos taken by adults or students that is printed and displayed on a bulletin board or saved to a monitor or tablet that can be used to run as a slideshow, with captions written or recorded by the students

- **Let student work be the focus.** When setting up this canvas, our space, keep in mind that children and their work will add color and design during the school year. It's not always necessary to prepare your classroom using commercially made posters and displays. When you have too many of these posters, they can quickly start to look like wallpaper or even neon signs. I've seen too many classrooms that, although designed with good intentions, provide such visual overstimulation that it is hard to see the trees amid the forest.

So don't feel obligated to fill the space when preparing for the new year. Start with an open canvas that says, "*Welcome!* We're ready for you!"

Supplies and Materials

First graders are enthusiastic and energetic, often in a hurry and full of ideas. Their space should reflect their growing creativity and need for frequent change of pace. As a first grade teacher, prepare for an often loud, messy, and joyful space. First graders *love* having various materials, especially those they feel are grown-up or new. Keeping new items covered with an "Opening Soon" sign sparks curiosity while setting a boundary. It will let you play up how special new writing tools are, and when you do an Interactive Modeling lesson, you can maximize your students' willingness to follow procedures so they can use the marker pens during writing workshops.

While schools and classrooms differ with regard to supplies (who provides, what's available, and whether students share them), keep a few things in mind as you select and curate supplies for first grade.

- **Choose materials with multiple uses.** By selectively choosing materials that encourage children to be creative, use their senses, ask questions, and engage in hands-on inquiry, we are setting up first graders for active and engaged learning. Children can understand and express their learning in various ways, and they will need a variety of tools to do so, no matter the setting or discipline. Writing tools and clipboards can be easily found and used when they are located in a writing area, and they provide children with logical and natural ways to plan and reflect on structures they have built with blocks or LEGO bricks. A class camera or tablet kept near a teacher's workstation will also allow children to capture an art project or dramatic play (and then share it in parent communication, with the appropriate photo credit).

See the appendix, p. 333, for more on Interactive Modeling.

- **Be explicit about how to use materials with independence and purpose.** Given that six-year-olds tend to dive into things and then hop right out, and that seven-year-olds can be quite focused, it's essential to use Interactive Modeling when introducing new materials and procedures, followed by a consistent soundtrack of reinforcing language when your students remember the actions you taught.

- **Remember that development matters.** It's important to keep expectations in check with developmental hallmarks. Finding an organized system that suits your needs and that can be accessible to students based on their developmental level can be a tricky juggle. One year, my partner and I read about yoga balls as alternative seating. We found funds for enough yoga balls to replace all of our first graders' desk chairs, and we provided Interactive Modeling lessons. We then began using the new seating, and soon students were bouncing, rolling, laughing, and, of course, falling off their yoga balls. It was bedlam. When we regrouped, we realized our first mistake was that we ignored the fact that six-year-olds tend to fall backward out of chairs (and yoga balls). First graders are often better standing, and we set up a workspace that allowed students to stand or lie prone. The yoga balls went to third grade classrooms, where nine-year-olds are restless but have greater physical coordination.

By choosing developmentally appropriate materials with multiple uses and introducing them with Interactive Modeling, we set students up for successful and deep engagement with those materials. Our ability to articulate our confidence and curiosity in employing these materials supports our faith in our students' skills and fosters student choice and accountability.

Organizing Work in Progress

When we use Interactive Modeling to show first graders how to place papers in a pocket folder, they will be able to store pieces safely in their own folders. But it may prove challenging to get those folders neatly and accessibly stored in a desk or magazine box. My first graders' folders for writing, math, and reading were each a different color. A large basket was used for work in progress and labeled "WIP" for any work I did not need to check. This basket was big enough to hold all the folders but not necessarily in a tidy stack. In addition, the basket had a top handle so it could be easily moved to areas where we could access it (often the Morning Meeting area) or stored on a shelf when not used. As the year progressed, we separated folders into baskets for each subject, and several students enjoyed the challenge of offering classmates reminders or sorting folders into the appropriate basket. Any finished work I needed to check was placed far away from our WIP basket to avoid confusion. A colleague used a similar system but by midyear had added a hanging file box for finished work that allowed each student to add their finished work to a file labeled with their name.

Classroom Displays

Displays of first grade learning reflect the very lively and fluid nature of life in the classroom community. There is always something (or lots of somethings) happening in first grade. Displays celebrate our efforts, both individually and as a group. Creating space to document the learning positions us to make meaningful connections to the curriculum while also generating enthusiasm and pride in learning. As shared earlier, our physical environment is both the map that lets us visualize our path and the canvas on which children add color and texture.

For this reason, we need to design displays with student engagement in mind. Learners of all ages need white space, especially if we want them to be drawn to specific anchor charts or truly useful or aesthetically pleasing items on the wall. Displays that are filled with commercially bought items designed by exacting adults convey the message that the adults are the creators and that children are the passive observers. Classroom walls shouldn't be too busy, but rather more like an inviting museum exhibit that lets the observer interact and engage with what's on display in ways that are meaningful, accessible, and pleasing.

The Great Tree Project

One December, the students in my first grade class were working on measuring, and there was a lot of buzz about the holidays and the rare sighting of snow in our city. We had read several books about evergreen trees, and there was much discussion about how you could build one from triangles. We decided to measure a hallway bulletin board, which ended up being easily divisible by three. We sectioned off the bulletin board and decided our class would fabricate a snowy tree scene. This required planning, since we would need to gather supplies, and cooperation, as tasks and roles were divided.

The work commenced. As expected, our "Great Tree Project" was met with zest and zeal—and a messy, active frenzy channeled by short periods working in an acutely defined space. There were a few bossy voices but a deep sense of caring to ensure that everyone in the group got to build part of the tree. We were fortunate, too, that mother nature was on our side and allowed us to pause our work sessions for a rare romp in snowflakes. It allowed us to stop and examine the live trees dusted in the snow with the same boisterous and enthusiastic language overheard as we worked on the Great Tree Project.

As the year progresses, observe how students engage with displays and invite them to be co-creators. First graders can suggest work to display, help create borders, and use push pins to secure and create areas that allow them to reflect on their work and that of their classmates. Be sure to snap photos of your displays throughout the year, too. You'll want to see how you as a teacher grow in this area, and these photos can often provide reflection points during the year for first graders to think about their own growth!

Creative two- and three-dimensional displays allow us to capture the work we do together each day. Jobs can be posted for the week, allowing first graders to learn the job expectations, practice multiple times, and develop a sense of ownership. A list of those jobs can also be placed on the wall, and photos hung to indicate who has which job. Maintaining charts of "Greetings We Know" (or energizers) helps the class to see how these lists have grown over time and allows them to go back and revisit favorites. A chart of "Books We've Read" enables us to see our shared reading, mainly when displaying these books on a dedicated shelf or basket.

Displays can also be used to support classroom management. When students engage with displays, contributing to them and reflecting on them, they begin to understand their role in the classroom community. We can design our displays so that they draw students' attention to the importance of cooperative behavior approach to classroom management, which values cooperation over compliance. Here are three strategies for focusing displays to encourage cooperation in the classroom.

1. **Use visual clues to support students in following routines.** Charts cocreated by adults and students serve as reminders of routines, procedures, and expectations. These reminders reinforce Interactive Modeling lessons, capture the essential steps for classroom practices and procedures, and highlight our expectations. For example:

   - Routines to follow when choosing a book or packing up at the end of the day

   - Ways that we can show we take care of others

   - Behaviors a listener demonstrates

   These steps empower students to have a voice and an interest in using displays they cocreated. It reflects the shared power and control in the classroom. The steps also guide classroom management by providing a shared infrastructure that doesn't always require a teacher to be involved.

2. **Document the learning process.** Learning is a fluid process. While we may teach the same lesson on persuasive writing each year, that predictable path will be peppered with different observations, challenges, and successes. Our displays can show our goals (an "I Can" statement or a hypothesis we are investigating) and the unique steps we follow on our path of learning. Two- and three-dimensional work samples displayed on walls or shelves (or even hung from the ceiling) show we value student work and will build a sense of community as we observe and reflect on the displays. As work concludes, reflecting as a class on what we've learned, what skills we developed, or what questions we still have will allow us to connect our work to the curriculum and celebrate individual and group success.

3. **Remember that voice and agency matter.** With first graders, adding student voices as often as possible is key to helping students see their agency and capabilities and where they have room to grow. First graders can often write all or part of the captions for displays. They can certainly dictate an audio recording describing a display or ask an adult to type captions or explanations. Their pride in doing such essential and grown-up work builds community and relationships, not to mention skills.

Classroom Library

Once I was asked to take a long-term substitute position in a first grade classroom. The children were enthusiastic, kind, and diligent with their work. There were many exciting parts of the classroom space, with many excellent resources woven throughout it—except for the classroom library, which looked like a forgotten and overgrown trail that had not seen many visitors. Shelves of books sporadically aligned and inaccessible to students may as well have been marked with orange danger signs saying, "Keep Away!" The library was uninviting, challenging to navigate, and overlooked.

See the appendix, p. 350, for a list of recommended K–2 books.

I spent the first week dedicated to getting to know students, keeping an eye on how the library was being used. Spoiler alert: it was not used. A small part of my heart broke as I watched those lonely books. The children would reluctantly pull one when nudged, but then would mindlessly flip through the pages and leave the book haphazardly in the vicinity of the class library.

In my second week, I set to work culling books that were in terrible shape or woefully out of date. I recruited a few curious readers to sort small stacks of books into categories and smiled at the children's glee when they discovered something unique. Soon we had a few baskets of leveled or "just-right books" first graders could choose and read independently. We had science and sports books in labeled baskets and used several other ways to sort books in an accessible and appealing way. To support this activity, I recycled a flimsy cardboard book easel and found four baskets at the craft store for under ten dollars.

Part of this process included recruiting students to sort and label books. At the hardware store, I was able to pick up laminated tags that had a hole at the top that a ring could fit through to secure it to the basket. My first graders knew how to use marker pens and labeled the tags.

Once we reconfigured our library, there was much excitement. We talked about it while it was "under construction," but we didn't use it for several days. We admired from afar, visualized and dreamed about how we'd use the books, and discussed what we found intriguing. Finally, the anticipation peaked. Using Interactive Modeling, we learned to select, read, and, when finished, reshelf these books that we had worked so hard to curate and organize. Our remodeled classroom library was popular, and we had to expand its physical space after a few weeks.

Technology

Much of technology depends on what you have access to. Work with what you have, and leverage it in manageable pieces. Here are some ways to use technology to support first grade learning:

- Maintain a digital file of student photographs that can be printed out when assigning work and classroom jobs and when creating displays.

- Provide tablets with audiobook apps that can be listened to during quiet time or meditation apps that can be used in a peace corner.

- Set up digital reading over the course of a few days as one of the academic choices for a set period.

Schedules, Routines, and Procedures

Each year, as I plan my class's daily schedule and how to teach routines and procedures, I invest a small chunk of time in revisiting developmental considerations for six-year-olds as a reminder of how fresh these first graders are when they arrive. They will be excited and then exhausted. They will want to move and construct and then stare into space as they mindlessly eat snacks. Everything will be exciting!

Schedules

Many of our schedules in schools are determined without teacher input or are based on a myriad of competing priorities. Most of us, even if we have a voice in our schedule, have to work with what we're given. Consider what is outside of your control (arrival, specials, lunch, and dismissal), and then set your sights on making the most of the time inside your classroom. In one school where I taught, I was fortunate to have most of our specials in the afternoon, yet sometimes I thought, "What will we do all morning?" The trick for me was to think through the pieces I could control, accept the pieces I had to work around, and then employ the most predictable and consistent routines. Our day started with Morning Meeting in each classroom, and then I would add some movement, perhaps a quick energizer or a kinesthetic English/language arts lesson. I kept mini-lessons brief and designed our activities to give students the opportunity to practice them for a stretch of two to five days—and to help slow down the propensity of first graders to race through everything. We went outside in the morning, even if it was simply for an organized walk or to take our snack outside as a picnic. There were some years when lunch came before recess and others when the order was reversed. I found it worked better to get outside before eating, but by keeping the schedule predictable either way we were able to plan accordingly. I held firmly to a fifteen-minute quiet time, but made it longer when kindergarten was half day and my first graders were in school for a full day for the first time. I let those who fell asleep, sleep, and communicated my reason with families and colleagues. For the most part, those who napped at quiet time did so just a few days a week or adjusted and slept less or not at all by October. Our afternoons varied based on special schedules. I found that packing up before specials allowed us to use those last five to ten minutes of the day for closing circle, a ritual that let us bookend our day and celebrate our time together.

See the appendix, p. 341, for sample schedules.

Routines and Procedures

Everything is new in first grade. Using Interactive Modeling around routines and procedures will prove to be one of the best investments you can make. When your eager learners can see and practice how things work in your classroom, they will be empowered to act and interact with materials and classmates in positive ways. The skillful and frequent use of reinforcing language reminds them that you see their efforts and that they are on track.

Don't assume that first graders know how to use pencils or crayons, and consider whether or not they have all had that experience. Determining your students' level of experience may involve a quick reflection, or it may require a thorough examination of equity among your students. Either way, where these tools are used and how they are cared for will vary from classroom to classroom. For example, I'll acknowledge that students may have experience with scissors by holding a pair up and asking, "How many people have used these?" I'll take a few responses to determine how they know about scissors and where they've learned to use them. I'll then validate those responses by saying, "That's fantastic! So you know they cut things and we have to be careful! I want to show you how we take them out in first grade, what they are used for, and how we put them away." As I model using scissors, I emphasize how cool and useful they are, but also how it's a big responsibility to use them on materials they are meant for and to always, always handle them safely. If I do see any students using scissors in a way that is unsafe, they will lose the privilege of using them for that day, and I assure them that we'll try again another day.

Cutting Without Scissors

Once, when I took scissors from a math thinker who was preparing cards for a game, he asked me how he was going to cut up his math work. I responded by saying, "Hmmm. How *will* you solve that problem." A classmate showed him how to fold the paper over the edge of the desk and tear it. I don't recall that child—or any other student in the class—walking with the blades pointed outward again.

Classroom Management and Responding to Misbehavior

One fall, my co-teacher and I were focused on practicing reinforcing language and Interactive Modeling. We were doing Interactive Modeling for routines and procedures seemingly every hour. We mixed up groups between the two classes, because we knew we'd collaborate for math and reading groups and we wanted to make sure we were providing the same modeling. Sticky notes with sentence starters for reinforcing language were tucked in places around our rooms and in our plans so we would remember to use these often. With all the repetition, we started to feel like a broken record and had a few good laughs at ourselves.

But it worked. We still talk about that year and how, despite having larger-than-usual classes and some real behavior challenges, we did some incredibly deep learning and truly enjoyed our classes. By practicing routines and hearing explicitly what was working, students gained our trust as well as trust in themselves, in each other, and in their teachers. At our fall conferences, one parent shared that their child had made the "oddest observation," saying, "I notice that you look like you are angry but you are remembering to talk calmly to me."

First graders thrive on encouragement and can easily—but usually only temporarily—be crushed by criticism. They are motivated to learn and will take on new tasks when guided by calm, caring adults who make the time to model and nurture positive actions.

Setting up kids for success matters, but it is not a guarantee of anything. In first grade, we should expect to repeat ourselves often—and should do so calmly, if not cheerfully. When students make mistakes, I keep in mind one of the best pieces of advice I received. Chip Wood, the author of *Yardsticks*, reminded me to focus on the deed, not the doer. By depersonalizing the mistake, we let children see that they are not bad or good but rather that they are in control of their actions and they can embrace the opportunity to fix mistakes and learn from them. It was an important lesson for me. I learned to focus on the small actions I could improve or fix when my teaching was not what I wanted it to be—rather than to catastrophize that I was a horrible teacher.

Grade

Classroom Arrangement and Organization

I begin each school year by asking myself questions to guide me as I consider how to arrange and organize the classroom. I reflect on how I would like the classroom to feel in the new year and what has worked well for my second grade students in past years. This thoughtful, self-reflective question-and-answer session allows me to really tease out what matters to me and what might work best for this year's students.

Setting Up the Space

One year I found myself at odds with how I wanted the classroom to feel and what was developmentally appropriate for second graders. I wanted our space to feel collaborative and to say to students, "We're a community." After many hours of consideration, I decided to put together the room's small square tables to create large table groups of at least eight students, allowing for large spaces for group work.

After the first week of school, though, it was clear I needed to rethink my classroom design. Students were having trouble navigating while sitting at the large tables. They struggled while trying to share the table's community supplies, and it was difficult for them to assert their needs when they wanted to work quietly and others were talking loudly. These were skills the students would learn and practice during the year, but at this point, they were not ready for this setup. I had not placed enough emphasis on a key component of classroom design: developmental appropriateness.

I redesigned the space in a way that met their developmental needs. I went back to the smaller tables and arranged them in smaller groups of two to three. Almost immediately, it

Repurposing Material

Going through older lesson plans, materials, well-loved books, and resources can be a challenging and often daunting task. Consider if any materials could be repurposed and used by a colleague before tossing it away.

was clear that students were more comfortable sharing a learning space with one or two other students and that they were better able to manage table supplies and learning. By the middle of the year, after much learning and practice on collaboration, we were able to move some of the tables together to create groups of four. That proved successful, and toward the end of the year, when we were working on larger class projects, we arranged our tables of four into tables of eight. Our learning and practice over the course of the year resulted in the students being able to now work in tables of eight.

Flexible Seating

Using flexible seating replaces traditional classroom seating and offers students options on where they can sit during learning times. It will also give students chances to rock, wobble, bounce, lean, or stand while working. By giving second graders a choice of where to sit, we provide them with opportunities to practice the important social and emotional competencies of self-control and responsibility. To help ensure success with flexible seating in the classroom, consider the following:

> ### Popular Flexible Seating Options
>
> - Rocking chairs
> - Wiggle seats
> - Therapy balls
> - Scoop rockers
> - Pillows
> - Crate seats

- **Have a plan.** Take your time introducing flexible seating choices to students. Think through which choices might be best to introduce at the start of the school year and which ones might be best saved for later in the year.

- **Identify the purpose.** Really consider each option's purpose and function in your space. Ask yourself, "Which of these choices will best serve the students in this space?"

- **Outline the expectations and procedures.** Consider using Interactive Modeling and anchor charts when introducing each flexible seating choice to students so they have a clear understanding of the expectations and procedures.

- **Be proactive.** Once you have developed a plan, identified the purpose, and outlined the expectations and procedures, consider using role-play to model potentially tricky situations related to flexible seating. For example, ask your students, "What if more than one person wants the same seating option?" or "How do we set up and clean up responsibly?"

For second graders, stability and structure in the physical space is key to their success. They need a well-designed classroom where they know where their personal items are stored, where they sit, and where to find the things they need. Whatever setup you decide on, plan to stick with it unless any glaring concerns arise. While small changes in the classroom's setup and organization throughout the school year shouldn't cause any disruptions, it is important to keep these changes to a minimum and to share any upcoming changes with the class. For example, if a seat change is necessary, you can let students know that tomorrow is "New Tablemate Day," and they will get to find their new table and tablemate when they come to school the next day. This brief announcement will prepare students for the change so they are not caught off guard the next day.

Learning Spaces

When considering student seating and workspaces, think about additional learning spaces that would be beneficial for second graders. Ideally, your classroom would have a space large enough to gather the entire class comfortably for your daily Morning Meeting, read-alouds, and whole-class

Organizing Work in a Second Grade Classroom

- Gathering area large enough for Morning Meeting and whole-class learning
- Classroom library
- Technology
- Creative (art, music, dramatic play)
- Math manipulative storage (student accessible)
- Indoor recess materials (games, puzzles, intricate coloring pages)
- Exploration area (science, social studies)
- Time-out space
- Small-group learning space (guided reading groups, guided math groups)
- Teacher workspace (optional, dependent on your needs)
- Student storage (cubbies, storage drawers, backpack hook)

lessons. Bringing everyone together in one space provides second graders with a sense of safety, security, and community. A whole-class gathering space also meets second graders' physical development, particularly related to their vision. Because information at a distance can be difficult for second graders to see and read, seat students closer to the display of any information on a digital whiteboard, television screen, or dry-erase board so their eyes are better able to focus on the information.

As you think about other learning spaces in your classroom, keep in mind that second graders benefit from spaces that foster their developing mastery of their environment. Make sure the items in learning spaces around your classroom are well organized, labeled, and introduced so that students will have a clear understanding of their purpose and guidelines for use in the classroom. Proactively modeling such spaces and materials will benefit the classroom community in the long run.

Supplies and Materials

Second grade is a year when students are more aware of their role in taking care of their own personal learning materials. To help second graders practice being responsible for their learning items, offer a balance of individual supplies and community supplies. Individual supplies might include pencils, colored pencils, markers, and erasers, while community supplies might include items that the group shares, such as glue, paint, and dry-erase markers. By offering a balance of the two, you allow students to practice caring for their own materials while also fostering a sense of togetherness through the use of community supplies.

One classroom supply you will need is a large stock of erasers. Second graders are perfectionists and will erase and redo their work several times before feeling comfortable with the final product. To avoid torn papers and students spending a majority of their work time erasing and redoing their work, plan to use Interactive Modeling to teach students how to erase properly and move on to the next task quickly.

When purchasing school supplies, remember to base what will be community supplies or individual supplies on what might work best for your students and their families. For example, I use a lot of sticky notes in my classroom and know to add that to my list of items to be donated to our classroom. If you are looking for support in purchasing items for your classroom, consider discussing your needs with your Parent Teacher Organization/Association, contacting local businesses for support, reaching out to the families of students in your class for donations for certain items, or looking into a setting up an online wishlist or fundraising page.

Classroom Displays

When I begin thinking about items to display on the walls, I ask myself two questions: "What can we create together?" and "How will this space represent us?" These questions allow me to think more deeply about the purpose of the posters, anchor charts, and displays that will hang in our classroom. While it may be tempting to cover the classroom walls with beautiful premade displays, your space will be better served with those created by you and your students together and that represent the students in your classroom community. As you plan your classroom displays, consider the following guidelines:

- **Each item hanging in your classroom should serve a purpose.** Before hanging anything on your walls, be clear on its purpose and function for students and their learning. When your wall displays, anchor charts, and bulletin boards serve a clear purpose, students will see the classroom walls as tools for learning rather than as decorative spaces. Ask yourself, "What purpose will this serve for students in our community?"

- **Change displays throughout the year.** We have all been there—you display something students did in October and it is still hanging there in December. The year can go by quickly, and before we know it, two months have passed since you've displayed any new student work. While some displays might be specific to a time of year and some will serve as a yearlong reference for students (for example, classroom rules or a birthday chart), think about your walls, bulletin boards, and displays as representations of what is happening at that moment in the classroom.

- **Display work at all stages.** Students work at different paces. Some students will have already finished two pieces of writing while other students are editing their first piece. This is true for many academic content areas. When displaying student work, make sure to include work in all phases: "Just Started" (beginning), "In Progress" (middle), and "Finished" (end). Set aside a space in the classroom for student work because it is very helpful for students to observe the work of their classmates at different phases. Due to the personal nature of students' work and the sensitivity that comes with being a second grader, give students a say on what to display. Ask, "What would you like to display for others to notice?" I'll get responses ranging from "I want everyone to see how I drew the main character of my story" to "I want everyone to see how I solved all of these math problems using the number line." Students can then hang what they wish the class to see. I've also had students respond by saying, "Nothing," which tells me they might not be ready for others to see their work, they might be less confident in what they are working on at that moment, or the situation makes them feel too vulnerable. Some students would

> ## Keep It Readable
>
> Due to the difficulty second graders have focusing on things that are far away, remember to hang items on the walls at eye level and encourage students to walk up to any charts or posters they might need to reference.

rather their work stay private, and that is okay. Honor their feelings around their work, and know that eventually, and with your support, they will begin to see themselves as competent, confident learners in all areas.

Classroom Library

See the appendix, p. 350, for a list of recommended K–2 books.

A robust library is another significant space in a second grade classroom. Second graders are transitioning from learning to read to reading to learn, and they are beginning to gravitate to chapter books that are a part of a series. You might notice less interest in picture books as the year progresses. As you see this transition happening, think about storing books that are no longer interesting for students so that you can make space for more engaging reads. Second graders are also becoming increasingly interested in their communities and cultural similarities and differences between them and their peers. They will often ask the most pointed questions as they try to find meaning and connect on a deeper level with their classmates. Second grade is the perfect year to explore these questions, and diverse literature can assist with those conversations.

Suggested Book Topics for Second Graders

- Chapter books that are a part of a series
- Joke and riddle books
- Graphic novels
- Children's magazines (*Scholastic News, Time for Kids*)
- Nonfiction books about famous people, animals, and science

Second graders also enjoy cozy spaces where they can curl up and read a good book, write a story, or draw. Walking into a second grade classroom during an independent work time, you will find students huddled in corners or underneath tables. One colleague of mine understood this about her second grade class. She placed a pile of pillows in each corner of the classroom and created a "fort" by draping fabric over a couple of tables. These cozy, comfy spaces were the most popular flexible seating choices for students.

Consider setting up the classroom library together as a whole group at the start of the year. Second graders enjoy classifying items and are able to identify books that might "live" together in the same shelf or bin. Once students have helped put similar books together, they can create labels to identify the contents of the bins and expectations for the use of the books in the library. Assembling a classroom library together provides students with ownership over the space, and it leads to increased care for the books in the library as well as for the organization of the library.

Technology

As technology becomes increasingly important in teaching and student learning, consider the role it can play in your second grade classroom. Second graders have grown up in a highly technological world and navigate the technology space well. When I am having trouble with technology during class, I always invite the group to help me problem-solve, and they are usually able to figure out the issue before I am.

While second grade students are skilled with finding apps to explore and know how to effortlessly change their virtual backgrounds, an area of needed learning and support is their role as digital citizens. As second graders become increasingly aware of the endless possibilities social media and the internet offer, they need specific learning opportunities on how to use such platforms in a way that fosters responsibility and respect. As you introduce ways in which technology will be used in the classroom for learning, consider integrating lessons around digital citizenship too. Using technology in the classroom, though, does not mean we throw out other tried-and-true tools and practices that support peer socialization. We want to provide students with plenty of opportunities to socialize and play, while also providing opportunities to interact with the digital tools around them.

Schedules, Routines, and Procedures

Structure and stability are important for second graders, and they will do best when you stick to a predictable schedule and establish clear routines and procedures. This predictability will offer them a sense of comfort and control of their environment.

Schedules

When creating your daily schedule, consider the following:

See the appendix, p. 341, for sample schedules.

- **Plan for the best time to learn.** Second graders are curious and begin the day with gusto. They are more equipped to take on any "heavy lifting" learning concepts at the start of the day rather than in the afternoon. Plan academic content that requires sustained thinking and work in the morning, and schedule more energizers and breaks in the afternoon. In addition, second graders will need longer periods of work time to produce their best work. Make sure students have at least thirty minutes of work time for each content area. Allotting forty-five minutes for each learning block would be ideal because it would allow fifteen to twenty minutes teaching and the remaining thirty to forty minutes could be used for student work time or small-group instruction.

- **Organize the school day around fixed time slots.** Some components of the day will have time slots that cannot be changed (for example, lunch, recess, and specials). Begin planning a schedule by first noting the fixed time slots and then adding specific learning blocks.

- **Build in nonnegotiable practices.** Think through any practices that occur during the school day at a specific time, such as Morning Meeting, and closing circle. These practices are essential to your students' development, and therefore they need to be slotted into specific time slots.

- **Take into account the needs of individual students.** As you create your ideal schedule, remember to note any special considerations students may require. For example, you may have students that have scheduled additional math support three times a week. You may need to modify your schedule to accommodate their absence.

- **Schedule time for movement.** Second graders need time to move in structured ways through the use of energizers during class and through unstructured ways as part of recess. You might consider offering students two recesses, one in the morning and one in the afternoon. Frequent use of energizers can also offer opportunities for movement throughout the day and can be particularly helpful when transitioning from one learning opportunity to another.

- **Be flexible.** Once the year begins, you might need to modify your original schedule based on the needs of your students. They may need more time to work on writing than you had anticipated, or you might realize that a second recess in the afternoon would serve them well. Use the first few weeks of the school year to try out the schedule and make any minor changes. At the beginning of the year, I'll say, "We are trying out this schedule to see how it works for us. Just know that I might make a few changes to make our time at school even better." When a change is needed, I'll say to the class, "We get to do math right after Morning Meeting today. We are going to see how this works for us!" We'll then spend time reflecting on the change before it becomes part of our daily schedule. Having the teacher model flexible thinking can benefit the sometimes rigid-thinking second grader, and being flexible with the daily schedule is a great place to start.

Routines and Procedures

Students come to second grade from many different prior learning environments, and their understanding of routines and procedures at school are based on those previous experiences. With this in mind, do not assume they know your expectations in the classroom. Instead, view the teaching of routines and procedures as an opportunity to create an equitable classroom community built on shared knowledge and experiences. Using Interactive Modeling will break down routines and procedures into small parts and allow students opportunities to observe, discuss, and try out each behavior. When students are able to see and experience an expectation, they will remember it.

Key Routines to Teach Through Interactive Modeling

- Participating in emergency drills
- Lining up
- Making transitions between activities
- Getting materials for learning
- Cleaning up materials
- Keeping items in cubbies organized (coats, book bags)
- Organizing workspaces
- Understanding signals for attention
- Turning in work
- Reading with a partner

Classroom Management and Responding to Misbehavior

In my first year of teaching, my enthusiasm for starting a job I had dreamed about since I was seven years old was paired with a wonderful mix of students. I told my parents, "I cannot believe they pay me for this! I would do this job for free!" My parents responded, "Hold on to that enthusiasm because one day the shine will wear off and you'll need to remember why you're doing what you're doing." I chuckled and continued to share all the awesome details of teaching that first year.

I began my second year of teaching with the same enthusiasm I had felt the first year. I could not wait to meet the new crew as I thought about the fun that would unfold that year. Very quickly into the year, though, things went awry, and I faced management and behavior issues. I remember one day looking around the classroom, wondering what was happening and what I was doing wrong. I followed all the suggestions from colleagues on how to manage this group of students. I tried to be tougher, I took away recess or anything that seemed remotely fun for them, and I used candy and stickers to reward those students who followed the rules. I soon had a behavior plan for each student and employed a color-card system that assigned a color to each student based on their behavior. But all this system did was publicly show the class who was behaving badly and who was considered good. In fact, students began naming their classmates using these labels. I was also spending an exorbitant amount of time filling out the behavior plans.

After making it through that year, I regrouped. I knew there had to be a better way. That summer, I had dinner with a good friend and shared my struggles of the previous year. She had done her preservice teaching experience at a school where teachers used *Responsive Classroom* practices, and she loaned me several books on these practices. It was love at first read, and the rest is history.

After much reflection on that second year, I realized two things. First, I had very few strategies to support students demonstrating difficult behaviors. Second, classroom management is much more than responding to misbehavior. I look back on that second year now as a gift. I learned more about myself as a teacher than I ever expected and became a better educator because of that year.

Classroom management is not about managing the students. It is about supporting students in ways that help them develop skills to manage themselves. When we focus on student needs and dig into the ways we can support students' social-emotional and academic development, we can create an environment where students feel empowered and intrinsically motivated to make appropriate choices. When we focus on the language used with students, and interact with students from a place of respect and understanding while modeling these interactions for students, students will learn to use reinforcing and reminding language.

Second graders benefit from language that reinforces expected behaviors and promotes positivity. They can often get caught up in thinking, "Am I doing this right?" or "This is too hard; I can't do this." The more we can reassure them that they are in fact demonstrating their understanding of our class expectations, routines, and procedures—and yes they *can* do this—the more successful they will feel in the classroom. Reminding language is also beneficial for second graders because they can forget these expectations. Second graders are trying to remember everything, but just as adults can forget things, students can forget the expectations for classroom routines and procedures too. Be proactive and consider how you might use reminding language to support students in remembering the classroom expectations, routines, and procedures. The language we use has the power to help students see themselves as confident and competent learners with the ability to make choices for the good of the classroom and school community.

My second grade teacher inspired me to become a teacher. I don't recall what we actually learned that year, but I do remember how she spoke to us: her kind tone, uplifting words, and smile are etched in my fond memories of that year. What we say to students matters and has the ability to impact them far beyond what we might see in the classroom. What my second grade teacher may not have realized is that the way she talked to me built the foundation for the rest of my years as a student and learner and impacted my own teaching. I've experienced firsthand as a student the power that words can have on student success. I think about her at the start of every school year as a reminder that we will all learn the typical academic stuff this year, but what really matters is how students feel about school. What do you hope your students will remember about second grade?

Chapter 3
Positive Community

• •

Overview

One summer, I taught a weeklong workshop for a school in Massachusetts. With my husband and two preschool-aged young daughters, we left western New York for what should have been a six-hour car ride. We were enjoying a peaceful trip when the engine suddenly cut out and our car had no acceleration. Fortunately, there was a service plaza just up ahead and we were able to coast into it.

We had few options. We could get the car towed, but it would leave us stranded at the plaza. The nearest rental car company was over fifty miles away, and any relatives were a couple of hours' drive from where we were. After some research on the internet, my husband figured out a way that we could drive—as long as our speed stayed between twenty and sixty miles per hour. Any speed below or over that, and the engine would cut out and possibly not turn over again. We decided to go for it.

Not wanting to tax the car any more than we needed to, we kept the air conditioning off and the windows down, hot air blowing in, the road noise making conversation impossible, and the wind in my ears making me motion sick. For the next five hours, my husband managed to keep the car going between twenty and sixty miles per hour—on the interstate and through towns, driving on the shoulder and coasting through E-ZPass tolls. But we made it.

As grateful as I was to be safe, I was exhausted and beyond stressed when I arrived at our hotel. As I approached the front desk, the young woman behind the counter greeted me: "Hi, you must be Amy. Welcome! We're glad you're here. We have your room all ready. Is there anything we can help you with to make your stay more enjoyable?" I'm not sure how she knew my name, but to be welcomed like that made me feel significant, valued, and cared for at a time when I really needed it. Fighting back my tears of gratitude, I told her that she had no idea how much I needed a warm welcome.

Positive Community Starts With Hello

Whenever I talk about the importance of positive classroom communities, I think about that horrendous trip and the power of a kind hello. It's important to set a positive tone from the start. Students come into our classrooms from diverse backgrounds and unique experiences. Some walk in with the right frame of mind for learning and playing together, but some will come in on the heels of a challenging morning. It might be something such as not being able to find the clothes they wanted to wear or a fight with a sibling over the TV. It could be something much more stressful—violence at home, a family member leaving (again), or the lack of basics such as food, shelter, and stability.

Just as I felt at the end of my rope after that car ride, students sometimes feel at the end of their rope when they arrive at school. But then they enter a classroom that says, "You belong here. This classroom is yours and *ours*. You can find success here. You are safe here." They're greeted with a smile and a hello from their teacher and peers. The student feels valued, significant, and cared about. Whatever stress—big or small—that had been weighing on them feels lifted. They know they can start their school day and will be able to face whatever comes their way.

Positive Community Embraces Discipline

At the heart of a positive community is an equitable, fair, and just classroom where there is mutual respect and dignity for all. Cultivating a feeling of belonging and significance for students takes careful consideration and purposeful planning on the part of the teacher. There are certain key practices that can be used throughout the day to help create safe, predictable, joyful, and inclusive classrooms where all students feel valued and engaged in learning. Students feel known by you and their classmates, not just by their names but by their interests, likes, dislikes, strengths, and challenges. Relationships are vital, and they can be strengthened by helping students make connections with each other.

We create a positive community when we approach discipline primarily in a proactive way. In Chapter 2, we talked about effective management being like a pie with a big proactive slice and a much smaller reactive slice. The same analogy applies here when we look at discipline, with the proactive slice of the discipline pie being the larger slice.

When you think about the word "discipline," what comes to mind? I used to think discipline was simply and only "what I do when a student misbehaves." In other words, discipline was my reaction to something negative a student did. But I've learned to think about discipline in a much broader way. The word "discipline" comes from the Latin word *disciplina*, which means teaching, instruction, education. In other words, we should associate discipline with acts of learning rather than punishment. If discipline is integral to teaching, then discipline is a good thing, and discipline leads to learning.

See the appendix, p. 334, for more on logical consequences vs. punishment.

My mom, a former teacher, always had favorite chapter books she liked to read to her class. When she retired, she said that was the part she'd miss the most—sharing a treasured story, knowing what parts would make the students laugh, pausing at a cliffhanger and hearing the students say, "Noooo, keep reading!" and revisiting those passages that would make her tear up even though she had read the story every year.

Although we all have things we love to teach, have you ever thought of yourself as a teacher of discipline? Just as we see ourselves as teachers of reading, math, and science, we also need to see ourselves as teachers of discipline.

Teaching discipline requires being both kind and firm. Being kind means having empathy toward the students individually, culturally, and developmentally, and understanding what they need. Being firm means that there are structures and boundaries in place to set developmentally appropriate limits that help each student and the class maintain self-control.

When I started teaching, I knew that part of my job was to discipline students, but I didn't want to spend a lot of time doing that. I found myself getting frustrated and saw discipline as taking away from my "real" job of teaching. I know now that discipline can and should be taught. It's not my job to discipline students; it's my job to teach discipline. By knowing my students individually, culturally, and developmentally, I can design active, interactive, and appropriate learning experiences to teach discipline.

How Many Times . . .

Over the years, I have found myself, often out of frustration, saying to students, "How many times do I have to tell you to line up quietly?" "How many times do I have to tell you to slow down?" "How many times do I have to say stop talking?" But I would never use the phrase "How many times," though, when it comes to academic skills. I couldn't imagine myself saying with a frustrated tone, "How many times do I have to show you how to do double-digit addition?"

When it comes to academic skills, I have always had a different mindset. When students were struggling, I would say to myself, "Okay, they are not getting this concept—how can I show it in a different way? What part of this are they getting? Let me reinforce that and build on it. Let me give them more time and practice."

I've now learned to use this same mindset with behaviors, routines, and social skills. I've replaced "How many times" with "Let me show you again . . . let's practice."

Proactive Discipline Starts With Rules

The way I approach establishing rules has changed over the years. I used to use a preprinted poster with rules that our school provided. It listed the character traits our school promoted, and beneath each trait we were to write some basic rules for our class. For example, under "Respect," I would write, "Don't talk when others are talking," "Don't get out of your seat," "Don't hit or push." No matter how many "don'ts" I came up with, there were always things the students did that were not on my list. Once a student cut the wires to the new earphones. I didn't think to put that on the rules poster. I also didn't really like the aesthetic of the poster. So instead I would go over the rules on the first day, and then hang the poster behind the door and never really mention it again.

Learning about the rules-creation process as taught in the *Responsive Classroom* approach changed how I went about setting up rules. I established the class rules collaboratively with the students and connected the need for rules back to them—their hopes, dreams, and learning goals. Including students in the process gave them a vested interest in following the rules and in being positive members of their class community. Before setting the rules, we would talk about what we hoped to do and learn and what we wanted our class to be as a community.

Rules Versus Procedures

Rules are different from procedures. Rules are general global ideals that articulate how we should live and be in our classroom. Procedures are the steps or expectations that support those rules: counting to five while getting a drink is the procedure; taking care of others is the rule. In my teaching, the rules have become a living document in the classroom that we talk about and reflect on often, not a dusty document hanging on the back of the door. I use phrases such as "our rules say," "one of our rules is," and ". . . is following the rule of." Just as students change and grow throughout the year, so do their hopes and dreams. It's important to revisit those goals, set new ones, and reflect on how the rules are helping students to meet those goals. When developed well, the rules become an anchor to so many good proactive practices, including Interactive Modeling, role-play, and teacher language.

Once classroom rules are established, they need to be translated into expected behaviors. These expected behaviors need to be taught so students know how to follow the rules. Just as they do in any other content area, students will need direction and instruction in prosocial behaviors, as well as opportunities—lots of opportunities—to practice them. Then we can use our teacher language to support the following of the rules. Envisioning language will help students see themselves successfully following the appropriate behavior. Reinforcing language will tell students they are doing the right thing and help them see connections between their actions, their positive behaviors, and the classroom rules. Reminding language will help students remember what they have learned about following the rules so they can remind themselves of the expected behavior. Redirecting language will help guide students back to the correct path when they veer off track. (Teacher language is discussed in more detail under each grade level in this chapter.)

Rules Process

What follows are steps to build a foundation for rules and support students in learning how to create and follow them.

Begin With Hopes and Dreams

Within the first two weeks of school, help students set personal learning goals for the year:

- **Set the context.** Paint a picture for students about what they will be learning. Use a slideshow of pictures from previous years, a tour around the classroom, or letters from the previous year's class describing their experiences.

- **Express your hopes and dreams.** Set the example for this activity by sharing something for which you are hoping for in the new year. For example, "This year, I hope that everyone will be kind and caring so we can all do our best learning every day."

- **Have students express their goals.** Providing students with examples of goals can be helpful. To support students in choosing appropriate goals, ask guiding questions framed using specific language. For example, rather than asking, "What do you hope to do this year?" ask, "What do you hope to learn about in our classroom this year?"

Connect Goals to Rules

Next, work with the students so they can see how the rules are helpful:

- **Cocreate rules.** Help students see the importance of rules by connecting the need for rules back to their goals: "If these are some of the things we hope to do this year, what might be some rules that could help us?" Students are likely to answer with "don'ts," so be ready to turn them into "dos." When they say, "Don't hit," turn that into a positive action by saying, "You're right, we don't want to hit. We need to be safe with our bodies."

- **Consolidate.** Help students to think about all their ideas and then make a final list of three to five rules that express taking care of ourselves, others, the classroom, and our work.

You can support students in deepening their investment in the process by having them express their commitment to following the rules. Celebrate and share the rules by making a classroom display, book, or poster for students to sign and decorate.

Build Discipline in the First Six Weeks

Use the first six weeks of school to establish rules, routines, and procedures. At the start of the year, begin the process of establishing rules and teaching students how to follow the rules, while you support the process through directed use of teacher language. Doing so will help in maintaining a positive community throughout the year.

Maintain a Positive Classroom With Morning Meeting

Starting each day with a warm and welcoming Morning Meeting will help create and maintain a positive community—and it will give you and your students an opportunity to review and update the class rules as the year proceeds.

See the appendix, p. 335, for more on Morning Meeting.

Not only does Morning Meeting honor the power of "hello," but it also gives students a consistent time and place to explore and to practice important social skills, the opportunity to connect with each other in prosocial ways, and a way to warm up for the upcoming day of learning. When students' needs for belonging, significance, and fun are met in

Morning Meeting and Inclusion

An inclusive classroom says your voice matters, your experiences matter, your culture matters, and you matter. Morning Meeting provides a daily opportunity for students to see that they matter and gives everyone equal value in the class community. Through greetings, sharing, group activities, and a morning message, students can make connections with each other, learn about cultures and experiences that are different from their own, and see different perspectives. Not only does Morning Meeting merge social, emotional, and academic learning, but it's also an opportunity to elevate each student's voice and culture, celebrating diversity, inclusion, and equity.

positive ways, classrooms will not be filled with students' misguided—and often negative—attempts to get those needs met. And their energy will be more available for learning, which is why positive community and engaging academics are such an integral part of teaching discipline. (For more, see Chapter 4.) By modeling the social and emotional competencies (cooperation, assertiveness, responsibility, empathy, and self-control, or C.A.R.E.S.) every day, and providing students the opportunity to practice these competencies, you will equip the children in your class with the skills they need to navigate their learning environment successfully.

Teacher Language: Planting the Seed of Student Potential

We create a positive community when we use envisioning language to plant the seed of student potential, which will take root and allow students to believe in themselves and their capabilities. They will learn to set goals, work hard, and problem-solve. When a student shows persistence in completing a challenging task, you might say, "You're a hard worker and you're continuing to try to figure that out." Addressing students by acknowledging their specific identity reflects what we value in our classrooms—creativity, kindness, critical thinking, persistence, and responsibility—with the hope they will carry the spirit behind these words beyond the walls of our classrooms: "Kind kindergartners, we are about to work with partners for math centers. Let's think about how we will take care of our partners when we play math games." Through our language we name positive actions in the classroom and positively label how students work through academic and social challenges: "You both figured out a way to work together on this—that's teamwork!" Carefully chosen words conveyed with a fair and friendly tone communicate inclusivity and allow us to shape each student's sense of belonging and significance.

Equitable Responses to Misbehavior

We create a positive community when we respond to misbehavior in ways that are equitable, that are respectful of the individual student, and that preserve the dignity of the group. Once we have filled the proactive slice of the discipline pie by engaging in good practices such as the rules-creation process, Morning Meetings, teacher language, and Interactive Modeling, we don't want to then lose it through the way in which we respond to misbehavior. Discipline that preserves dignity is crucial to maintaining a positive class community. It helps students develop empathy when we, as teachers, model it. It conveys to the students that the behavior, or the damage done, is the problem—rather than any individual student.

Even when we have that proactive piece of the pie, we still need to have a reactive slice that we'll use for discipline. In busy classrooms, students will go off task: playing with things in their desks, daydreaming, or sitting and doing nothing. These behaviors are not necessarily disruptive. But left unchecked, these behaviors can lead to more disruptive actions such as blurting out, talking back, or responding defiantly. To keep these off-task behaviors from escalating and get students back on track quickly, use strategies such as establishing proximity (just moving closer to the student); providing visual cues (pointing to an anchor chart, a checklist, a picture schedule); and offering reminding language (giving guiding directions such as "Tell me what you are going to do to get started on this work").

Even with the proactive steps we take to guide them, our students will still misbehave. They will break the agreed-on classroom rules, they will forget, they will move too fast. They will test limits, which is part of growing up. These behaviors are disruptive to the classroom and to learning. When responding to these kinds of misbehaviors, keep the following guidelines in mind:

- Stop the misbehavior in the moment and respectfully help students get back on track.

- Give students the opportunity to recognize and fix their mistakes, and help them to repair the damage.

- Help students develop self-discipline by learning internal control of their behavior.

- Guide students to grow in their abilities to use positive behavior skills.

When we approach misbehavior with these goals in mind, we can stop problems from escalating and help prevent similar problems from happening again in the future.

Redirecting language, or what I think of as "lifeguard language"—clear, simple directives in ten words or less—can help get students back on track quickly by telling them what to do: "Benjamin, walking feet in the classroom" or "Sophia, cleanup time. Books go back in the bag." The key is to intervene immediately before the misbehavior escalates into bigger disruptions. For example, if we don't rein in Benjamin's running, it can result in someone getting run over or someone's work getting trampled; if we don't get Sophia to clean up, this inattentiveness can turn into fooling around with friends and missing directions for what's coming next. Small misbehaviors can quickly become bigger disruptions if we don't get to them early.

There are two guiding principles to keep in mind in order to address student misbehavior equitably. First, it's important for students to understand that misbehavior will result in logical consequences. Second, as teachers, we must understand that there is no single response to misbehavior and that we must treat students as individuals when they make mistakes or break rules.

Logical Consequences

To better understand logical consequences, let's first look at what they are not. Logical consequences are not nicely packaged punishments. These two approaches to discipline, logical consequences and punishments, are actually quite different both in theory and in application. Logical consequences are meant to help students fix mistakes and get back on track. If students feel bad because of making a mistake or losing control, that's not a bad thing—that's their conscience speaking to them. Logical consequences are not meant to make students feel bad, but rather to stop the misbehavior and give them the opportunity to restore the positive behavior quickly. If you ever find yourself wondering whether disciplinary action is a logical consequence, ask yourself the following questions:

- Is this *respectful* of the student? Am I focusing on the specific behavior rather than on the student's character? Am I being both kind and firm?

- Is this *related* to what has happened? Does this help the student actually fix the problem?

- Is this *realistic* for the student and for me to follow through on?

In general, logical consequences fall within one of these three categories:

1. **Break it, fix it.** This is about taking responsibility for an action, whether it be intentional or not, and doing something to fix the mistake. A student is running in the classroom and knocks over the science materials. The student then is responsible for picking those materials up and putting them back the way they were.

2. **Loss of privilege.** Think of a privilege as an opportunity to follow the classroom rules autonomously. Using classroom materials such as markers or scissors is a privilege. Sitting next to a friend is a privilege. Running an errand to the office is a privilege. When a student is not being responsible with that privilege, the logical consequence is

for the student to lose that privilege. Keep in mind, though, that it's not just about losing the privilege—it's about giving the opportunity to try again.

3. **Time-out.** This third category is about a chance to regain self-control in order to be a positive member of the class community. It's not about going somewhere, sitting down, and feeling bad about what happened, which would be a more punitive approach to a time-out. Telling students to think about what they did isn't as helpful as asking them to think about what they are going to do now, at this moment: how are they going to regain control? Teaching students the ways to self-regulate is an important part of using time-out as a logical consequence.

No One Response to Student Misbehavior

It would be wonderful if there were a magical book that said what to do and how to respond when a student misbehaves. You could just open it up and find out exactly what to do when a student (again!) interrupts or cuts the wires to the new earphones. A one-size-fits-all approach may seem like

Discipline and Issues of Equity

When looking at issues of equity, discipline should be a part of that conversation. Discipline can be one of the biggest promoters of inequity. There are students with less developed social skills, and there are those who possess a different set of skills that don't always work best in a school setting. Students who experience higher levels of external stressors and who are more likely to struggle to meet the social and behavioral expectations of school tend to experience more punitive measures in response to misbehavior. Examining our beliefs around discipline—our goals and how we view our students—will allow us to approach discipline in a way that will make the situation more equitable and more effective. When we view discipline as teaching, our approach to discipline becomes not only a vehicle for us to build and maintain a positive community but an opportunity for students to learn valuable skills such as exercising self-regulation, taking responsibility for actions, and making reparation, all of which will ultimately make school a more successful experience.

a good idea, but it isn't the best way to respond to misbehavior. Every student and every situation is unique, and the reason behind the behavior will be different for each student. Instead, responding to misbehavior should be about consistency when intervening. Even though the misbehavior will vary from student to student and from situation to situation, your response needs to be consistent.

I look at responding to misbehavior in terms of a wheel rather than as an escalator with limited options. The escalator approach tends to be a one-size-fits-all model in which we keep upping the ante: the student does this, I do that, and when the student does that, I respond with this, and up we go until we reach the top—out of responses but full of frustration. With the wheel approach, we have different options of responding to the same behavior. We take what we know about the student and the situation to decide our best first guess in how to respond. Sometimes we nail it, and the response stops the misbehavior and restores positive behavior quickly. But if the first response doesn't stop the behavior, we can go back to the wheel and try another response.

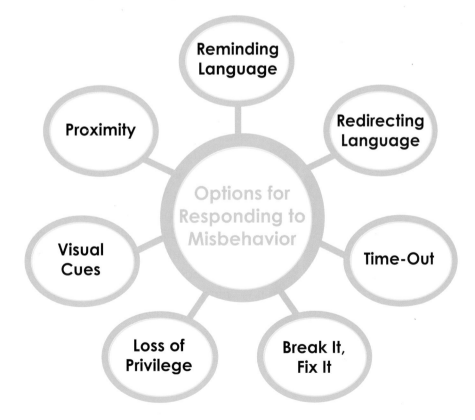

It's not always about finding the magical logical consequence. Sometimes it's about changing what *we* do. When my daughter Ella was three years old, she used to kick the back of my seat when we were on long car rides. My husband didn't appreciate the leather seats getting scuffed by little feet, and he would get upset with Ella. Then I would get upset with him, and it made for an unpleasant car ride. At first, I would say things such as, "Ella, show me how you should be sitting in your car seat." When that didn't work, I tried saying, "Ella, feet down!" That also didn't work, so I then moved to saying, "Ella, if you keep kicking my seat, when we get to the hotel you'll lose out on swimming in the pool." That didn't work either. When you're three years old and trapped in a car seat for a long time, you're going to want to move your legs. Then one day, an epiphany: I had an automatic seat! I pressed the button and the seat moved forward. Ella could now move her legs without hitting my seat. This led to another epiphany: sometimes it's not about finding the ever-elusive, magical logical consequence. It might be more about changing your expectations or about looking at the situation and managing the environment to help manage the behavior.

Equity in a Positive Community

We create a positive community when we provide opportunities to succeed that are equitable, fair, and just. Creating equity can be a complex issue. We want high-quality education for every child every day, but that can be a tall order when our students come from diverse backgrounds, cultures, and experiences, thus leaving big gaps for historically marginalized groups. Reflecting on our classrooms and the messages we send is a good place to start. The practices we do to build a positive community should create an environment that says to *all* students:

- I belong in this space.

- My teacher and classmates know me—what I like, what I'm interested in, what I'm working on right now.

- I am a member of this social and academic community.

- The work I do here is important to me and this community.

- This environment is designed for me to do my best learning.

- I can find success here.

We create a positive community when we teach student-to-student problem-solving strategies. We can only begin to teach these strategies when we address students' basic needs:

- **Belonging.** Most children have the desire to be a part of a group and to have a sense of connection with others.

- **Significance.** Children desire to feel important in a group, to know that they matter.

- **Fun.** Children desire to find joy in themselves, within a group, or in an activity.

Students will seek ways to get these needs met—either in positive or negative ways. Misguided attempts to gain a sense of belonging, significance, or fun can lead to conflicts with peers: trouble sharing materials, using a mean tone of voice, excluding others, teasing, or playing too roughly.

The teacher's response can help stop the misbehavior (as it should), but it won't necessarily repair peer relationships. This is where student-to-student problem-solving is effective. Student-to-student problem-solving skills allow students to resolve conflicts peacefully and restore positive relationships. A classroom cannot maintain a positive community without it. Here are some strategies to develop student-to-student problem-solving skills:

- **Students need to be able to differentiate which problems are safe for them to solve by themselves and which ones will need an adult to resolve the issue.** The number-one rule in problem-solving is safety. If a problem is scary, dangerous, and may cause someone to get hurt, students need to tell an adult. For problems that are bothersome and might be upsetting but not dangerous, students should resolve the issues themselves. You can call these "Big Problems" and "Small Problems" or "Grown-Up-Size Problems" and "Kid-Size Problems" or something along those lines to distinguish the size of the problem.

- **Students need to know the difference between telling/reporting, tattling, and asking for help.** Telling/reporting is letting an adult know about a big problem so the adult can help resolve it. Tattling is letting an adult know about a small problem just to complain and get someone else into trouble. Asking for help is asking an adult to assist in resolving a small problem that the student has tried to solve but that isn't going away.

Several problem-solving strategies can be taught through children's books, think-alouds, Interactive Modeling, and role-play. Students should understand that problem-solving can be resolved promptly and peace can be restored quickly by using our words, changing what we are doing, changing our thinking, and taking care of our feelings.

Imagine this scenario: Ben, David, and Sarah are playing with building blocks. David and Sarah are working on building a castle, but Ben wants to build a fort with the blocks and feels as though no one is listening to his ideas. Ben's voice is getting angrier, and David tells Ben he thinks forts are boring.

Here are some strategies to teach students to consider in such a situation:

- **Choose something else.** Teach students that if what they are doing isn't fun or isn't going well, choose something else to do. Ben is upset when David and Sarah won't listen to his ideas, so he could instead decide to go and do a coloring activity with Emma.

- **Talk about it.** Teach students to say how they feel and what they need. Ben could say to David and Sarah, "I feel *mad* because *I want to do some of my ideas too.* Can I get to pick something for us to build?"

- **Let it go.** Teach students that sometimes others will say or do things we don't like. Rather than being stuck on thinking about David's comment that forts are boring, he could tell himself to let it go and move on. Ben says to himself, "I like forts and I don't think they are boring. I'm going to keep having fun building my fort."

- **Compromise.** Teach students that sometimes we have to be flexible and let someone else choose or decide. Ben says, "I really want to make a fort, but it's okay. We can do the castle this time."

- **Say "stop."** Teach students to be clear and firm when telling another student to stop. When David takes the blocks Ben was using, Ben can firmly say to him, "David, stop taking the blocks from my fort. I'm using those right now."

- **Share and take turns.** Teach students how to ask for and offer a turn. Ben says, "Hi, can I build blocks with you?" Sarah responds by asking, "Ben, do you want to play with us? We're building a castle." Teach students how to give a polite no. Ben says, "No thanks, I think I want to build a fort today. Maybe tomorrow."

- **Take a break.** Teach students that if they are really mad and upset, they should take a break and settle down their feelings. Then they should think about how to handle the problem. Ben takes some deep breaths as he watches the colors change on the sensory bottle at the break spot.

After explicitly teaching these strategies, you can help students develop student-to-student problem-solving skills. You might consider these options:

- **Share children's books on the subject.** Here are some I've found useful:
  - *Help! A Story of Friendship* by Holly Keller
  - *Matthew and Tilly* by Rebecca C. Jones
  - *Best Day of the Week* by Nancy Carlsson-Paige
  - *Don't Squeal Unless It's a Big Deal* by Jeanie Franz Ransom
  - *It's Mine* by Leo Lionni
  - *The Rainbow Fish* by Marcus Pfister

● **Display visuals of the problem-solving strategies you've taught.**

● **Create a peace table.** A peace table is a specific place where students can go to work out a conflict, either on their own or with teacher guidance.

Actively developing and maintaining a positive community in your classroom is time well spent. In the grade-level sections ahead, you will find specific and age-appropriate suggestions for creating a safe, predictable, joyful, and inclusive environment where all students have a sense of belonging and significance.

Grade Ⓚ

I was having one of those days. I had had a long, exhausting meeting before school, left my coffee in the copy room, forgot my lunch, and arrived at my classroom only four minutes before students were to arrive. I tried to take a deep breath before getting ready to greet my students, but my heart was not in it. And then the first student arrived. Jenny greeted me with an enormous grin and a piece of paper in her hand. "Ms. Howard!" she called out as she practically danced down the hall. "I am so glad to see you! I made you this picture last night! Look at your hair!"

Her joy was palpable. I looked at the picture: she had drawn me with purple hair because the week before I had put on a purple wig to celebrate something ridiculous. I couldn't help smiling, and my exhaustion soon melted away. Later, I looked around my classroom at the children playing and learning in their stations, and I felt a surge of gratitude for our community. That is the power of a positive community for everyone, children and adults. We create a space where we are safe to feel and express all of our emotions and come together as a group of people who will hold us up when we need it.

Teacher Tone and Demeanor

Language is one of the most powerful tools we have as teachers. Unlike technology, which we have to rely on our school system to provide, it is a tool we already have and can practice with immediately. We have the power to build students up and to help shape how their inner voice will talk to them and how they will talk to each other. The words we choose send deep, lasting messages and empower students to learn, grow, self-correct, and reflect. We can use our words to empower students to resolve disputes together, to remind them how to help clean up safely, and to reinforce their kind words and actions.

Kindergarten students are resourceful and learn many things almost by absorption, often realizing how clever they are. Our job as teachers is a gift: we can help them feel that sense of capability, show them when they are behaving appropriately, and empower them when they get off track.

Positive teacher language includes the same characteristics, regardless of the age level in the class: it's always direct, encouraging, action oriented, and to the point—and it incorporates thoughtful silence as well as the spoken word. Although word choice or context will differ depending on the grade level, the intent remains the same: to empower our students. The following table provides some examples.

Guidelines for Positive Teacher Language	
Guideline	Example
Be direct and genuine.	• "You let Javier walk in front of you. That was a kind thing to do."
Convey faith in children's abilities and intentions.	• "Pause. We use kind words in our class. Try that again." (If need be, give an example of kind words: "May I please have the crayon?")
Focus on action.	• "I saw your eyes on me and your heads nodding. I could tell you were listening!"
Keep it brief.	• "Maria, walk."
Know when to be silent.	• Put a finger to your lips. • Provide students with wait time before sharing their responses. (This models and provides important think time.)

Keeping these guidelines in mind not only helps us to choose what to say, but can also help us figure out what to do when things go wrong. Young children—especially kindergartners—take our words at face value. If we say, "Are you ready to clean up now?" they truly think we are asking them that question. Most of them will answer honestly: "No." Even tacking on some of those extraneous filler words such as "okay" can make our language sound like a question: "Put your pencils down, okay?" A well-intentioned kindergartner may truly think you are asking a question.

Kindergartners and other young children are not always capable of stopping or responding to something immediately. Sometimes they need a few seconds for that executive functioning to kick in: to process, to understand, to do. Others may feel like they need to save face: they might do that thing one more time before they stop because then the choice feels like it's made on their terms.

Types of Teacher Language

There are four types of positive teacher language to use with your kindergartners:

- **Envisioning language.** We use envisioning language to get children to create a mental image of themselves doing things that surpass what they can already do. Perhaps more than children at any other age level in elementary school, kindergartners are ripe for this. They have such powerful imaginations that we can tap into to help them envision themselves as capable of what *we know* they can do. This type of language can be helpful when starting things you know might be tricky for them.

- **Reinforcing language.** This type of teacher language allows us to notice what children are already doing well and point it out to them so they know what to keep doing. It is especially important with kindergartners to avoid labeling. Keep in mind the characteristic of being genuine and specific about behaviors. This is an important distinction for many children. If you notice a child doing something kind and you say, "You are so kind!" they may immediately think of a time earlier that morning when they weren't kind to someone else. It can overwhelm them. Instead, be specific about what you saw them do: "You saw Kendra crying because her milk spilled and you went to get her another one. That was a kind thing to do."

- **Reminding language.** We use reminding language with children to set them up for success or to help just as they get off track. Four-, five-, and six-year-olds are impulsive and will often start something without thinking about it. Expect to become very good friends with reminding language. Using reminders in a friendly, firm tone shows your faith in the children's abilities and doesn't sacrifice your relationship: "Before you use those scissors, remind me how you will use them and keep everyone safe."

- **Redirecting language.** This is one tool we can use to support children when they get off task. Use redirecting language when the off-task behavior is just beginning so you can guide children back to on-task behavior quickly, safely, and without judgment: "Jayden, pause. Carry the chair in front of your body." Do this early, before off-task behavior can escalate.

Teacher Language Examples in a Kindergarten Classroom

Type of Language	Scenario	Language Example
Envisioning	• It's the beginning of the school year and you would like children to envision their hopes and dreams for kindergarten.	• "Close your eyes and make a mental picture of you learning and having fun in kindergarten . . ." (Pause.) "Open your eyes. Turn to your partner and tell them something you hope to learn in kindergarten."
	• You want to start a conversation about children using words to share materials.	• "Imagine you were going to color a blue ocean, but you noticed someone else was already using the blue crayon. What could you do?"
Reinforcing	• The class walked quietly in the hallway.	• "Kindergartners, our class was safe, calm, and quiet in the hallway. When we do that, we help all of the other classes get their own work done."
	• Mandy sometimes gets frustrated when she is drawing. Today you saw her focus, take a deep breath, and complete her drawing.	• "Sometimes drawing is frustrating for you. Today you finished your whole picture. What helped you do that?"

Type of Language	Scenario	Language Example
Reminding	• Maria is walking to the circle area during cleanup time.	• "Maria, what is your job right now?"
	• Your class is talking about an afternoon time when you will be at a meeting and there will be a guest teacher.	• "Remind me what you will do when our guest teacher rings the chime and tells you to clean up."
Redirecting	• Aaron is poking the student next to him on the carpet.	• "Aaron, hands in your lap or at your sides."
	• During math time, several students have started tossing the Unifix cubes at each other.	• "Everyone, pause. We use these tools in safe and careful ways. Show me you know how to do that."

No matter what language you use, remember that the relationship with each student and the class as a whole is at the core of your language. When you truly see the best in each student, when you take a breath before you respond, the children will hear that.

Getting to Know One Another

Children, especially those in preschool and kindergarten, find safety and joy in the familiar. Our job in those first few weeks of school is to create and build on the familiar for all of our students. One of the first times I took my kindergartners to the school library, I overheard one of my students say, "Oh! We have this book! I'm going to check this one out!" At first I was pleased that he was inspired by one of the books we also had in our classroom library, but when I looked at it, I realized it wasn't one we had.

"Who has this book?" I asked him.

"We do! At my house," he answered excitedly.

I waited a moment to see if he would understand the redundancy, and we talked quietly for a moment to clarify that yes, he did have that exact book at his house, and yes, he wanted to check that exact same book out of the library. It was early enough in the school year that I was still learning all about him. I didn't want to step on his excitement, so he checked that book out of the library, along with two others. I wrote his family a note of explanation, and made a mental note to do a mini-lesson about thinking about what *kind* of books you have and like and how that can help you choose books that are *like* those books, but not the same ones.

It wasn't a one-time experience. After it happened a few more times (my five-year-old daughter made a trip to the library once and returned with a book we already had at home!), I thought through what that behavior was telling me. Children are jazzed by familiarity, so much so that they want to *hold onto* it, even if they already have it.

Getting to Know the Teacher

Before the school year starts, reach out to the students in your class. Mail a short letter or postcard introducing yourself (include a picture) and telling them something about yourself. There are so many ways to connect with students ahead of time: record a short video introducing yourself, create a short video tour of the classroom, or do home visits. Many schools have a kindergarten playdate for families and children before the first day of school. The goal is to make yourself a familiar face *before* they walk into the classroom for the first time.

Getting to Know Classmates

Photos are a very useful tool. Pictures of children taken on the first day of school can be used for many purposes, such as labeling their coat hooks, cubbies, and folders, or including them in their surveys of favorite foods and favorite colors. Ask families to email a photo ahead of time and print out the photos on adhesive labels to use throughout the first weeks of school. Create a name chart early, and place students' photos on it, along with their names, so that children can touch, talk about, and refer to them.

One year, our class got into the habit of regularly taking class photos. We made "Welcome to Kindergarten" hats on the first day and took a group photo. Before we came in for recess one day, we took a group photo, and we did the same when we met with our reading buddies for the first time. These pictures became documents of our learning and growth as a community. It all happened very organically, and by November we already had ten class photos in a binder. It was very motivating. We looked at those photos dozens of times. It made our group feel more connected, and looking at pictures of a community being built made it feel that much stronger.

Starting the Day With Morning Meeting

Morning Meeting is one of the most powerful ways for everyone in our class to get to know each other. We have Morning Meeting every day, at the same time, in the same space, with the entire class. The sense of the familiar is important for kindergartners. Morning Meeting proceeds through four familiar components: greeting, sharing, group activity, and morning message.

See the appendix, p. 335, for more on Morning Meeting.

Each component provides an opportunity for us to get to know one another, but nothing more perfectly than the sharing part. The goal of sharing, especially at the beginning of the year, is to provide multiple opportunities for children to learn about each other and make connections. Also, because sharing occurs at the start of the day, it can serve as a point of connection later in the day. For example, two students who learn they both have a new baby sibling have a connection that they can follow up on later.

Ending the Day Positively With Closing Circle

Just as Morning Meeting opens the day with a positive connection, closing circle ends the day with positive reflection. You have observed the children's work, energy, and learning throughout the day, and closing circle can be used to help everyone reflect. For example, every day your students are performing small acts of kindness that can be shared at the end of the day. Or, when your class has a set of rules, you can use them as a reflection question: "How did you see someone following our rules today in kindergarten?" Consider a simple statement, chant, or song that can become a ritual to close the day together. Rituals build a sense of community spirit and connection, and provide a simple, predictable way to end your class's time together each day.

"The Wish"

One year I taught at an extended day school. Many students stayed and transitioned into the extended day with a different teacher, and I wanted a way to mark the transition. One day I had everyone join hands, I made a statement, and the children echoed. This impromptu experience became known in my class as "The Wish" and became a ritual in every class I've taught since:

> The time has come
> To say goodbye.
> We learned a lot today.
> Some of us will go,
> And some of us will stay,
> And we'll all be together tomorrow:
> To work, to have fun,
> To be in our kindergarten community.

Projects That Support Positive Community in Kindergarten

As the school year progresses, the classroom community needs and deserves continual nurturing. Consider and plan for regular partner work and class projects that will support your existing community and continue to deepen the positive connections you all have built.

Beginning of the Year	Middle of the Year	End of the Year
• Draw a map of your city or town on wood or heavy cardboard, and then have each student glue a photo of where they live to keep in the block area.	• Contribute a page to a class book.	• Contribute a page to a class book that will be copied for every student or put into digital format.
• Make a puppet or photo block of themselves.	• Undertake a service project to help the school or community.	• Write a letter for the next year's kindergarten students, telling them what to expect about kindergarten.
• Take lots of surveys with photos and invite children to come up with some of the questions.	• Create a mural of the school.	
• Make books in which each child contributes a page about what they shared during Morning Meeting.		

Birthdays, Holidays, and Other Celebrations

Celebrations are fun! They are especially fun with kindergartners, because no one is better at looking forward to things than five- and six-year-olds. More than once I have had a student say to me, "Oh, Ms. Howard, I cannot wait until my birthday!" when it is more than four months away. Kindergartners have perfected the art of excitement.

Birthdays

There is nothing more exciting than birthdays! Turning six! Holding up fingers on more than one hand! Birthdays are in full exclamation marks in kindergarten. At the start of the year, put together a birthday chart: the children can decorate it with cakes hanging over each month, forming a graph of birthdays.

Choose what you feel comfortable with for birthday celebrations, and stay consistent. For children with summer birthdays, consider celebrating them on their half birthday, or choosing a week near the end of the school year to celebrate all the summer birthdays.

Holidays and Other Celebrations

Your school community may have holidays that get celebrated every year with joy and excitement. It is also important to plan for learning celebrations for your class. When doing so, consider the following questions:

- **What is the purpose of this celebration?** Asking yourself what the purpose is will help you clarify for students what they are celebrating, and why.

- **What will we do at this celebration?** Sometimes the simplest celebrations are the best. One year we had a writing celebration. The children each shared a page from a book they had created, which we followed with a "class reception," during which we walked around, drank lemonade, and talked with each other about our books.

- **Who will we invite?** Does it make sense to include families? Do you want students to invite a buddy to class? Will you invite other adults and teachers? Or is this a celebration just for your classroom community?

- **What preparation do the students need?** If children will be sharing work, give them the opportunity to practice ahead of time.

Lunchtime and Recess

Lunch and recess should be a break in the day filled with joy and fun, but it can also be a challenging time for students. Just as we specifically model and plan for classroom structures, the same care needs to be put into lunch and recess. A few minutes of reminding and reinforcing language can support students as they transition into and from these noninstructional activities.

Lunch

The more casual downtime of eating together is a great opportunity for students to get to know each other. Consider having "lunch buddies," and assign or have students choose lunch partners for the day or the week. These partner teams will give each student someone to sit with and talk to. Before going to lunch, suggest one to two topics for the children to talk about in case they get stuck. This time may be a lunch break for you as well, and if it is, consider staying and eating lunch with your class every once in a while. Sometimes I laugh harder with my students at lunchtime than at any other part of the day.

Recess

At the beginning of the year, plan to provide both structured and unstructured time during recess. Plan and teach some large-group games such as Duck, Duck, Goose or Freeze Tag, and balance those activities with unstructured free play for the children. Before you send them off to recess, model and practice how you will call them back together. For example, when I taught kindergarten, I found it easier to call my class back together in a circle, rather than a line. I'd blow three whistle blasts, and then I'd call out, "Kindergarten, circle up!" My class would run to form a circle and all join hands, and then we would raise our hands and say, "Together!" Then I'd have the children drop their hands and rest them on their knees so we were bending in together toward each other, and I could give them any proactive reminders and let them know what we would be doing next. It was a calming way to come back together.

Establishing Rules and Investing Students in the Rules

Kindergartners bring both ends of the spectrum when they think about hopes and dreams for the future. They have wide, sweeping goals ("I want to be a firefighter ninja fairy when I grow up") as well as those that are far more focused on what they want to happen in the next five minutes ("I want to play in the home corner").

Over the first two to three weeks of school, preview many of the things that the children will be learning and experiencing during their kindergarten year. Provide examples of what children did the previous year if you have them, including photographs of children working and their work, physical work examples, and short video clips, which can provide children a baseline of what they can hope to achieve in the coming year.

Giving the children a chance to brainstorm and think through what their hopes and dreams are can take from a couple of days to a little over a week. Here are some activities you might use to support students in this experience:

- Read a book that envisions school as a positive, encouraging place. (See *Jamal's Busy Day* by Wade Hudson, or *A Fine, Fine School* by Sharon Creech.)

- As you introduce materials and areas of the classroom, share some of the learning that will occur in those areas, and show examples if you have them.

- Invite children to share something they hope to learn in kindergarten during a "lightning share" at Morning Meeting.

- In small groups, ask the children to draw things that they hope to experience in kindergarten and what they dream kindergarten will be like. And there's no need to set a limit: if they want to draw four to six things, that's fine!

- Next, give the children their papers back and ask them to choose one thing to be their hope and dream. Everyone shares their hope with the class, and then their hopes and dreams are posted in the classroom.

When we take this time to help children really think about and take ownership over their own goals, it allows them a way in: this is the place where they are going to achieve these hopes and dreams. It's a motivating and a positive way of framing their path forward, and it will allow them to create and sustain a positive self-image as community members dedicated to learning.

The work on children's hopes and dreams is a key component in helping children become invested in the classroom community. When they feel like an integral part of the community—when they feel a sense of belonging and significance—they will feel more connected to the community as a whole.

Another key use for these hopes and dreams involves connecting them to a set of classroom rules. You have the option of working with your students to create a classroom set of rules or to start the year with an established set of rules. Whatever works best for your teaching is the best choice for you, but be sure to deliberately connect these hopes and dreams to classroom rules. The classroom rules will help everyone achieve their hopes and dreams. When we make that connection, children see their importance and will be more invested in the rules.

The classroom rules become the backbone of our community. When we refer to the rules constantly, children will get comfortable with them and they will become second nature. I post my rules in a place where children can see and touch them. It's not uncommon to see a child high-five a rule that they followed. You might even encourage students to acknowledge their achievement this way: "You saw the colored pencils spilled on the floor and you cleaned them up. Go high-five the rule that says, 'Take care of our tools.'"

The rules of the classroom provide a sense of safety and security for the children. They know what to expect. One year our class created physical motions to go along with each rule. We would recite the Pledge of Allegiance, read our classroom rules with our fantastic motions, and then

Keeping Hopes and Dreams Alive Throughout the Year

Children's hopes and dreams should be fluid. As children achieve them, recognize and celebrate them. Creating new hopes and revisiting old ones will emphasize and show children that learning is cyclical. You could plan to revisit and create new hopes and dreams during naturally occurring times of the year, such as the end of a quarter or when the class returns from a school break.

Do not let your students' hopes and dreams fade into the background and become decoration. When you regularly and deliberately refer to children's hopes and dreams and how the class's work and community support everyone working to achieve those hopes and dreams, you are modeling for the children that their ideas matter—that a positive community notices and celebrates everyone's achievements, and that working to achieve something, celebrating that achievement, and then using that knowledge to create new goals is a worthwhile and valuable process.

everyone would use a moment of silence to think about the rule they wanted to work on the most that day. This approach not only gave many students a frame for jumping into the day, but it also gave us a link to use during our closing circle at the end of the day. Once a week we would partner-share about the rule we kept in mind and how we followed it that day. A parent once told me during our conference about a time at dinner when their kindergartner asked, "How did you follow your rules at work today?"

Proactive Approach to Discipline

I always look at proactive discipline as backward planning. I think, "What do I want my students to be able to do independently? Okay, so what do I have to teach them so they can get there?" If we want children to have meaningful conversations about what they are writing, we have to teach them how to have those meaningful conversations about writing. If we want children to put tools away carefully, then we have to make sure all of the tools have a clear home, and teach the children how to put everything away. If we want children to ask connected questions during sharing time, then we have to teach them what connected questions are. If we want children to be able to resolve a conflict in the block area, then we have to teach them ways to address problem situations.

Children are brilliant. They come to our classrooms with so many different experiences, with so many valuable ideas. So make it the norm in your classroom to ask for their thoughts and ideas. When children know that their ideas and voices are valued, it cements their connection to the community.

See the appendix, p. 333, for more on Interactive Modeling.

Use strategies such as Interactive Modeling to model skills and routines so children know what to do. Use role-play to offer strategies for situations that have multiple solutions.

One class I had was trying hard to resolve disputes about the use of blocks, but it proved difficult for them to talk about the problem when the blocks were *right there*. They were better able to discuss the issue away from the source of the problem.

Our solution was to create a conflict corner, a space the children could go to if they were having a problem. Each child made a puppet of themselves (to be used if they felt more comfortable being one step removed). We created steps for how to solve problems and posted them in the conflict corner. There were paper, crayons, and pencils there to use as needed: to create a plan, to draw out the problem, or create a drawing to show how they solved the problem. We introduced the children to the space and taught them how to use it. The conflict corner quickly became a well-loved space. It was comfortable and allowed children the independence to work something out together, and as a result they felt empowered. Being able to solve a problem together can be magical for strengthening the positive community. Its message: solving problems together makes us stronger.

We eventually added a binder in the conflict corner containing pictures of the students' solutions, documenting the work they did there. An unexpected result of keeping this binder was that it allowed my coteacher and I to see common themes where children were having conflicts, letting us know what the children needed from us proactively so we could better support them going forward.

I've spent time over the years reflecting on why this was such a success and continued to be a success in subsequent classes. First, the children wanted to be able to solve the problem. Community mattered, and they wanted to support it. Second, the children felt like they had a voice. They knew that others would listen to them. Third, they enjoyed the process. It wasn't always easy, but coming to a solution often brought such a rush of joy to them that it wasn't uncommon to see them spontaneously hugging each other after they had worked something out. Each of these motives connects to needs that all people have: to feel a sense of belonging, significance, and fun. When we make sure that children are getting those needs met in positive ways, it adds layers of connection to our community.

Maintaining a Strong Community

I had a professor in college who told me that one of our (many) jobs as a teacher was to become a "professional child watcher." He urged me to observe without judgment—to notice. When I gave myself permission to stop, breathe, and just watch, I always found elements of good.

During the first six to eight weeks of school, we put so much of our energy into teaching students the routines and expectations for the school year. We spend hours planning and setting up our classroom and then filling it with learning. We help children get to know each other and make connections with each other. Once we get swept up in the curriculum and content, it can be hard to remember to go back to the work of maintaining these connections.

Meaningful personal relationships need to be nurtured. It's the same with our classroom community. When we nurture the classroom community throughout the school year, relationships deepen and grow.

Morning Meeting and closing circle are two very natural times during the day when we nurture our classroom community. As the year goes on and you are integrating academic content into your Morning Meeting and your closing circle, remember to plan for community building. Just as we use curriculum to plan learning experiences for the week, use the classroom community to inform what you plan for community building.

Managing Students Instead of Teaching Students

I once had a picture of a large stoplight in my classroom. Everyone's name started on green, but I'd move names to yellow if students needed to better control their behavior or to red when they were having a lot of difficulty. Sometimes I would invite students to move their own names up to green as they regained self-control. I told myself that this was helping my students manage their behavior.

But then one student kept removing his name from the board. He told me he didn't like having his friends see when he was having a hard time. I later asked myself, "Was that stoplight helping my students? Or was it helping me?" Over the next few days I observed through that lens.

I was managing their behavior instead of teaching them how to manage themselves. They knew when they were having difficulty. I was just making public what they already knew. My students needed me to *teach them* how to handle things when they were feeling overwhelmed, upset, or out of sorts.

My solution was to create a "feelings board" where children were in charge of their own name cards. They would place their name under the feeling that described how they felt that day—happy, worried, sad, excited, angry, frustrated—and they could change their card as needed.

One day I had an especially frustrating morning. I arrived at school, dropped off my bag, and went to the feelings board. I felt a great sense of satisfaction moving my name card under "angry" and realizing that I had a group of students that would be willing and able to help me with my own big feelings when they arrived in class thirty minutes later.

One year I had a very energetic class who loved to move. Whenever it felt like everyone was on edge, we'd stop everything and have an impromptu dance party. Taking the time to dance with abandon, to be silly and laugh together, seemed to help my class reset and recharge.

Your class will show you what their resets are. It won't be the same for every class. A different class was not a fan of dance parties, but they could sit and listen to read-alouds and look at books for hours. With that class, we would sometimes have a "Book-ternoon." We'd plan for an afternoon of reading, and the kids would suggest read-alouds and find stories on CDs from the library. During our Book-ternoon reset, our class would do just that: have an afternoon full of books, books, and more books.

Prioritize a reconnect when your class returns from a break or after a difficult event in the community. The children will need a safe space to process, practice familiar routines and skills, and come together to see friendly faces.

Here are some strategies for maintaining a strong community:

- **Hold Morning Meeting and closing circle every day.** These are natural community-building opportunities. They are times to build a repertoire of familiar and favorite greetings, activities, and reflections. Having these shared rituals will deepen connections.

- **Make and read class books together.** Choose these books for read-alouds, sometimes to encourage reflection: "Remember when we were new kindergartners?"

See the appendix, p. 344, for more on preparing for a guest teacher.

- **Plan for guest and substitute teachers.** Having their teacher away can make young children anxious. Set up a familiar routine before you plan to be away so the children know what to expect. Plan your Morning Meeting and closing circle routines so they will remain the same when you are out.

- **Set up recurring learning partner teams so children get to know each other.** They might have the same writing or math partner for several weeks. This will allow relationships to grow.

- **Pay attention to what your class is interested in.** Let the children's interests inform classroom displays and materials. For example, have a basket in the class library on a favorite topic, or allow children to make posters or books to teach others about their interests. Children are more invested in the community when they feel like they have a voice.

- **Encourage reflection.** Plan regular reflection that encourages the children to think about why something went well, or why a game was so fun. When the children reflect on what the community is doing well, they will recommit to doing those things.

- **Work together.** Choose projects that will have everyone working together toward a common goal. Projects might include making a class quilt, preparing a book of recipes, or creating a basket of how-to books.

- **Celebrate growth.** On a regular basis, invite students to look back at what the class has learned and celebrate it.

- **Focus on gratitude.** Many studies have shown that practicing gratitude increases people's happiness, instills an overall positive outlook, and improves relationships.

Every day, children do small, beautiful things to take care of themselves and the people around them. When we take that role of "child watching" seriously, it gives us so many examples of things we want to reinforce to the children. Children, too, learn from us. What we choose to model and say sets the tone for what they notice and how they speak to each other. One of my students once said to the class during our closing circle, "You know, I miss my family when I'm at school, but I miss my class when I'm at home. My class is like . . . my school family!"

Which felt exactly right.

Grade ①

Many years ago, my school held training for staff. The consultant used several energizers with us, knowing that we were already close and many of us had worked together for years. Our existing sense of community was buoyed by our work together, and several nuggets from this training stuck with us for years.

We played the energizer Famous Pairs, and as it turns out, the shoe fit for so many of us. To this day, my then partner and I still refer to ourselves as Lucy and Ethel. Other pairs from that training referred to each other as Bert and Ernie and Lewis and Clark. Maybe it was fate or a self-fulfilling prophecy, but I think it was really more of teachers genuinely knowing each other and seeing each other for who they are and who they might become that allowed us to take these fictional pairs and see threads of truth in each other.

The community of teachers knit among the adults is the model from which first graders build their own relationships. For us as teachers, knowing each other's likes and dislikes, strengths and weaknesses, and how individuals work together is essential. Finding meaningful and often playful ways to connect allows us to show grace and humor when things are working and while we work hard to climb the hills together.

Teacher Tone and Demeanor

Our thoughts have tremendous power and influence over our words and actions. In turn, those words and actions become the habits and models we share with students—and often become our legacy. I was often dubbed "Loquacious Lisa," as words always came easily to me and often slid right out of my mouth without much of a filter. But what I learned in my early years of teaching was that it's often our economy of words, the willingness to pause and our subsequent word choices, that allow us to have a positive impact and set an important example for children.

Like our breath, our teacher language is always with us, is always free, and has a powerful impact on how we self-regulate and exchange energy with our class. That might sound lofty or ethereal, but it's fundamentally true. Most of us rarely think about our breath, but science and experience tell us that when we control our breath, we can better manage our emotions, health, and relationships. The spoken and nonverbal language we choose to use in our classroom and with our school community profoundly impacts our relationships. We know that words matter and that sometimes our intentions don't quite line up with the outcomes, so being aware of our language is the first step in making sure these are in sync. No matter where we are in our teaching and personal life, being intentional about witnessing our thoughts, words, and actions has a way of becoming our destiny. As such, it is well worth our while to pay attention to our thoughts and words.

We know that the characteristics of teacher language are aspirational and, with practice, they become habits. When my partner Lucy and I were first working together, she was new to the *Responsive Classroom* approach. Technology was just coming into our school lives, so we relied heavily on sticky notes and pastel-colored sentence strips. We judiciously placed sentence starters around our space that said things like the following:

- Connor, you remembered to _____. That keeps the _____ safe.

- I noticed we remember our rule _____.

- I see your [eyes/bodies/hands] _____.

- Use *brevity*, and *pause*.

These prompts were visible reminders and helped us reinforce habits in ourselves and among students. It laid the groundwork for our community and allowed us to regularly and enthusiastically reinforce what was working.

First graders thrive on new tasks and responsibility, and the students in our class appreciated hearing what they were doing well. It didn't take long before we heard them reinforcing each other with phrases like "Way to go, Marcus! You moved *all* that sand into the truck!" Likewise, proactive reminding language functioned like a pause button when we suspected or witnessed behavior starting to slip. Our sense of playfulness helped us take a light but firm approach as we asked questions such as "Which of our class rules will help us use our new watercolors safely and carefully?" while wearing a Matisse smock and beret. This practice might feel artificial at first, but with practice and the ability to witness how children respond to these prompts, you will see the gains.

Similarly, when we used real tools such as glass jars for paint and water or real cameras to photograph our classroom, we'd refer to our students as painters or photographers to communicate that we saw them as multifaceted and skilled learners and community members. As the year progressed, we helped activate their past learning memory when we needed to bridge into introducing a new experience or tool. For example, months after our photojournalism unit, our students were studying Mexican culture. My teaching partner and I were so busy that we had little time to document our learning—something we did routinely for display panels in the hallway and for our class newsletters. We began a conversation with our students in Morning Meeting by asking, "What do you remember about using the digital cameras?" From there, a rotation for students was arranged to either photograph our studies or to write a few sentences about the photos. Our first graders were thrilled to have these responsibilities, and my teaching partner and I were 100 percent confident they could use the cameras and were grateful the students saved us a few steps as we moved into the last six weeks of school with so much on our plates.

Types of Teacher Language

The skillful use of teacher language has the power to help create and maintain a positive, encouraging, and respectful classroom community. As with kindergartners, there are four types of positive teacher language to use with first graders. Whereas with kindergartners we use teacher language that taps into students' imaginations about what we know they can do, with first graders we use teacher language to strengthen students' confidence in their capabilities as learners and as community members.

- **Envisioning language.** Using future-oriented language helps first graders see what's possible and reinforces your faith in their abilities. Referring to first graders as "painters," "scientists," or "friendly friends" lets them see themselves in a different light. Comments such as "I bet we're going to take our class guidelines with us to PE today!" let them know you're 100 percent confident in their ability to transfer what they do in the classroom space to other learning spaces.

- **Reinforcing language.** From the start, use reinforcing language when you notice first graders taking care of themselves, each other, and the learning environment. This serves as a reminder to you to be observant and lets students know you're watching and noticing the goodness. Once the classroom guidelines are set, you can use reinforcing language to strengthen the agreed-on classroom rules.

- **Reminding language.** Most of us need reminders during the course of the day. First graders are no different, and when we use reminding language we help them stay on track and learn the habits to self-regulate. When used proactively, reminding language lets students remember or use resources to remember.

- **Redirecting language.** As shared earlier, redirecting language is your lifeguard language. It's direct, short, and gets right to the heart of the off-track behavior. When a student begins to get off track, a simple neutral statement is an effective way to them get back on track. When I see a first grader start to go hands- or headfirst down the slide, I'll use a statement like, "Beth, feet first on the slide."

Teacher Language Examples in a First Grade Classroom

Type of Language	Scenario	Language Example
Envisioning	• The classroom teacher has a planned absence for the next day.	• "I see people following our classroom rules every day. I see each of you taking care of yourself as you read. I see you taking care of each other at recess, and I see you being safe and careful with our learning tools. I know that while I am out tomorrow and Mr. Marcus is here, you will show him the same things!"
Reinforcing	• During the first week of school, first graders walked the perimeter of the playground, and there was Interactive Modeling on using the slide.	• "I see people having fun running and digging within the boundaries of our playground. I see people walking up the ladder with hands on the railing and then sitting feet first to go down the slide. I even saw people moving away from the end of the slide as soon as they got there. Those are important ways we can all have so much fun out here and stay safe!"
Reminding	• Students are getting ready to transition to the working portion of writing workshop after having an Interactive Modeling lesson the day before about choosing a place to work.	• "Writers, as you think about where you will write today, who can think of one way you will take care of each other as you make that choice and then work?"
Redirecting	• During silent reading, a first grader, Sal, begins kicking the leg on his desk.	• The teacher walks over to Sal and silently taps the desk to establish eye contact and says, "Sal, bodies quiet."

Getting to Know One Another

First grade is in many ways one of the easiest places to get to know children. What you see is what you get. And if you don't see it, ask and they will tell you. In the years I taught first grade, it was rare for a first grader not to seize the opportunity to share their ideas or wishes with me. And if they were reluctant to speak, I knew with some careful if not slightly distanced observation, they would show me what they needed. First grade is where I truly honed and learned to crave "kid watching," when I got to assume the role of Harriet the Spy and delight in observing and noting what I saw in first graders, and without intervening, helping, or solving. They are competent learners who are eager to engage with playmates, their environment, and the tools of learning. It was by kid watching that I learned what they needed me to facilitate, starting with how to interact with each other.

Before the start of each school year, I would send a welcome letter to each child and their parents. I would share important information such as what I envisioned for first grade, some things I loved about teaching, and a few personal details. Once we met face-to-face, then, there would be all sorts of questions about my dog, my skateboarding son, and my personal library. I also encouraged the children to write back before our welcome visits.

I cherished our welcome visits. They were private meetings (well, with parents in attendance too) when I was able to give the incoming first graders my undivided attention. They usually came ready to share something exciting or to check out the (nearly all set up) classroom. For the shy ones, it gave me an opportunity to read them and gently ask questions that allowed them to let their guard down. All of this was such helpful data for our first days together as a class. Gathering information from a previous teacher or school can be helpful as well, but I often gave myself and the students a little time to get to know each other first.

Once the school year began, I found one of the easiest vehicles to get to know students, beyond observing them, was to read—to read the best books I could find, to read often, and to pause to engage in conversation. We kept a careful log of our books, started by me and later added to by first grade writers, which gave us a road map to go back to and discuss books we had already read. Some of my most accessible and captivating read-alouds for creating community at the start of the year included these books:

- *The Kissing Hand* by Audrey Penn
- *Kindness Starts With You* by Jacquelyn Stagg
- *Wemberly Worried* by Kevin Henkes
- *Help! A Story of Friendship* by Holly Keller
- *A Frog Thing* by Eric Drachman
- *Sylvester and the Magic Pebble* by William Steig
- *Appelemando's Dreams* by Patricia Polacco
- *More Than Anything Else* by Marie Bradby

Each of these picture books proved to be relatable to first grade and let us talk about being together in school and all the feelings that came with that. When I read them in this sequence, it allowed us to build on the feelings of individuals and to think about and help others. Simultaneously, as we got to know each other, we were overtly creating notes about interests and strengths (sometimes charting these, other times discussing them) and I was (covertly) taking notes of strengths, disposition, behavior, and needs. As we moved into talking about hopes, each of these books allowed us to see what characters hoped to do and often how adults supported or discouraged those hopes. Ultimately, I could use these stories and our discussion to help excavate the children's hopes and how we'd all be there to support them.

As much as most first graders love to be read to, they also need to move and have fun. Our read-alouds and work time were punctuated by deliberately planned opportunities for movement, cooperation, and laughter. Energizers we used inside, just like the cooperative games we enjoyed for outdoor recess, were planned weekly and reflected the important data we picked up from kid watching, our physical environment, and our knowledge of development. At times, they also reflected what was going on around us, such as back-to-back hurricanes (rain became a big theme). At other times, they connected the name of energizers to our local community by renaming Land, Sea, Air! to Army, Navy, Air Force! since we lived in a (mostly) navy town.

Birthdays, Holidays, and Other Celebrations

Birthdays provide an opportunity for students to be seen and celebrated as valuable members of the community. Recognizing birthdays also offers a way to build community. In first grade, everyone knew that we celebrated birthdays, and I made sure it was clear with families from the beginning that we would celebrate in class and take care of everything and stay safe. What does that mean? Basically, the students were in the driver's seat and made choices from some options and families did not have to assume the obligation of sending treats. Their contribution was to share their child with us, and the class did the honoring and celebrating.

Be sure to plan for holidays and other celebrations. Consider the following questions:

- **What is the purpose of this celebration?** Make sure it's clear to students what they are celebrating, and why.

- **What will we do at this celebration?** Sometimes the simplest celebrations are the best.

- **Who will we invite?** Should families be included? Do you want students to invite a buddy to class? Should other adults and teachers be invited? Or is this a celebration just for your classroom community?

- **What preparation do the students need?** If children will be sharing work, give them the opportunity to practice ahead of time.

Establishing Rules and Investing Students in the Rules

One year I created a metaphoric map of first grade at the start of school. The map showed what we would do over the course of the year and included space for the class to imagine what our hopes and dreams would be and what our responsibilities would be. As the students contributed to the map, they became invested in rules that were needed for the class to function as a positive community.

Examining the Map

In the first five days of school, I read books to the class that introduced the concept of hopes in first grade. These were interspersed with books about the start of school and friendship, and books about feelings. By day five, I used the language of hopes and dreams and how we take care of each other. Reinforcing language was vital. I called attention to simple yet essential tasks such as pushing in chairs, holding the door for others, active listening behaviors, and inviting a friend to play. I asked the children to look around the room to see what they noticed and what they were curious about since many areas of the room were taped off and marked with "Opening Soon" signs that indicated we weren't quite ready for everything. I repurposed documentation panels and photos from previous years, and displayed them on the bulletin boards. This led to curious discussions about what had happened in previous first grade classes. (As the year closes, you could also have interviews between your students and kindergartners as a way to introduce first grade to incoming students. Don't underestimate the power of a seven-year-old to tell a six-year-old all about school.)

These strategies not only create mystery and intrigue, but they also generate a sense of communal importance: "Don't those paints look lovely stacked and closed up? The students who used them last year took such good care of them, knowing that we'd want to use them too! I can't wait to show you how we'll use and care for them!"

Mapping Our Path

By creating interest in the topography and shape of first grade, we can begin to chart our own path for our first grade community. For the most part, first graders are full of hope and grand ideas of what they want to accomplish. But since every class is different, the path will be different every year.

In that first year when I created the map, we took big ideas from our readings and our predecessors and began to make them our very own. As our read-alouds and discussions turned to hope, it was important that we considered the connotations around that word and came to a working definition of our own hopes. In later years, we'd call it a dream or "Ways We Want to Be," but we always worked together to decide on the terminology. We sometimes used a container to hold the hopes for what we wanted for first grade. (See "Brainstorming Hopes" on the next page.) At the beginning of the year, students would write or make drawings about their hopes, and place them in the container.

Brainstorming Hopes

One of the ways we helped create the hope container was to brainstorm possible hopes, which included:

- Reading books by myself
- Playing with friends
- Writing my whole name

- Going to music class
- Swinging high
- Not having rest time

During the first go-round, everything was fair game. We'd come back to it the next day informally, during settling-in time, at transitions, or in passing. We could talk more about each one and see how it might or might not work. I would chuckle at the hopes for a swing because in first grade they had graduated to a different playground from the one the students had played on as kindergartners. Neither playground had swings (for insurance reasons), but every year there would be one child who was certain we would be able to swing in first grade. Our walk around the playground perimeter when we modeled it doused this hope, but on occasion, we had permission to walk to a nearby public park in order to perfect our swinging skills.

The process of illustrating and writing about our hopes varied from class to class and took into account the developmental and unique cultural and individual traits of each given class. Graphic organizers helped students to sketch their hopes and begin to write words or a sentence. I'd conference and review these, using open-ended questions to dig deeper. The next day, we might read another book and revise our sketch or words, which also gave me insights into the students' attitudes and interest in the process of writing. I'd refer to the idea that adults sometimes try to minimize or not believe children, and I'd encourage children to make sure they followed their hearts and understood that as a class we were there to support each other.

A final pass at our hopes would take different forms, using fine black sharpies and watercolors or markers or crayons. Mounted in black mat frames or a monochromatic cardstock, their art was placed where our class (not just adult passersby in the hallway) could see them. I would type their hopes in large fonts that encouraged literacy as we'd use these often in our day-to-day life. I treated their hopes as precious art because they were.

Creating the Key to the Map

That first year, I made copies of the hopes the children had written about and illustrated, and I placed them in a pocket chart, often as a provocation to look at before Morning Meeting. We'd take a look and notice each other's hopes. Later in the day, we'd come together to talk about what was similar and different, and to acknowledge each person's hopes. I'd often let that percolate before coming back the next day to say, "If we wanted each person to be able to *accomplish* these *hopes*, what are some ways we all need to try our very best to be each day?" In this way, the students themselves became invested in establishing our classroom rules.

I have continued to use this process for twenty years with students in nearly every grade, and it's never the same. It's about reading the audience, encouraging them to coconstruct the rules, and working within the school leadership framework. In some years, I had to delicately navigate the students' input to match schoolwide rules. In other years, we had a more fluid conversation, which led to the hopes falling into three categories:

- Taking care of ourselves

- Taking care of each other

- Taking care of our learning space

No matter how the conversation went, the goal was to have our rules finalized by the tenth day of school. Once finalized, our rules would go on a large chart or in a repurposed picture frame, and we'd make hanging it on our wall a big event. Copies of the rules would go to our specialist teachers and in our newsletter that was sent home to students' families. One year, we made two sets of the rules and carried one on a hanger (the kind with clips) every time we left our classroom, with the mantra "Rules go in our hands, our feet, our bodies, and our minds!"

The framed version became a part of our environment, our vernacular, our reflection, and our daily life. It often took days to get there, but the return on the investment lasted all year long.

Proactive Approach to Discipline

When presenting *Responsive Classroom* workshops, we often ask participants what connotations they have around the word "discipline." It's a question I often pose to students too. Both groups tend to think of discipline as something negative, but as discussed in the overview to this chapter, "discipline" is derived from the Latin *disciplina* and refers to instruction and education, and is actually anything but negative.

As noted earlier, it's not our job to discipline children but to teach discipline. That statement always makes me exhale some of the pressure away. We don't have to rule with a heavy hand or feel that we need to fix misbehaving children. Our job is to calmly model and reinforce habits that teach children discipline, and to follow up by teaching them how to fix mistakes and to learn from their mistakes.

A multilayered process contributes to the proactive discipline that makes up a classroom using the *Responsive Classroom* approach. The physical environment and tone of a classroom should welcome all learners in a way that sets everyone up for success. It's easier, more effective, and more joyous to set everyone up for engaging learning. Here are some strategies for setting up proactive discipline:

- **Witness everyone.** We all have an innate need for belonging and significance. Observe students with a curious and neutral lens so you can see them for who they are and articulate what you notice, affirming as much as you can and offering proactive reminders when it looks like they need support.

- **Create the space.** Consider how the space you've set up reflects development and encourages interaction and engagement. When materials invite children to engage, they are invested in the care and keeping of those materials, and the shared responsibility becomes an investment in the community.

- **Lean into the rules.** Co-creating rules with the class and displaying them prominently will make it more likely that these rules will become an essential part of students' day-to-day experience in the classroom. Referring to the rules, and having children refer to them, will keep them meaningful. It will also encourage the students to work collectively to uphold the rules, rather than you as the teacher having to ask for compliance.

- **See the forest for the trees.** Keep an eye on the long-term outcomes. When we have a vision for where we want children to be, we can model habits and behaviors that support long-term goals such as autonomy, independence, and kindness.

- **Keep it lively.** It is essential in first grade that frequent movement breaks occur with regularity and, at times, spontaneously. This is easily accomplished with interactive learning structures and outdoor games at recess. Plan breaks, but also be open to taking breaks if you see one is needed to get the children back on track. First graders also appreciate when adults show a sense of playfulness, so don't forget to enjoy yourself as well.

- **Don't be afraid to flub it.** Mistakes are a vital part of learning. Make sure your relationship and conversations acknowledge mistakes and how individuals have the ability and agency to fix mistakes and learn from them. Be sure to show how you also can make mistakes, and point out how you then fix these mistakes and what you have learned from them.

Maintaining a Strong Community

Building a strong community of learners is not a continuous task. It's a daily commitment that requires us to see children, to collaborate and share, to admit when we make mistakes, and to celebrate our wins. Each day we have the chance to start fresh, commit to doing our best to live our class rules, and make the most of each day.

Here are some strategies for maintaining a strong first grade community:

- **Start each day with Morning Meeting.** Each day, we get to recognize and see each other. We share and listen, and we have fun with an activity. As we get to know each other, we practice skills and add to our repertoire.

See the appendix, p. 335, for more on Morning Meeting.

- **Assign class jobs, or have students volunteer.** Jobs in first grade work well when they are assigned for a week. Children get to learn the job, practice it, and demonstrate proficiency. They play an active role in maintaining the learning space and supporting the learning, whether it be to organize the library, set the schedule for the day, or to help refill the water pitcher. (For more, see Chapter 1.)

- **Appoint student ambassadors.** Whether it's to welcome adult visitors or students, or to help communicate the learning in first grade, students make the best ambassadors. They are, after all, the experts on first grade, and when given the opportunity to explain to visitors or guests how things work in their classroom, they rise to the challenge.

ⓘ

See the appendix, p. 347, for more on whole-class problem-solving meetings.

- **Incorporate project work.** First graders thrive on interactive work that allows them to collaborate and make connections across content areas. Surveying students to see what they are interested in builds investment and allows them to make choices about their learning. It tells them we value their curiosity and trust them to be in control of their learning. Giving them the opportunity to reflect on the process, and to share their work, lets them explain their thinking, whether within the classroom or as part of a whole-school Morning Meeting.

- **Provide catch-up time.** Schedule regular time toward the end of the week, especially when approaching a vacation break, to allow students to catch up on any unfinished work. My first graders loved the play on words ("Ketchup Time") and learned quickly that if they used their time effectively and completed tasks, they had time for free play at the end of the week. This time allowed me to meet with students individually or in small groups to confer on academic or social issues to make sure everyone's needs were met.

Grade

What I look forward to the most each school year is seeing our classroom community develop. I am always in awe that we begin each year as individuals, some of us as strangers, and end the year with such a strong, family-like bond. Our school schedules an open house a few days before the first day of school. This gives families an opportunity to visit the classroom, meet their teacher, tour the school, and see if students already know any of their classmates. I find it to be one of the most important days of the year.

The open house is more than just a time to meet the students and families I will get to learn with that year: it's the start of the classroom community-building process. Positive community building begins with that first interaction with students and their families. Whether this is a "welcome to our class" postcard sent before the year begins or a warm introduction at the open house, our first interactions with students and their families are foundational in building a positive community of learners.

Teacher Tone and Demeanor

What you say and how you say it matters. To be effective in your communication with students, your words, tone, body language, and facial expression need to work together to send a message. Second graders are keen observers and quickly pick up on discrepancies between what we say and our tone and facial expressions. What follows are some tools for using your tone, demeanor, and word choice to reinforce the values of the classroom community.

Leading by Example

During my first year of teaching second grade, I had an experience that highlighted the notion "Do as I say, not as I do." Second graders took a computer-based standardized assessment a couple of times during the year. This assessment was something new to me, to students, and to the families. I prepared the students ahead of time and presented lessons on persevering through challenging tasks, keeping a growth mindset, staying positive, and relying on specific strategies when feeling frustrated or in need of a quick break.

Unfortunately, I failed to model those skills outside of those lessons. Students noticed my frustration when some of the computers died in the middle of testing, and they remembered my annoyance earlier in the year when they were asked to read content that contained words far beyond their reading levels. I realized my attitude about this assessment was subsequently reflected in the behaviors of the students. All of the "mindset" work we did in preparation for this test was forgotten. Second graders rely on their teachers to be the constant model—*of everything*. They are always watching us and often choose their behaviors based on their observations of the adults in the community around them.

Open and Honest Communication

See the appendix, p. 347, for more on whole-class problem-solving meetings.

Second graders care about their school and classroom communities and are willing to help solve concerns related to those communities. If the entire class is struggling with an expectation, routine, or procedure, then consider a whole-class meeting to bring this concern to the group. Whole-class problem-solving meetings can be effective in discovering the root cause of a whole-class issue and finding ways to remedy the concern.

In one class I noticed many of the students were struggling in the transition from recess to reading workshop. Our routine was to come back from recess, make a reading workshop choice, and then set up our space and get to work. Instead, I noticed students were coming back from recess, chatting with each other, using the restroom, getting a drink, hanging out by their backpacks, and needing to be reminded to make their reading workshop choice.

A whole-class problem-solving meeting was arranged, and I began by being honest with them. I said, "I notice that when we come back from recess it is taking us a long time to make our reading choices. Has anyone else noticed this? Why do you think this is?" The result was a great discussion that eventually led us to understanding that after recess many of us needed some time to take care of ourselves before settling into a reading choice. Based on that need, we decided as a group to add five minutes between recess and reading to take care of ourselves and our needs, and then I would play a short song to signal it was time for everyone to transition to making their reading choice.

These changes worked for us and met the needs of the entire group. By approaching the problem with honesty, we were able to have a very real discussion and problem-solving meeting that kept our community intact and addressed the needs of the entire group.

Fair and Impartial Communication

Speak with all students from a place of kindness, grounded in respect. By speaking with students in this way, you model for the class how the students should be speaking with and to each other. Consider if there are any inequities in your communication with students that might hinder the full development of a community of inclusive learners.

Types of Teacher Language

The skillful use of all four types of teacher language—envisioning, reinforcing, reminding, and redirecting—has the power to help create and maintain a positive, encouraging, and respectful classroom community.

- **Envisioning language.** Envisioning language is future oriented and can help students think about what's ahead in order to make those events successful. For example, at the beginning of the year you might use envisioning language to help students formulate their second grade hopes and dreams.

- **Reinforcing language.** Once the classroom guidelines are set, you can use reinforcing language to strengthen the agreed-on classroom rules. For example, one of your rules states, "Place books back on the shelf when you're done reading them," and you notice a student carefully setting two books back on the shelf after reading them. You might say to this student, "I notice how carefully you placed the library books back on the shelf. You are following our 'Place books back on the shelf' rule."

- **Reminding language.** We all need and benefit from reminders to keep on track and move forward in our daily lives. Second graders are trying to keep track of so much—classroom expectations, social rules, new academic learning, among other things—and they will forget. Reminding language can be used to assist students in remembering social and academic routines and procedures. For example, one day during science block the class had a hard time respectfully finding a partner. The next day, you might remind students about the expectations for partnering before asking them to find a partner for that day's science lesson.

- **Redirecting language.** Redirecting language is useful when students get off track. This was once explained to me through the analogy of the rumble strip on the side of the road. When you are driving and drift to the right side of the road, the rumble strips are there to help you get back on the road. When students begin to get off track, redirecting language can be used to help them get back on track. For example, when you notice a student running across the classroom, you might redirect them by saying, "Stop, walk."

Teacher Language Examples in a Second Grade Classroom

Type of Language	Scenario	Language Example
Envisioning	• It's the beginning of the year and you are helping students dictate their hopes and dreams (goals) for the year.	• "What do you hope to learn this year in second grade?"
	• Students are playing basketball at recess and a student shares with you that they were told they could not play basketball with the group.	• "How might it feel to be left out of a game at recess?"
	• The class is about to embark on a challenging math task.	• "Mathematicians, yesterday we worked on counting coins. Today we will use those skills to learn to count mixed groups of coins."
Reinforcing	• One of your classroom rules says, "Take care of our classroom materials." You notice a student putting the dry-erase markers away gently.	• "I notice how carefully you put the cap on the dry-erase marker and gently put it in the container. You are following our 'Take care of our classroom materials' rule."
	• The class is working on using a number line to add double-digit numbers. You notice a student who had trouble with this skill yesterday showing success with it today.	• "I see you remembered to label your jumps when adding the numbers together. This will help you get the correct sum."

Type of Language	Scenario	Language Example
Reminding	• Yesterday, students had a difficult time getting into student choice partnerships. Today they will need to choose a partner and you want to ensure everyone has a partner.	• "Remember to have your hand up to pair up when choosing a partner."
	• You notice a student forgot to add ending marks to their writing.	• "What goes at the end of your sentences?" or "Remember to add ending marks."
Redirecting	• Everyone is meeting in the carpet area for a word study lesson and a lot of students are talking to each other rather than showing they're ready for learning.	• "We will start once everyone is quiet and looking at me."
	• Everyone is cleaning up from a science experiment and you notice a group of students being silly.	• "We are cleaning up. Put the science materials away now."

"We" and "Our"

To further signal that our individual selves are a part of a larger community, consider using the terms "we" and "our" when referencing the group, rather than leading with "I want" and labeling the group as "my class" or the classroom materials as "my materials." By replacing "I" and "my" in this way, we say to students that the teacher is also a part of this group and reinforces the concept that the classroom belongs to everyone.

Phrase	*Replace With*
My class . . .	Our class . . .
I want you to . . .	We will . . . or Let's . . .
The classroom library books . . .	Our classroom library books . . .

Getting to Know One Another

Second graders learn best in environments that feel physically, mentally, and emotionally safe and in spaces where they feel connected to their classmates and their teacher. Teachers know the power of relationships (peer-to-peer and student-to-teacher) and how they correlate with student success. When students feel they belong and have a significant role in the community, they are able to do their best learning and bring their best selves to school. While the foundation of safety and connection begins at the start of the year, community and relationship building is always in progress and ongoing. Second graders will benefit from class rituals such as a daily Morning Meeting and closing circle, both of which help students and teachers get to know each other, make deeper connections, and form friendships.

The Power of "Sharing" in Morning Meeting

Morning Meeting offers specific practices that allow students to get to know each other. They learn the value of a friendly "hello" and take comfort in participating in a unifying activity. The sharing component of Morning Meeting provides an opportunity for the entire community to get to know one another in ways they might not otherwise. Students will light up when another student shares about a similar interest and when new friendships begin to form. Teachers will see a new side to students. The sharing component reinforces the message of "we all belong here."

See the appendix, p. 335, for more on Morning Meeting.

Ending the Day Together With Closing Circle

Bringing students back together at the end of the school day for a five-to-ten-minute closing circle allows students to come back together as a community, reflect on the day, and participate in a fun end-of-the-day activity. Just as Morning Meeting begins the day on a positive note and allows for students to interact with each other first thing in the morning, closing circle offers a calm way to end the day and say "see you tomorrow" to the group.

Special Projects to Support Classroom Community Development

As the school year progresses, the classroom community needs and deserves continual nurturing. Consider and plan for regular partner work and class projects that will support your existing community and continue to deepen the positive connections you all have built.

Special Projects for Second Grade		
Beginning of the Year	**Throughout the Year**	**End of the Year**
• "All About Me and My Family" poster or video	• Twenty Questions interview	• Classmate interview and presentation
• Five Favorites paper bag activity	• "Who Am I?" visual art project	• "All About Me" paper or video for next year's teacher
• Self-portrait poem	• "All About Our Class" poetry	• End-of-the-year reflection project
• Family survey	• Our class timeline	
	• Service projects	

Birthdays, Holidays, and Other Celebrations

Second graders love celebrations. They are often eager to celebrate their birthday, holidays, and school-based accomplishments such as a recent story they authored.

Birthdays

Birthdays are at the top of exciting events for second graders. They are turning another year older and are often counting down the days until their big day. Consider creating a class birthday display at the start of the year so students can see the different birth dates of their classmates. A class-created "Birthday Book" is another way to involve the class in celebrating birthdays. On the morning of a student's birthday, each student would work on a page for the book, which might include a picture, letter, or poem. Once the pages are complete, you can put them together to present to the student to make their second grade birthday memorable. If you have students with summer birthdays, think about celebrating their half birthday or setting aside a day near the end of the year to recognize summer birthdays.

Holidays and Other Celebrations

As you consider various events that might take place in your classroom, take into consideration what you know about the celebratory preferences of the students and their families, and what celebrations will be purposeful and meaningful for students.

- **Keep it simple and have a clear purpose.** Not all celebrations have to be extraordinary events that take up a lot of time and energy. Sometimes the simplest celebrations are the most memorable. Think about the purpose of the celebration, who benefits from it, and what you hope comes from the celebration. Clarifying the purpose will help you decide on the other details related to the event.

Second Grade Celebration Options

- Publishing party
- Author or genre celebration
- Math game day
- "My Best Work" museum: students display their best work to be admired by others
- School-based festivals (fall, winter, spring)
- Cultural celebrations

- **Prepare and allow for students to practice.** When your celebration involves students presenting their work, remember to allow time for them to practice. This will help settle any nerves or jitters and instill confidence in their presentation skills. Consider how the skills students have practiced in Morning Meeting can assist with their presentation skills.

- **Invite others to share in the joy.** There is no doubt students will be excited to share with important people in their lives. If appropriate and possible, consider inviting your colleagues, other classes, special area teachers, lunch teachers, recess teachers, or families to certain celebrations throughout the year.

Lunchtime and Recess

Lunch is a ritual that helps to foster and deepen the classroom community. Second grade students, though, will benefit from some extra time and attention to this time of the day. By second grade, many students are already familiar with the process of eating lunch at school, but don't assume they remember all of the routines and procedures. Here are some guidelines for helping students with lunchtime routines.

- **Teach expectations.** Ask yourself, "What skills do students need to be successful during lunch?" Once you have a list of skills, break down which of those can be taught and when.

- **Provide assigned seats.** To assist students in finding a place to sit and to lower their anxieties of "Where do I sit?" and "Who do I sit with?" give students an assigned lunch spot until you have modeled and practiced inclusivity during lunch and are confident that students can easily choose where and with whom to sit.

- **Teach conversation skills.** Second graders are learning how to make and maintain friendships, and at the same time they are continuing to develop and refine their speaking and listening skills. To support students' conversations with one another, consider providing a set of laminated conversation cards for students to use during lunch. Some popular questions and topics include:

○ "What's your favorite part of the school day, and why?"

○ "If you could be any animal in the world, what animal would you be, and why?"

○ "What's something new you've learned this week?"

○ This or That: Put two pictures on a card and students can discuss which of the choices they would choose, and why.

Lunchtime Skills

First day of school

- Lining up to get a hot lunch
- Paying
- Packers
- Where to sit
- Lining up to leave the cafeteria

Second day of school

- Responding to a signal for attention
- Staying in your seat
- Cleaning up your space

Third day of school

- Restroom procedure
- Handling spills
- Asking for help

Ongoing

- Appropriate conversations with peers
- How to initiate a conversation with a tablemate
- Choosing a spot to sit
- Welcoming others to sit with you

Similar to lunch, recess is an important event for students. This is a time when they can laugh and play together, try out new friendships, connect with existing friends, and navigate complex social situations. In addition, recess allows second graders opportunities to further develop and explore their rapidly developing gross motor skills. Allowing students to participate in recess yields a number of benefits throughout the entire school day. Like other parts of the school day, recess requires special attention to be sure this time runs smoothly for all students. You can support your students in having an enjoyable and interesting recess by taking the following steps:

Working With Lunch and Recess Support Staff

Work together with staff to identify common recess and lunch expectations, signals for quiet and lining up, and how to respond to and communicate about misbehavior. When adults are on the same page, it will benefit students.

Class rules that travel with the students (traveling rules) will also work well as they transition from space to space and adult to adult. Your traveling rules can include your class rules, a class list, and any special notes related to rules and behavior.

- **Teach expectations at the start of the school year.** Consider breaking down the playground into zones and spending the first days of the school year using open-ended questions ("What might we use this area for during recess?") and Interactive Modeling to teach students appropriate ways to play in each zone.

- **Explore different recess options beyond what is provided on the playground.** Consider teaching students group games that the class can play together, providing sidewalk chalk and bubbles, teaching the game Four Square, and taking stock in additional activities that might be of interest to the group.

- **Model essential recess behaviors and skills.** Recess is a socially complex time and requires the use of multiple skills. Consider using Interactive Modeling and role-play to teach the following:

    ○ Making a recess choice

- Joining a game already in progress

- Handling a disagreement

- Asking for help from an adult

- Helping when someone is hurt

- Taking care of recess materials

- Responding to signals

- Cleaning up and lining up

- Reentering the building

● **Observe and support students during recess.** Take time during recess to observe students and notice areas of strength and those that may need support. This is particularly important as the year goes on and the classroom community evolves.

There will be different options to teach for indoor recess. Have the class come up with a list of possible indoor recess choices. This will serve not only as a beginning list of indoor recess choices, but it will allow students to get to know their classmates' interests. Ask, "What choices might we have for indoor recess this year?" and "What indoor recess choices did you enjoy from last year?" Once a list of ten or so choices has been created, decide on two to explore first. Model each one and then send the students off to experience both choices. Use a few days each week to introduce more indoor recess choices, and soon you will have a list of choices with clear expectations outlined for each one. Throughout the year you can add to the list and rotate items based on the interests of the group. Some popular indoor recess options for second graders include:

- Puzzles

- Board games (Checkers, Candy Land, Guess Who?, Chutes and Ladders, Trouble, Sorry!)

- Card games (Go Fish, Old Maid, Uno, War, Memory, Odds and Evens)

- Coloring pages and blank paper

- Dry-erase markers and boards

- Reading

- Dramatic play

Establishing Rules and Investing Students in the Rules

Working hand in hand to develop rules that will govern class behavior is an important process in defining how "we," the class, will function as a community. This process begins with the use of envisioning language to help students articulate their hopes and dreams (their big goal) for the year. Once students have landed on their second grade hopes and dreams, it's important to take time for the group to hear the hopes and dreams of their classmates in order to better understand that each of us is working toward something special during the school year.

Once everyone's hope and dream is noted and displayed in the classroom, the conversation around classroom rules can begin. The rules-creation process takes time and does not have to be done on the first day of school or even the first week of school. Give yourself and the students time to settle in, learn something about each other, generate some excitement about the year, and share their hopes and dreams.

A great way to initiate a conversation around rules is to connect them to the hopes and dreams by saying, "If these are our hopes and dreams this year, what rules might we need to follow so everyone can achieve their goals?" or "How do we want our class to be so everyone can accomplish their hopes and dreams?" or even "What rules might we need to follow so everyone can be successful with their hopes and dreams?" From there, go for volume and positively list all of the suggestions given by students.

Students might offer rules stated in the negative, such as "Don't hit" or "Don't run." In cases like these, make sure to flip these statements so they are positive. One way to do this is by simply asking students, "If we won't hit, what will we be doing?" Offering a list of rules stated in the positive gives clear expectations for behavior.

Over the next few days, have the class identify similar rules and then pare the list down to just three or four global rules. The rules-creation process is a collaborative one that values the voices and contributions of all students. Once you have a final set of rules, consider the ways in which the rules will come to life to support the success of all students in the classroom.

Tips to Help Students Articulate Their Hopes and Dreams

- **Set the stage.** To keep the hopes and dreams focused on school, consider sharing information about what students will learn during the year and show pictures of projects from previous groups of students. This gives students an idea of what will be in store during the year and provides them with many examples before formulating their own hope and dream.

- **Share your own hope and dream.** Think about your goal for students for the year and share this with them. Your hope and dream for the year might say something like "I hope everyone enjoys learning" or "My hope is that we all support each other this year."

- **Use qualifiers.** When we say "hopes and dreams," some students may take it literally. I had a student who expressed her hope and dream for the year as "I hope balloons will fall from the ceiling." Use qualifiers to help students specify an attainable goal for the year. For example, "Based on what you know about what we might learn this year, what is your hope and dream for this school year?"

Proactive Approach to Discipline

Proactive discipline involves skillfully being able to think ahead and "see" the future in order to provide students with the skills they will need to be successful with what lies ahead. Ask yourself the following questions:

- "What's coming up?" (socially, academically, routines, procedures)

- "What skills do students need to be successful with this task?"

- "How can I support students in developing the skills they need to be successful with this task?"

The more proactive you are in your thinking, the smoother it will go for everyone, and less time will be spent reacting to student misbehaviors and misunderstandings.

Another part of proactive discipline is the effort put into creating classroom rules and building the classroom community. Creating classroom rules together encourages discussion around what expectations might serve the class community well during the year and allows for equal voice. Everyone has a say in the class rules and reasoned discussions are encouraged. When students feel they contributed to and had a say in the class rules, they are more apt and willing to follow those rules. Second grade is the year when students begin to consider how their actions affect the group. They will want to follow the rules and will view the class guidelines as law. To further build investment in the rules, consider using role-play to bring the rules to life and reinforcing language to make connections between classroom behavior and the agreed-on rules.

The classroom community is built over time and will continue beyond the first weeks of school. Practices such as Morning Meeting and closing circle will reinforce the significance students hold in the classroom. The four components of Morning Meeting offer opportunities for you and the students to learn about each other on a deeper level and beyond what we might observe throughout other times of the day.

Maintaining a Strong Community

Naturally, more time is spent at the beginning of the year on building the foundation of the classroom community, but it is important to make efforts to continue to build the classroom community as the year progresses. There are other times during the year when it will be important to take additional steps to maintain a positive classroom community:

- **After breaks.** Extended periods of time away from school can be challenging not only for classroom routines and procedures but also for peer relationships. After a long weekend or extended periods away from school, consider using additional community-building activities to allow students to re-acclimate themselves to the classroom.

- **Arrival of new students.** The addition of a new student offers the perfect time to review classroom routines, procedures, rules, and consequences, and to plan activities to assist the new student to get to know the class and for the class to get to know the new student.

- **Highly stressful times of the year.** There are certain times of the year that feel a bit more stressful than others. Maybe it's the end of the marking period, when grade cards are due, or a time of the year when statewide testing is taking place. Be proactive and keep in mind your needs as well as those of the class during those times. Consider ways to keep the community intact through lighthearted and fun activities.

  My former colleagues and I relied on each other during stressful times of the year and would plan ways to support each other so we could be our best selves for our students. One year the other teachers in my pod and I designed a spring break day on the day before our weeklong holiday. Each teacher planned a fun activity for students, and we spent the entire day rotating from one class to another facilitating the activity we planned with different groups of students. It was not only awesome but preserved our sanity—students and teachers alike!

Chapter 4
Engaging Academics

● ●

Overview

Imagine the quintessential, picture-perfect classroom. When I do, I see my friend Jean's kindergarten. It is totally child centered, from the furniture to the class materials to the learning activities. One of my favorite parts is a large credenza just inside the door. It's a long, wide bookshelf that's perfect for students to stand and work at, to place large art projects on to dry, and to display thematic items throughout the year. There was always something new and fun happening at this bookshelf. One day, I walked into her classroom and I was greeted by fifteen houseplants of all shapes and sizes sitting on the shelf. A student's grandmother had volunteered and was so thankful to be invited, and so impressed with the classroom, she sent Jean an African violet as a thank you. Jean had it set on her desk and, as you can imagine, the inquisitive five-year-olds wanted a closer look at the plant with its beautiful colors and soft, fuzzy leaves, so it was moved to the bookshelf. The next day, another houseplant appeared on the shelf. A student had told his family about the African violet plant and asked if he could bring in a plant from home. By the end of that week, there was a collection of houseplants to look at, talk about, and explore as students contributed plants to the collection.

This collection led the class to ask questions about the houseplants, and soon the class was doing research on them. They were excited when they discovered books from the school library that Jean placed alongside the plants. Rich conversations followed, and Jean was impressed by the students' vocabulary and the concept words they were learning and practicing as they discovered together. The class eagerly wrote about and drew the plants, and they were thrilled to create the new classroom job of plant caretaker. Who would have thought that one little African violet would spark so much excitement and such rich learning opportunities?

Know Your Students

Making academics engaging for students starts with knowing our students, and one of the best ways to get to know our students is to observe them. Jean is a master observer: she uses what she sees and knows her students well enough to guide her instruction. We can't help but see our students as we interact with them in Morning Meeting, during recess, or when they come to show us things and talk to us. But surface-level seeing is not enough—we have to deliberately and intentionally take time to actively observe our students. As you get to know your students, take note of the following characteristics:

- **Relationships.** Who gets along with whom? Which students are like oil and water when they interact? Who is a peacemaker, and who is an instigator?

- **Self-control.** Who is a risk-taker, and who is not? Which students get quickly frustrated, and which ones exhibit good emotional control?

- **Attention and focus.** Who has a lot of energy, and who is more settled? Who can remain focused, and whose attention wanes quickly?

- **Language.** How well do students express themselves? Do they understand others easily? Who struggles to find their voice and share their ideas?

- **Learning styles.** Is it easier for them to learn with verbal or written explanations? Who learns best with visuals? Who needs to move to learn?

Observing students is not a onetime task or something that is scheduled like an assessment or a report card. Observation should be an integral and automatic part of our daily practice. There are a few ways in which to incorporate observation into your teaching:

- **Make time to observe both the whole class and each individual student.** Your classroom setup is important here because you want a physical space that allows you to move easily around the room as you observe. Focus your observations on the learning that is going on rather than using this time to look for off-task behavior or to redirect misbehavior. Keep a journal or notepad handy to record what you see.

- **Provide in-the-moment feedback.** Moving around the room as you observe will offer opportunities to provide immediate feedback to students that can help them better understand and reflect on their own learning. Use reinforcing language with students that focuses on the specifics related to the learning and goes beyond general praise, such as "Looks good!" Help students develop a growth mindset by focusing more on process rather than end results. Use open-ended questions to assess your students' thinking, clear up any confusion or misunderstanding, and make adjustments to the instruction when needed.

- **Reflect on your observations.** Take a few minutes at the end of each day to review and reflect on your observations while they are still fresh in your mind. Use these observations to make instructional decisions and to adjust plans so you can provide more support or more challenges. Look for patterns and measure progress.

Clipboard Trick

Another teacher once showed me how she tracks her observation of students. She writes her students' names in little boxes and bubbles on a piece of paper, and then places the paper on a clip-board. As she observes throughout the week, she makes notes about each student—something funny they said or did, an interest they're exploring, a strength they discovered. The clipboard reminds her to be on the look-out and to observe every student, and it provides a record of observations to go back and reflect on. Using the clipboard has become a regular part of her day, like taking attendance, doing the lunch count, and writing dismissal notes. Once, when a student was taking notes on a book and noticed the teacher nearby with her clipboard, the student asked, "Are you going to write this down about me?" Even students know the power of observation!

Faced with canned curriculum and programs, we need to be careful not to fall into the trap of spending more time looking at spiral binders with pre-made lesson plans than at the students. The information we glean through our ongoing observations should be used to help guide our instruction. We can design or structure lessons and learning activities that offer appropriate risks, play to students' strengths and interests, capitalize on their learning styles, incorporate the right amount of movement, and create pairs or groups that support each student. Just as with other aspects of teaching, observation will come naturally with time and practice. Taking time to observe your students will help you plan more effective instruction and create more opportunities for engaging academics.

Purposeful and Meaningful Learning

When Jean welcomed a collection of houseplants into her kindergarten classroom, she was capitalizing on the natural learning cycle. Educational theorists such as John Dewey and Jean Piaget found that learning follows a natural three-part cycle that begins with a sense of purpose or a goal for learning. This, in turn, leads to a period of exploration as students follow leads and interests, gather information, and try out new skills. The cycle ends with students taking time to reflect as they consider what they have learned and still want to learn. They then revise their goals or set new ones, and the cycle starts again.

Generating ideas and goals

Reflecting on experiences

Actively exploring, experimenting, problem-solving

Within the requirements of the curriculum, we should strive to set goals that are meaningful for the students and that connect with their interests and needs. My friend Jean didn't have to say, "Today we are going to be learning about plants." Instead, the learning grew naturally out of the students' interest and excitement. Learning happened because the teacher observed her students, saw an interest, and capitalized on it.

Setting High Expectations for Learning

Lessons should provide an appropriate level of challenge so students spend most of their time in what psychologist Lev Vygotsky (1978) termed their "zone of proximal development." Or, as I like to call it, "the rubber band." You want to have just the right amount of tension on the rubber band, at the point where learning can take place. Too much tension could mean too much of a challenge for the student, and they'll "snap"—push away the paper and shut down. Too little tension could mean not enough of a challenge for the student, and they'll check out—hurry through and daydream. Each student's level of challenge will be different, but identifying students with similar levels can help you to guide groupings and differentiation so that each student is appropriately challenged. Then you can build on what they already know while encouraging them to push to the next level of knowledge and skill. Setting high expectations for students will:

- Encourage questions, promote engagement, and deepen students' thinking.

- Foster a growth mindset in students and help them to know when it is okay to make mistakes, how to ask for help, and how to learn from challenges.

- Promote higher-level thinking as students make choices, engage with interactive learning structures, respond to open-ended questions, and find meaningful ways to reflect on their learning through carefully designed lessons and activities.

- Give students a belief in their abilities to learn new things and reflect on their work, supported by their teacher's reinforcing feedback.

Active and Interactive Learning

Students need structures to be active and interactive with content and with each other. Interactive learning structures are fun and purposeful ways to get students moving, playing, exploring, talking, collaborating, and sharing in ways that are safe and productive. There are some key points to keep in mind when using interactive learning structures:

- **A quiet signal is an essential tool.** I used to think the gold-star classroom was the quiet classroom, but in reality, the gold-star one has a healthy buzz of conversation and movement. Gaining the attention of a class working and learning together is needed when students are active and interactive.

- **Interactive learning structures need to be taught.** Think about how you will teach the skills needed for students to be able to participate successfully in a partner chat, table talk, Museum Walk, or Inside-Outside Circles.

- **Directions need to be clear, and materials should be ready.** Interactive learning structures can have a few working parts, so it's important to think about how to scaffold the skills, how to explain what to do, and how to get the needed materials.

- **Activities may need to be adapted, depending on the developmental readiness of the students.** For example, when doing a partner chat with six-year-olds, you will need to help them with procedures such as determining who talks first and how much to say. Some interactive learning structures require reading and writing skills that young students may not be ready for, so you may need to adjust the activities to their level.

- **Timing and space need to be considered in planning.** Some interactive learning structures can be completed quickly and don't take up a lot of space, while others may take longer, require a bigger space, or call for good traffic flow.

If we want to make learning active for young students, approach it in the spirit of play. Remember what young children enjoy doing:

- **They enjoy playing, pretending, and performing.** I often use puppets when I teach my guidance lessons. Students love to act out the stories with puppets and put on puppet shows to practice skills we've been learning. It doesn't have to be a big production or take a lot of time. I usually pick a few students to be puppeteers, and they stand around me as I sit in my chair with the rest of the class as the audience. Sometimes I give them the lines, and other times we'll generate the lines together. These short, fast-paced puppet shows keep students engaged time and time again. Through movement, students not only have the opportunity to go deeper with the content of the lesson, but they are able to practice collaboration, use their voice, and engage in storytelling.

- **They enjoy building, creating, and constructing.** I had a large arts and crafts center in my counseling playroom, nice and neat and organized. But students often didn't use it. One year I instead put out a bin of unorganized art materials and told them they could make whatever they wanted. It became one of their favorite activities. When given the opportunity to make things, students will gain practice with problem-solving, using supplies creatively and responsibly, and turning a mistake into a success.

- **They enjoy telling things to the teacher and to each other.** Children like to talk about what they know, what they want to know, what they think, and what they wonder. I use a listening exercise with students in which I tell them a story about a pet I would like to get someday. My story is full of details; for example, I want to get a chocolate Lab, name him Snickers, and let him snuggle with me on the couch. When I'm done telling the story, I ask the students to think about why I would name my chocolate Lab Snickers. To hear

the explanations of these six- and seven-year-olds is just fascinating. Strong speaking and listening skills are foundational to learning. When students are given the chance to share their thinking orally or through writing, they are able to practice taking turns, public speaking, listening, and observing social cues.

Collaborative Learning

Academics are engaging for students when learning is collaborative; creating opportunities for collaboration is thus an essential part of teaching. There are many benefits to setting up collaborative work. For example, learning involves risk-taking, and for many students working with a partner or in a small group provides a safe place to try new things, make mistakes, and ask questions.

While each student is a unique learner, there are some commonalities that can be used when grouping students together. Differentiating by learning styles, interests, strengths, or needs can increase students' engagement by best meeting their learning needs. Great cognitive growth can occur through social interaction, and offering students the opportunity to work in partnerships and groups throughout the day not only meets their need for connection but can help deepen learning.

When creating opportunities for collaborative work, keep these guidelines in mind:

- **Be flexible.** Common abilities can be used as the basis to form partnerships or groups, but groups can also be organized according to students' interests, learning styles, friendships, or skills. They could be teacher created or student selected as well. Considewr the purpose of the activity, and use what you know about your students to guide how, when, and what type of collaborative groupings to use.

- **Be creative.** Consider trying an approach other than "Find a partner" or "Let's count off by 2s." There are many creative ways to form partnerships and groups that will get students up and moving, make for quick transitions to partners or small groups, and be fun. (See the chart in Grade 2 for examples and explanations.)

- **Be proactive.** There is a core set of social and emotional skills that need to be taught when students will be working with each other. This "language of learning" will be the key to successful collaborative work because it gives students the thinking and communication tools needed to successfully engage with each other and with the work. Learning in and of itself can be hard. Asking students to engage in appropriately challenging work and utilize skills such as cooperation, turn-taking, and waiting can be a tall order. Use Interactive Modeling and role-play to teach the social and emotional skills needed to navigate working with partners and in small groups.

When to Teach Language of Learning Skills Suggested Timeline K–2

Weeks 1–4	Early in year to midyear	Midyear to end of year
• Focusing attention • Showing interest • Taking turns • Speaking confidently	• Sustaining attention • Developing listening comprehension skills • Speaking confidently • Core question skills • Staying on topic • Speaking with clarity • Answering questions	• Staying on topic • Speaking with clarity • Asking purposeful questions • Answering questions • Organizing thoughts • Distinguishing facts from opinions • Presenting evidence • Agreeing • Disagreeing

Adapted from *The Joyful Classroom: Practical Ways to Engage and Challenge Elementary School Students* by *Responsive Classroom* (Center for Responsive Schools 2016).

Allowing for Student Choice

Choice—any kind of choice—is powerful. For young students, it's who you sit with, what order you get to do things in, how you practice something, where you work, and what you learn. Choice gives students a sense of autonomy, increases their motivation, and reduces behavior problems in classrooms, all of which lead to greater student engagement.

But how much choice? What choices? When? Offering choices can quickly become overwhelming. Offering choice, though, doesn't mean choice in everything. Look at it as a balance between "have to" and choice. Think back to Jean's fifteen houseplants. There could be some have-to's, such as everyone has to write a sentence about plants or everyone has to browse books on plants during book center time. But within these have-to's there can be some simple choices. For example, deciding which plant to write about and draw is a simple choice, as would choosing which book on plants to look at during the book center time or determining two things to show the class that you've learned about plants. As often as you can, build in simple choices.

Lesson Design and Lesson Structure

Effective lesson design utilizes a three-part structure that reflects the natural learning cycle and that can be used for planning any lesson, regardless of how long the lesson is or the age of the students. Well-designed lessons are important because they keep students focused on learning, help them to stay connected to the learning, support them by setting an appropriate pace for learning, and provide them with time to reflect on their learning.

Here is how an effective three-part lesson can be structured:

- **Step one: Create purposeful *openings*.** Engaged learning is purposeful, and having a purposeful opening goes beyond just knowing your learning objective and what you want your students to be able to do when the lesson is done. Purposeful openings help students know what they will be learning and why it matters. Your role in the opening of a lesson is to set a positive tone for learning and set the stage for the engaged learning to come. Use envisioning language to inspire your students: "We've been doing a lot of investigating and observing of our plant collection. I have a favorite plant. Do you? Today, you're going to get to write about your favorite plant and choose how you want to do your illustration. You can use markers or watercolors." Ask open-ended questions to prompt students' thinking: "Think about what plant is your favorite from our plant collection and why you like it so much." Be thoughtful about the transitions students will need to make during the lesson in order to be successful; for example, if students are going to be choosing between markers and watercolors, how and where will the materials be set up?

- **Step two: Make the *body* of the lesson active and interactive.** There are several characteristics that make academics engaging, and the body of the lesson should reflect these so that the work is:

  - Purposeful

  - Appropriately challenging

  - Active and interactive

○ Connected to interests

○ Structured with opportunities for choice

While there is a place for direct teaching, keeping it brief and focused allows time for students to construct their own knowledge by asking questions, exploring, trying out ideas, and applying new learning. The teacher's role in the body of the lesson is mostly to observe, facilitate, and coach. Observing allows you to see where students are in their social and academic abilities and skills. These observations will help guide you as you facilitate and coach students as they work. Your goal at this point is to help students stay on task and work through points where they are stuck, to encourage them to stretch themselves, and to correct misunderstandings.

Coaching will work best when students want the help. Before offering direction or help, consider first asking, "Would you like some help?" or "Can I tell you something that has helped other second graders?" These questions give students the opportunity to choose to accept help or to keep trying on their own. If you notice several students struggling with the same academic or social challenges, reteaching an academic skill or classroom routine may be needed. Be sure to check in with each student regularly, including those students who are working well and on the surface may not seem to need your attention.

● **Step three: Facilitate student *reflection*.** Some of the deepest learning happens not during the work time but when students have a chance to think about and talk about the work they've done. That's why it is important to be thoughtful about this step by planning how students can engage in reflection and allotting enough time for meaningful reflection. The length of the lesson helps determine the length of the reflection. For shorter lessons, the reflection may be a brief restatement of the purpose of the lesson or a quick turn and talk with a partner. For longer lessons, the reflection piece may be more intricate and involve longer summaries, connections to other learning, and more talking points or movement. Your role in this final step of the lesson is to summarize what was practiced or learned, facilitate the reflection, and make connections to other learning. Open-ended questions are a great way to get students to think about what they learned about the content, the process, or themselves as learners: "What's one thing you learned about plants from our activity?" or "What's one new idea you got from looking at everyone's drawings and paintings of plants from our plant collection?"

Each step in this three-part lesson structure plays a role in making and keeping academics engaging for students. Think of the opening and reflection steps as important bookends around the work. Keeping that in mind will be helpful in not shortchanging these two important steps. Teaching with purpose leads to learning with purpose. Keep the purpose of the lesson at the forefront of your mind as you create an opening to the lesson. Consider posting the learning objective in kid-friendly language for the students on a whiteboard or other display area and on a sticky note for yourself as a reminder to refer back to the purpose during the lesson. When planning the body of the lesson, be thoughtful about choosing a learning structure that matches the goal of the lesson. When giving feedback, make sure that it connects students back to the purpose of the lesson to help keep students focused on the goal.

Some schools allow teachers autonomy in how they design their lessons, which will make it easier and more doable to plan your teaching in a way that uses the three-part lesson structure and honors the natural learning cycle. Teachers in schools where much of the curriculum is delivered through canned programs or scripted curriculum will find designing lessons more challenging. Even with limited opportunities to design your own lessons, though, you can still look for ways to include purposeful openings, to make work time active and interactive, and to offer reflective closings within the existing lessons.

Questioning Is Key to Stimulating Motivation

Young children are naturally curious. When we ask what they are thinking, what they want to know, and what they are wondering, we are showing them that their curiosity matters. Effective questioning is the ability to bring forth students' natural inclination to seek out learning experiences that inspire them and instill a lifelong love of learning. Whether it is to invite curiosity at the opening of a lesson, to help stretch their thinking while working, or to elicit reflective thoughts and ideas, consider the following questioning tips:

- Incorporate open-ended questions into your lesson design.

- Use a variety of questions.

- Offer different ways to respond to questions (with partners, through interactive learning structures, in writing, or through a poll).

- Use what you know about your students—their interests, their developmental stages, their strengths—to drive your questions.

- Remember the importance of wait time to allow for deeper thinking and more thoughtful responses.

Just as our use of questions can have a big impact, so can the questions students ask. Effective questioning skills are essential to students too. Asking effective questions is a developmental skill that has to be taught. Young students are still learning the difference between questions and statements, so they need lots of exposure and practice. Use Morning Meeting as a time to practice asking respectful questions. With students, create an anchor chart that has examples of respectful questions. Here are some:

- **Purposeful questions** connect back to the learning objective. They help students know the goals and purposes of the lesson: "When we spend time observing the plants in our plant collection, how might that help us in our writing?"

- **Diagnostic questions** are quick ways to assess students' knowledge and understanding of content or a skill, and can thus help us to identify misunderstandings and misconceptions: "What are the four different parts of a plant that we've been learning about?"

- **Open-ended questions** are ones that cannot be answered in a single word. Responding to these questions requires thought and detailed answers: "What are some different ways we can take care of our plant collection?"

- **Reflective questions** help students think about their learning, their work, and who they are as learners: "What do you want to learn more about?"

Developmentally Responsive Teaching, Effective Management, and Positive Community

To teach in a way that is truly engaging for our students, we must go back to what we have learned in the previous chapters of this book. What we know about our students developmentally, individually, and culturally has to be at the forefront of our lesson design. We can have the best-laid plans for making our academics engaging, but without the solid foundation that comes from effective management practices and the creation of a positive community, those wonderful plans can quickly fall apart. Teaching in a way that is engaging requires a classroom setup that allows for partner work, small-group work, and whole-group work. The classroom environment has to be equipped with materials that allow for choice and should be organized in a way that allows students to have a level of independence in accessing and using those materials. Lessons should be approached with an eye on inclusiveness and equity for all students.

Think back to Jean's kindergartners and their excitement about sharing houseplants with the class. Jean had to be thoughtful about so many things. She had to provide space for observation and exploration, and she needed to have the materials available that would allow students to engage in interesting learning activities. By not requiring students to bring in plants, she was also mindful of families who might not have had houseplants or who did not have the means to purchase one. Engaging academics can't stand alone. They must be supported by developmentally responsive teaching, effective management, positive community, and cooperation with families.

In the grade-level sections that follow, you will find wonderful stories and examples that illustrate effective lesson design for young learners and approaches to culturally responsive teaching. Tips and ideas for using open-ended questions, teaching social and emotional skills, making student groupings, and observing students are looked at more closely as they are examined through each grade level's developmental lens.

Grade Ⓚ

Early in my third year of teaching, I was sitting with two students at one of the center tables in the classroom, looking for colored cubes and counting what we found. I looked up and did a visual sweep of the room, saw all of my students engaged, and then returned my attention to the students sitting beside me. I felt a profound sense of satisfaction: children were writing a menu for the dramatic play area we were turning into a restaurant while others were building a town in the block area. Another student was painting pictures of food at the easel while others were using collage materials in the art area. There was a hum of industrious activity. I was overwhelmed by the beauty of it all—it was exactly what I had envisioned when I was in college and thought about teaching.

It was a landmark moment for me as a teacher. Later that day, I took time to think about why things were going well. I thought about what I had done to set up the kids for success and how I could keep that momentum going. That day taught me how to unpack what was going well and understand why. As I have grown as a teacher, I've become better at articulating why things went so well during that particular experience:

- **It was based on student interests.** We had recently taken a walking field trip to a local pizzeria and the students were fascinated, so we were reading books about restaurants, buildings, and playing and counting.

- **It was purposeful.** After our visit to the pizzeria, the class wanted to turn parts of our classroom into a restaurant, so many of the children were focused on doing things to accomplish that.

- **Children could make choices.** They felt a sense of autonomy in being able to choose what they wanted to do during that workshop.

- **It provided various levels of challenge.** Depending on how they were feeling, children might choose to challenge themselves to count really high, to write the words on the menu, or to create a collage made up of food images.

- **Children were active.** Those that wanted to move, build, and create could choose to do so.

- **Children could be interactive.** Some children were working together while others worked independently.

Designing Lessons

A three-part lesson structure is successful with kindergartners because it supports their short attention span and honors their need for active engagement. Remember: keep your introductory lessons short. No matter how engaging you are, kindergartners learn from the work and play they are doing, and by focusing your lesson plans on these activities, you can embed, facilitate, and extend your students' learning.

- **Opening.** The workshop begins with a small mini-lesson or hook to capture the students' attention and set the learning focus for their lesson.

- **Body.** This is the bulk of the workshop, when children do most of the work and the teacher facilitates, extends, and supports, often pulling small groups.

- **Closing.** The workshop ends with a structured reflection or sharing time to allow students time to process the work they've done.

Kindergartners are naturally curious and energetic. These characteristics can be productively channeled when we provide our students with predictable structure and routine, as well as fun, movement, and novelty throughout the day. As you think through the ebbs and flows of the day, there are other structures to incorporate to keep your students engaged:

- **Guided Discovery.** This structure introduces materials in an engaging way. Guided Discovery also provides a shared common experience and allows children to exchange ideas, knowledge, and insight with each other, so if a student has a clever idea, the other children get to see a demonstration as well.

See the appendix, p. 332, for more on Guided Discovery.

- **Interactive learning structures.** These provide important opportunities for kindergartners to build relationships with each other in an active way. Interactive learning structures have a give-and-receive structure and can be used with social and academic content. Optimally, children should be engaging with each other through interactive learning structures multiple times per day.

- **Energizers.** Teachers of young children instinctively know that students need to get up and move around regularly. Cultivate a repertoire of songs, dances, and activities that represents your student body. Use these energizers often.

- **Small-group learning.** Groups of three to five children work well for teacher-focused lessons on language arts, math, and social and emotional skills. This size group allows children to feel they are seen and heard, and it is manageable for teachers to get needed information about children's thinking. Small groups can also be a good way to provide children with choices for material or content, as well as allow you the space to join in briefly and engage with all students of a group.

- **Partner work.** Kindergartners delight in having a partner for so many things. It can be helpful for students to have a partner for several weeks so they can build a stronger connection with each other. Young children will need both instruction and freedom for partnerships. When left to their own devices, many kindergartners will start out on task but will quickly realize they have a lot to talk about. You may join them at a table during math and find them in a rousing debate over which video game character is best. If you're going to partner students for work or a game, be sure to model and teach them how to do the work so they know what to expect. Remember, too, to allow that flexibility for true five- and six-year-old conversations. Discussing video game characters is just as important to them as the math game they're playing.

Lesson Considerations for Kindergartners

The most important thing to remember when planning for kindergartners: process over product. For example, after a week or two of work, a kindergartner's writing project might resemble many things. It could look like a completed book with pictures on every page, a series of drawings with letters or words, or strings of letters. What matters, though, is that they feel a sense of ownership. Can they describe for you what is contained within their work? If they can, then it was worth it. Their work tells you what they already know: What do they understand about writing? Do the pictures match? Are they writing the first sounds of some of the words they're writing? Are they hearing more than one sound? All of these things tell you what they're learning through the joyful process of writing.

Kindergartners find joy in the magic of learning. Puppets or sets of small dolls can help with lessons or acting out a tricky issue. Puppets or dolls should have varied body types, ability types, and skin tones. Give each puppet or doll their own background and personality so children will be interested and invested in their stories. These puppets or dolls can be used to model problem-solving, teach social and emotional skills, and initiate wonder about upcoming events.

This "magic" can be used for the hook of your lesson. For example, incorporate something new or novel to build your kindergartners' excitement or interest, or put an item in a mystery box and have the children guess what might be inside by having them ask questions. It will be endlessly rewarding to harness the enthusiasm of five- and six-year-olds.

Culturally Responsive Teaching

Zaretta Hammond defines culturally responsive teaching as follows: "The process of using familiar cultural information and processes to scaffold learning. Emphasizes communal orientation. Focused on relationships, cognitive scaffolding, and critical social awareness" (2014, 156).

Kindergarten teachers should understand the power and importance of relationships: the teacher-student, the student-student, and the collective community relationship. Whether preparing to teach either new or familiar content, do so with a critical eye. As you review lessons, literature, photographs, videos, books, and other media, ask yourself, "Whose story is being told?" Find materials and books that let children see themselves and people of all different abilities, races, and genders represented. Keep in mind the following:

- **Diversify your own media.** If you are on social media seek out voices and representation from those not yet represented.

- **Examine your curriculum materials and class library critically.** Students should see representations of all abilities, gender expressions, races, and family structures. Are you reading books that only model a single type of child or family?

- **Continue to learn.** Seek out professional resources that challenge your thinking. Be willing to sit with discomfort and make mistakes.

Social and Emotional Learning

Social and emotional skills can be deliberately woven into the lesson fabric. When planning a lesson or workshop and considering what will be expected of the children, ask yourself, "What skills do children need in order to be successful with this task?" Consider embedding proactive modeling into your lesson or earlier in the day before the lesson so the children have the opportunity to practice during their work period. Many kindergartners need instruction and practice with skills that relate to others (taking turns, asking to borrow something) and skills that relate to themselves (managing their feelings, self-regulating, persevering when things get difficult).

Observation provides an opportunity for noticing what sort of social and emotional learning the class needs and will also allow you to support individual children in the moment. Effectively teaching social and emotional content involves a mix of proactive lessons and on-the-spot teaching as children need it.

Here's an example of how that once played out in my class. One day I was sitting with a small group during a writing workshop period when Mara, one of my students, came to me in tears. "Ms. Howard, I'm asking my friends for help, but nobody is helping me!" I looked over at her table and knew that any of her seatmates would have helped her. I wondered if she might have turned to a lesson our class had done the week before. "It sounds like you are remembering what we talked about last week about asking a friend for help," I said. "Sometimes people might not know that you are talking to them. Try choosing one person at your table to ask, and then say: 'Sarah, will you please read over my writing with me?'" We dried her tears and she went back to the table. I heard her ask Sarah and smiled when I overheard the response: "Of course I will, Mara!"

Mara remembered the lesson from the week before. When it didn't work, she realized that she had an additional level of support: her teacher. She reached out when the other students didn't respond to her first strategy, which was to ask all of them simultaneously for help. Then she was willing to try something new. And it worked! Mara's experience also taught me that I should add that important step to proactive lessons. The other children could benefit from knowing to include the person's name when asking a question so that the person you're addressing knows you are talking to them.

While there are many social and emotional skills that are developmentally appropriate for kindergarten children to learn and practice, observation will let you know what your students need. When you as the teacher take the time to get to know your students individually, culturally, and developmentally, you will be better prepared to support their social and emotional learning.

Social and Emotional Lessons for Kindergartners

Consider practicing these skills in fun ways during energizers and Morning Meeting. This will allow children to practice them before using them in academic situations.

- How to ask for help
- What strategies to use when you have a big feeling
- How to take turns with a partner
- What to do when you disagree
- What to do if you lose and feel upset
- What to do if you are working on something and it doesn't come out the way you want
- How to keep going when something gets difficult

Setting High Expectations

We want our students to reach the highest goals, and we want them to exceed all of their dreams. The first step to helping our kindergartners to achieve these goals is by building a solid relationship with each student, and knowing each one individually, developmentally, and culturally. When we know who they are, we are capable of holding them accountable to the high standards we know they can achieve.

Use your relationship with your students and what you have seen them do to guide regular reflective conversations. Talk about what they can do now that they couldn't do before, and ask how they were able to achieve those things. Ask how they can use that knowledge to learn new things, and what help they might need from you so they can achieve them.

When children get in the regular habit of talking about learning—of seeing themselves as capable and seeing their teachers as supportive facilitators—they get the message that they are capable of doing hard things, and that they are already doing hard things. To help achieve this, consider using differentiation and teacher language strategies.

Differentiation

A couple of summers ago our family moved and my daughter had to change schools. Her new school had a weekly hour on Friday afternoons called "Innovation Hour." During this hour, every student in the school, kindergarten through fourth grade, was engaged in self-directed projects of their choice. Children created games and game boards, recorded videos that taught others how to knit, made figurines out of polymer clay, and engaged in many other projects. My daughter bounded out of bed every Friday morning brimming with ideas for Innovation Hour that day.

The assistant principal beamed with pride when I asked her about Innovation Hour. She talked about the different projects she had seen children create and how much teachers learned about their students during this time. She also noted that they had almost no office referrals during this time.

Consider implementing something similar to Innovation Hour in your schedule. Then watch carefully and observe: What sparks your students' curiosity? What motivates them? What do they create? Use what you observe to make adjustments to your other learning times, and use what you see works well to inform the other times of day. Encourage the children to wonder how some of what they're doing and how some of the materials they are using can be used for other learning times. And be sure to wonder along with them. There are so many ways to differentiate—through content, materials, and even partners and small groups.

Teacher Language

In Chapter 3, we discussed how teachers can harness the power of language to build up children to help them deepen their self-concept and to see themselves as capable. Our language allows us to teach them about having a growth mindset and to see mistakes as necessary and important for learning. We want to be very clear that mistakes are okay. Kindergartners are often very aware of when they get things wrong, and they can be very upset when they think they've done something they shouldn't have.

One day I kept dropping materials. I dropped my marker multiple times. I dropped the bundles of ten straws. And then I dropped calendar numbers, after which I said, "Goodness, it's like my name is Droppy McDropDrop today!" The class burst out laughing. Later that afternoon, I was reading a story aloud and kept messing up the words. Sara, one of my students, said, "Ms. Howard, it's like your dropping brain went into your mouth brain." When I looked confused, she said, "Like when you kept dropping things and you were Droppy McDropDrop. So the dropping part of your brain went into the mouth part of your brain and you're messing up the words . . . like dropping." Many in the class nodded in agreement. While I'm certain I don't have a "dropping brain" that's separate from my "mouth brain," those back-to-back experiences ended up being a blessing. We became joyous when mistakes happened, often saying "Droppy McDropDrop" and laughing. It was an unplanned but very organic way of embracing mistakes as part of learning.

Open-ended questions are another tool in our language toolbox to support holding our students to high standards, especially to encourage reflection. Kindergartners are capable of true reflection when they know that they are free from judgment. The relationship we build with each child helps solidify their ability to be honestly reflective.

When my son was in kindergarten, he tended to be obsessive. At one point, he had become very interested in reading Dav Pilkey's *Dog Man* series to himself, and he wasn't always giving his full attention to his class, which was being done remotely at the time. So we had an honest conversation.

I asked him, "What happens when your school is going on and you're reading one of the *Dog Man* books?"

He thought for a moment and said, "I get distracted by the book and don't get my work done."

"I've noticed that too. Can you tell me why your teacher asks you to do all of the other learning things?"

"So I can get smarter in all the stuff!"

"Yes! Do you have any ideas about what we could do to help you pay more attention?"

"We could put the *Dog Man* books in my bedroom and I can read them after school."

We found a basket and put his *Dog Man* books into it, and he chose a special spot in his bedroom for the basket. A few times a week, we talked about his smart idea of putting the books in a special place until school was over, and he continued to wait to read the books in the basket until his schoolwork was completed. When we reinforce children's reflection and ideas, it reinforces for them how capable they are in so many ways.

There will be some students that consistently choose something that we know is too easy or too hard. This is when scaffolding can be utilized. Just as we build on students' learning by pointing them to next steps and providing them with opportunities that are incrementally more challenging, we can follow the same steps with children who need support choosing things at an appropriate level of challenge. This support might come in the form of having them choose to do one thing for part of the time and another thing for the other part. It could involve asking permission to let you choose their work for the next day and then talking about it. Some children need support in feeling a sense of challenge and knowing they can walk out onto that tightrope because they know we are there with a net to catch them if they fall. They also know that when they fall, we will be there to help them get right back up onto the rope.

Observing Students

The best and most effective teachers of young children lead with love and curiosity. They know that a strong relationship with each child is key to success. They understand that young children—especially four-, five-, and six-year-olds—are brimming with curiosity, enthusiasm, and energy.

One day, my son was in a breakout room during a virtual learning session with three other kindergartners, working on their writing and chatting with each other as they worked. At one point, my son looked at the screen and realized that one of the students was sharing their screen. He wanted to know immediately who had done that—and *how* they had done it. An explosion of kindergarten energy followed, and they took turns sharing their screens, giggling, and then they tried out the important next question—"What else can we do?"—and all writing was soon forgotten.

Not long after, their teacher popped into the breakout room to check on them. The students spoke over each other, enthusiastically sharing their newfound skills. She patiently let them explain, and then asked if they could share what they had learned with the rest of the class. Their teacher cleverly understood that their excitement was something to harness. Over the next few days, as children shared learning with the rest of the class, she let each of them take a turn sharing their screen as they worked.

This story illustrates the idea of approaching children and new situations with curiosity instead of judgment. Rather than jump in right away to correct the students, the teacher watched. She then wondered, "What is going on here? What is driving this?"

When we as teachers approach situations with an emphasis on trying to understand what is going on, it allows us to respond supportively and sends a message to students that we know they are capable, smart, and worthy. Try treating children's behavior as a message to you letting you know what they need rather than a reflection on you and your skills as a teacher. Their message could mean "I need connection," "I'm feeling vulnerable," "I'm not feeling seen," or "Look what I can do!"

As Ross Greene puts it in *The Explosive Child* (2014, 14), "Your explanation guides your intervention." This statement could not be more relevant or important for teachers. If a child scribbles on their paper, our explanation for their behavior has an impact on how we respond. How many of us have responded immediately, without pausing a moment to try to understand what might be going on, only to make the situation worse? I know I have been guilty of this. But when we treat behavior as a message, it allows us to look into the "why" and respond with warm, firm support.

To observe is to see things through our own lens. It's important to regularly examine our own internalized biases so we respond to children's behavior based on what it is rather than base our response on our assumptions. In a classroom where the message is that all are welcome and that all will be able to thrive, it's imperative that children see examples of themselves in the curriculum, and in the readings, photographs, and videos used. Some resources to help become aware of one's biases include the following:

- Harvard Implicit Association Test (IAT), available at https://implicit.harvard.edu/implicit/takeatest.html

- *Me and White Supremacy: Combat Racism, Change the World, and Become a Good Ancestor* by Layla F. Saad

- *Culturally Responsive Teaching and the Brain: Promoting Authentic Engagement and Rigor Among Culturally and Linguistically Diverse Students* by Zaretta Hammond

- *Blindspot: Hidden Biases of Good People* by Mahzarin R. Banaji and Anthony G. Greenwald

In addition, it is important to regularly engage in professional development centered on recognizing bias.

When conducting observations, talk to and engage with your students as well as watch them, take notes about what you see and learn, and then review and reflect upon what you have learned.

Talk to Children

As mentioned earlier, open-ended questions are a key strategy to use when we observe children, because it allows us to approach them with curiosity.

Sometimes the easiest way to find out what is going on with a child is simply to ask them: "Tell me about what is going on here." Or you might point out what you observe: "I see your eyebrows are all pushed together and your mouth is turned down. Tell me about your feelings . . ."

When children trust that we honor what they tell us, they become more willing to provide a window in. Be open to whatever the children have to tell. Similar to observing without judgment, listening to their true message is an important part of the respect we can give to children.

Take Notes of Students' Words and Actions

I've tried multiple ways of recording student observations, and one size does not fit all. As a classroom teacher with eighteen to twenty-six students, I found that carrying a clipboard, to which I'd attached a simple form with a grid and a box for each student, allowed me to glance down and easily see who I hadn't checked on yet and guide my rotation around the room. As a special education teacher, I used four-by-six index cards held together by a ring, with one card for each student and one to two of their Individualized Education Plan goals pasted at the top of the card, to help guide my observations and keep my notes focused. I do more things digitally now. I find it helpful to use a digital slide deck with a page for each student. I can write observations directly onto my tablet with a stylus. It saves my work automatically, and I find that I misplace things far less often.

Whether you prefer to write by hand or use a digital option, find a method that works best for you and is sustainable. Just make sure your method is easily accessible and allows you to look back through to see the progress and patterns of students.

Review and Reflect

The observations we make based on the lessons and curricula we plan, the proactive teaching we do, and the positive community we strengthen daily—all of these factors connect and can lead to an incredible amount of growth and learning in our students. We take countless photographs and videos, save work samples, make checklists, and record notes anecdotally. When we are in the day-to-day work of the school year, it can sometimes be hard to recognize the learning our students do.

This is why it's so important to make time regularly to review and reflect on what you've observed. You'll see patterns that can provide insights into where to go next. You'll want to share some of what you've seen with the children so they can see how they have made progress. And then you'll want to sit back and marvel at the sheer brilliance of these fast, messy, and beautiful young children.

Grade ①

For most of my teaching career, I taught in a progressive school that balanced traditional curriculum with project-based learning that included student-selected research projects. There was so much I enjoyed about this lively dance between teacher-directed and student-directed learning. It was a much different approach from what I experienced in my own elementary years in an open classroom taught by self-proclaimed hippies. As cutting edge as the environment was, though, it was still the 1970s and the pedagogy was still very teacher driven. We sat on log stumps in our wing while our teachers played instruments and we sang together. But once we went back to our "pods"—essentially wall-less rooms—we sat at desks with our basal readers and math workbooks. We admired our cool teachers with their fringed jackets and round glasses, but the excitement for learning stopped when we turned to our own learning.

I apprenticed under many master teachers, all of whom seemed to have pixie dust that made learning come alive in our little Boston school. A steady hum of work pervaded each classroom with occasional crescendo bursts when students sang or learned something new. It seemed that students were admiring the coolness of themselves, not just their teachers. Why? I realized that the teachers were curious about their students, which in turn gave the students the confidence to express their innate curiosity. Students were inspired when asked very basic questions that sought to unearth what they knew and what they were curious about in the world—a revelation that made my heart sing, just as when I was a young student on my tree-stump seat in our singing circle.

Designing Lessons

In my first teaching job, I co-taught a classroom of three- and four-year-olds that was project based. Units of study were generated by the observations we made of young learners, the resources we could obtain, and what children expressed an interest in learning about. It was a great deal of work when we started a unit, but then it was so worthwhile. When I moved to teaching first grade, I stumbled quite a bit when learning the curriculum. There was a path to follow and a destination we had to get to, following a map laid out from a preset curriculum and teachers' guides. I learned, though, that with some creative thinking and deep understanding of development, I could take my first graders on some off-the-trail paths and still get to our destination.

Even when I taught in schools that required me to follow teachers' guides, I always found that offering choices and inquiring about what excited or interested students allowed me to think creatively about what mattered to them. Doing so made our lessons richer. You'd be amazed at how excited first graders can get when deciding between whether to use a set of beads or a set of blocks to build a pattern.

As a parent, I experienced this sense of enthusiasm for learning when my daughter was in first grade. Over dinner one night, she announced she had homework. I raised a brow at my husband, keenly aware that my colleagues in first grade did not assign homework. Her class was studying the geography and culture of Mexico, and she proceeded with a monologue on what she knew about Mexico and shared that her task was to burn a CD of music from Mexico . . . *for the next day.* Most parents would have many questions about this "assignment," but my husband proceeded as if this was a perfectly normal assignment based on our daughter's convincing sales pitch.

As a proud melomaniac, my husband had hundreds of albums uploaded to his account, and the two of them set to work culling his library for music. The end result was a lively CD that her class enjoyed for days. My daughter's teacher got a big chuckle out of the whole thing. Apparently her statement to the class was, "Keep an ear out, you might find music from Mexico on the radio or in your family's music collection!" This simple statement to *notice* if what they were invested in studying was a part of daily life became an invitation to my daughter to dig into the music. While it would have been easy that night at dinner to question her claim that she had homework, by running with her interests, my husband and I, her teacher, and her class were able to more actively learn about in Mexican culture.

What I came to study and appreciate is that when we tap into intrinsic motivation we leverage the power of meaningful learning. This requires us to articulate the purpose of activities and to provide choice, to foster positive relationships with students and among students, and to give them autonomy to be responsible for their own growth. While we may have a set curriculum to teach and goals for learning that guide our path, the tools we carry along and utilize can make that learning journey richer and more meaningful.

Lesson Considerations for First Graders

When preparing lessons for first graders, there are three important factors to keep in mind. First, ask and listen. Next, design them in a way to build and sustain relationships. And last, create lessons that allow the children space and time to control what they are learning.

Ask and Listen

I often would let my first graders know why we were studying something, and I would sometimes ask a series of open-ended questions and chart their responses. For example:

- "We are going to begin our writing unit on real-life stories. Why might it be important to know what a real story is?"

- "Where or from whom have you heard real-life stories?"

- "How do we know stories are real? Does everything have to be real or true?"

- "What makes real stories exciting or makes you feel like you have to hear the whole story?"

First graders love a good story, and when we lay the groundwork for what role stories play in our lives and in our learning, they will understand the purpose. From there, it's a matter of finding choices that allow children to make meaningful decisions that let them explore this genre of writing. For example, choices might center on the mechanics:

- **Writing tool**—black pen, blue pen, pencil

- **Paper**—lines, no lines

- **Where to write**—desk, floor with clipboard

Once students demonstrate their success in making these smaller choices, we can then model how to make more significant ones, such as which real story to write or how they want to publish.

Sustain Relationships

Intrinsic motivation also focuses on relationships. The purposeful time invested in building community from day one continues throughout the year. When children are known and seen, they are motivated to share and take risks. Like most writers, first graders will be more willing to share their true stories when they feel safe, valued, and respected in their community.

Inherent in building this community of trust is knowing how individuals and the class work together. When I taught third grade, I knew my students preferred same-gender partners. In first grade, though, my students were typically game to work with anyone, and they particularly enjoyed groups of three or four. First graders also needed plenty of space when partnered so they could stand, sit, or lie on the floor. Some classes even benefited from having roles described and labeled to minimize the discussion and planning, and each group member knew what their job was. Often, these job descriptions would be defined in the morning message. Knowing that first graders can make quite a mess as they work on a project, I'd offer structures to keep track of time or ways to put a hold on work and save for the next time.

Give Students Space and Control

One of the hallmarks of the *Responsive Classroom* approach is its emphasis on the shared power and control between adults and children. When we invest in building community, and we structure the space and the day in a way that invites learning and allows us to articulate how we envision learning, we convey our faith in children. By being proactive in teaching how routines and procedures work to keep everyone safe and able to learn, we set children up for success, just as when we intervene with logical consequences when children forget to follow guidelines. These are examples of the adult's responsibility for maintaining the classroom community, but we will also have to let go, bit by bit.

If you've ever taught a teenager how to drive, you know what this experience is like (but when comparing teaching hundreds of first graders with teaching two teenagers to drive, the classroom is less risky!). We have already spent years modeling safe driving. We have talked about expectations and what rules to follow so everyone can be safe and enjoy the ride. We teach our teenagers to stay within the lines, and as they demonstrate competence and confidence, we let them drive a little farther or a little longer. I made a conscious effort to use at least twice as much reinforcing language ("Ah, you remembered to look in all three mirrors before backing up this time!") as I did reminding or redirecting language.

Interactive Learning Structures

Before using an interactive learning structure, I would introduce it as a Morning Meeting activity or outdoor game. For example:

- If we were studying authors of a particular genre, we'd learn Who Am I? before playing it to connect to the authors we were studying.

- If I wanted to use Inside-Outside Circles during academic times, we would play a game using that interactive learning structure in Morning Meeting during the sharing or greeting portion.

- If we were going to examine character traits or geography, we would use Four Corners as our activity so we could practice both moving about the room and quickly partnering up for discussion.

Teaching a teenager to drive involves modeling and practicing before turning over the keys and letting them drive solo. When humans feel connected to other humans, when they have experience and knowledge, and when they are given autonomy, they are more confident about taking risks and engaging with new learning—whether it's behind the wheel, reading a book, or tinkering in a makerspace.

Letting children have choices in the classroom means providing them with autonomy. More than once I've watched a first grader choose to sit on the floor to write, and I think, "Hmmm. That might not work. . . ." But I give the student a chance to try and thrive, and often they will rise to the occasion, even if it does take a reminder.

Here are some ways first graders can exercise autonomy:

- Choosing which biography they want to read from the library

- Refilling their water bottle and carrying it down the hallway

- Using towels to dry off playground equipment and then hanging them to dry

- With teacher guidance, considering options for resolving a conflict with a partner and then choosing one they want to try

- After watching and discussing teacher modeling, being tasked with packing their own mail, buttoning their own jackets, and clearing their own lunch trash

Active Learning in Math Lessons

We can use active learning strategies when introducing students to new concepts in math. For example, to practice single-digit addition, we would use the beanbag toss game and record our scores. We would usually do this at recess. After playing, we would use the tallies to practice computation (Dousis and Wilson, 2010, 45).

Another way to embed active learning would be to ask a question during Morning Meeting and then explore it later in the day. For example, if we were going to look at graphing and data collection, the Morning Meeting message would include a question and a table that we would use in the afternoon for math lessons (Dousis and Wilson, 2010, 51).

See the appendix, p. 332, for more on Guided Discovery.

Regardless of the units or themes studied, I made a point to outline potential interactive learning structures as well as opportunities for Guided Discovery, and social and emotional learning that would keep students engaged. Often, we would tap into these during Morning Meeting or mini-lessons. As I planned the week, I would include each of these approaches in our formal learning and sometimes in the conversations we'd have individually or in small groups. For example, if I were going to use Guided Discovery later that day, I might say, "Oh, we are going to be thinking about our character, Ramona Quimby, soon. I wonder what *materials* we could use to show what she is like." First graders would be full of ideas, including suggestions for fabric, dress-up costumes, yarn, and clay. While I often had ideas of my own, it wasn't uncommon for me to listen to their ideas as they worked hard to procure the media they thought would work.

Setting High Expectations

Setting high—and appropriate—expectations can be one of the more challenging aspects of good teaching. Some students arrive in first grade having experienced expectations that are beyond them—sitting still for too long, attempting math that they are not yet ready for, or articulating those tricky ending sounds like /s/ or /th/. Other children enter first grade having had many of their needs and daily tasks handled by adults who don't understand what a six-year-old is capable of. Families often don't understand what is developmentally appropriate for their young children. As educators, our job includes understanding what a five- or six-year-old can do in the moment and what they can learn to do with a bit of support (recall the "rubber band" in this chapter's overview). This also applies to how we communicate what realistic expectations are for first graders to their families. Through newsletters, blog posts, and formal and informal conversations, we can share the experiences we have had with this age group and how children can meet our expectations in the classroom.

Guided Discovery

In project-based learning, there is often a myriad of new materials to explore. When we studied photojournalism, we did several Guided Discoveries on the different styles of cameras. In other settings we'd use Guided Discovery for:

- Using pens in addition to pencils in writers' workshop.
- Using calculators to check our math calculations.
- Exploring modeling clay, which we later used to represent book characters.

Observing Students

As educators, it's important that we have a really solid understanding of development, which can come from our education, professional development, and self-study. We also gain an understanding of development from day-to-day interactions and observations as we work with first graders. It can be a delicate balance of drawing on our expertise as educators and having that "beginner's mind," observing from a place of curiosity and wonder, not authority. It also involves looking for patterns—within individual students, across the class, and across time. Look at it as building a mental library catalog of what we observe, but knowing and appreciating that the catalog is fluid.

When I started teaching, my first graders loved quiet time. They looked forward to that twenty-minute block when they could take a break and relax in the dimly lit room before resuming our work. But during my fourth year teaching, I noticed that my first graders struggled with quiet time. They dragged their feet getting to their spots and seemed to be challenged when they were expected to do something individually and quietly. Some of the children even complained. So I observed and made changes. I tried moving a few students, I offered a few more choices, and I would play an audiobook with one of their favorite characters.

I couldn't figure it out. I talked through my observations with a former colleague, who pointed out that my class had been in all-day kindergarten the year before, the first year it had been mandated by the state. Unlike students in previous years, these first graders were used to going to school all day for five consecutive days.

I followed up by asking my class what they thought of quiet time. I asked them individually so I could survey their feelings and thoughts and also so I could limit the propensity of this age to build on each other's ideas. Some of the responses were "It's baby stuff, like in preschool" and "I'm just not tired, Mrs. Wells!" Fair enough, but we still needed to have quiet time. We held a short class meeting, and I explained that I had noticed some things and had to do some "teacher learning." I shared that I had talked not only with them but with teachers at our school and at other schools. I told them that I understood now that this class had "lots of experience" being at school all day, and we would change our quiet time routine accordingly. We would now have a shorter quiet time (ten to fifteen minutes) and they could bring up to three picture books or a clipboard and pencil to their spot. To this class, a twenty-minute quiet time felt like rest or nap, and developmentally, they had the stamina to get through the day without sleep or a long rest.

Observing students is one of the sweet spots for me as an educator. I learn so much and it brings me great joy to see their curiosity, determination, and singular focus. I use a myriad of tools and ways to document my observations in the classroom. Some examples have been shared earlier in this chapter, and I can confirm that there is no one right way to observe students. In fact, if you do it one way and one way only, you're probably missing something.

Back to that beginner's mind.

Each day is different in first grade, and as my experience with quiet time illustrates, each class is different. As you observe, be open, be honest, experiment, and stay committed.

Be Open

If you have a willingness to observe students, it will inform your teaching and strengthen your relationships with your students. This willingness will let you witness each of their strengths, questions, relationships, needs, and personality. You might see them take risks or help someone, see them struggle, or see them share something tricky or hard. You get to see them being so very human.

Observation is also the perfect opportunity to set aside stereotypes, your own bias, and assumptions about individuals, small groups, your class, and your physical environment. Many times I've come to realize, after conversations with students, that what I set up in the pretend area is not working. (See the kindergarten section of this chapter for tools to examine your own biases.)

Be Honest

Observing is a valuable if not essential part of teaching. You are not "doing nothing," and if anyone suggests that, you can smile and say you are collecting data, which you are. Be honest with your students and tell them you are curious about what they are doing and want to learn from them. If you're taking notes, record what you see, hear, and observe, and not what you "know is happening." I often leave space in my notes for questions, especially if while I was observing I assumed I knew what was happening, or when I realized I needed to collect more data.

Experiment

There is no one way to observe, so be flexible in how you collect your data. I always kept a spreadsheet of names as well as a quarter piece of paper with the same names so I could quickly grab one for notes. I used to keep these on a clipboard or in a folder, but now I use apps for notes or even snapping photos. Start with what you're most comfortable with, but remain open to other possible ways to keep notes. Be sure to schedule time to review those notes each week so that you can use your observations when you talk to children, write your newsletter, share positive feedback with families, or collaborate with teachers to help solve tricky behaviors to better support students.

Stay Committed

Making time to observe students can be challenging. Making time to review and reflect on what you observe, either alone or with colleagues, is even harder. Both of these practices are essential to good teaching. Observing, and then reviewing and reflecting on those observations, is part of sustaining relationships because observing lets you get to know students and students know you are really seeing them. Observation requires you to have meticulous classroom management skills that allow students to work autonomously while you do the important work of observing. This practice will affirm what you know developmentally about students and let you fill in the details of who they are individually and within the class community. It may raise more questions, which will allow you to improve the physical space, make time for social and emotional learning, and enrich academic learning.

Give yourself permission sometimes to simply observe—to get absorbed in the moment of watching without feeling like you have to capture everything or do something with what you see. This is a practice that doesn't take a lot of time or resources, and it should remind you of the magic of childhood and learning. You should also give yourself permission to take a pass on this process when needed. Certainly if you're preparing for family conferences or writing report cards, you might need to spend more time on those tasks and skip observing. Stay committed, but allow yourself grace if it just doesn't seem to work at that moment.

Grade

Second grade is a time when students flourish. They are building on the skills they learned in first grade and are developing into confident readers, writers, mathematicians, scientists, and critical thinkers. Second graders are eager to learn and, although they are getting older, school continues to be a place of engagement and a source of happiness and fun.

A colleague shared a story that highlights the dichotomy between the innocence of seven- and eight-year-olds and the academic pressures they often encounter in second grade. It was nearing St. Patrick's Day and students were preparing to take an end-of-the-year computerized assessment. This type of standardized assessment began in my colleague's district in second grade and was taken a few times throughout the year to measure academic achievement. It can be an intense experience for students as well as for teachers, who want each student to show high academic achievement. During this final standardized test, a second grade student walked up to my colleague and wanted to know when the leprechauns were going to visit the classroom. My colleague smiled, acknowledged her wonder, and redirected her attention back to the test. This second grader was more concerned about catching a leprechaun than the content on her computer screen.

Second graders still believe in all things magical, from superheroes to the tooth fairy to leprechauns, and they thrive in spaces that balance academics and their imaginative spirits.

Designing Lessons

When planning engaging lessons for second graders, it is important to plan lessons that are purposeful, interactive, appropriately challenging, and that allow for student autonomy.

- **Purposeful lessons.** These connect the academic content to skills that students have learned before and to skills that students will learn later. Second graders benefit from knowing how their existing knowledge around a skill benefits their current learning. For example, to make learning purposeful for students you might say, "We've been hopping by ten using a number line. Now we're going to take that knowledge to add together mixed groups of coins," or "Let's take what we know about the table of contents in nonfiction books to improve our own nonfiction book writing."

- **Interactive lessons.** Offer students opportunities to further engage in academic content. Using learning structures will allow students to have discussions with one another and participate in noncompetitive games to solidify academic content in a way that fosters an inclusive community.

When planning to teach academic content that students will find both engaging and challenging, it is important to design lessons that include appropriately demanding work that meets the needs of the wide range of student abilities in the classroom and that also provides opportunity for student choice. Indeed, student choice and varying student abilities should go hand in hand in a developmentally responsive classroom. Consider the common goal, and then plan different ways that students with varying abilities can work toward that common goal. One way to go about this is to offer students a choice in what they do and how they do it that best meets their needs.

A Cautionary Tale: Competitive Games and the Classroom Community

One year, a community member came into the classroom to do a series of lessons with students as part of a community partnership program. During her last visit, she decided to split the class into two teams, boys versus girls, to play a game in an effort to review what she had taught them over the course of the past month. She explained the directions and told the students that they were on teams and would be competing for points. The team with the most points at the end would be declared the winner. Immediately, students started yelling, "We're going to win!" and at first it appeared to be a friendly competition. However, after a few losses by one of the teams, the classroom community that we had built over the course of the first few months of the school year came crumbling down. Suddenly, their friendly chants of "We're going to win" turned into "That's not fair!" and "I can't believe you got that wrong!" Their faces went from smiles to frowns, and the body language went from jumping up and down with excitement to shrugged shoulders, crossed arms, and disengagement. This was a stark contrast to the intended outcome of this activity.

While there is a place and time for healthy competition in a child's life (such as sporting events), the goal of the planned games played in the classroom is to further build an inclusive and supportive classroom community. Therefore, games planned in the classroom should be chosen to foster just that. We spent the time after this game reflecting on what had happened and began to repair hurt feelings.

Second graders have competitive spirits and, when given an opportunity to compete, will give it their all—they want to win! However, this should not be to the detriment of the group and class community. One way to build on their competitive nature and preserve peer relationships is through a whole-class competition around a common goal. For example, students might work as a class to reach a certain number of reading minutes or "beat the clock" when cleaning up from science.

Special Projects

Second graders enjoy opportunities to explore their interests in the form of whole-class community projects and individual projects. As a group, consider embedding whole-class community projects into the academic scope and sequence for the year. For example, have the class write letters to residents of a local senior home to develop a pen pal partnership, plan and create a community garden, or collect food donations for a local pantry. Connecting whole-class projects to the community reinforces students' understanding that they are contributors to a larger community.

Second graders have many individual interests and enjoy learning about those interests. Providing opportunities for students to explore these interests can increase their engagement and help them to learn important research and presentation skills. Consider setting aside time each week for students to explore an idea or area of interest that they can learn more about and then, after several weeks, share what they have learned.

I like to plan this type of project three times a year. We spend an hour at the end of each week for about eight weeks when students can explore an area of interest, a passion, or something that makes them wonder. Prior to the first hour, we have conversations about what each student is interested in, passionate about, or just curious about. Students have explored everything from "Why do bees die after they sting someone?" to "What makes comics so funny to read?" After each student has an idea and turns that idea into a question to explore, we formulate an action plan consisting of materials they will need to investigate, all of their questions, and ways to present their findings to others. After eight weeks of research, we present our findings to each other, our families, and our school community. Students discover so much about themselves and about their classmates during this process.

See the appendix, p. 332, for more on Guided Discovery.

Guided Discovery

Second graders are curious by nature, and the practice of Guided Discovery allows students to explore new materials in a way that fosters creativity and teaches them about the appropriate use of materials. Take into consideration what materials are new to students in second grade and what materials they have used before but might use differently this school year. To streamline the use of Guided Discovery, think about combining like materials into one Guided Discovery experience. For example, you might use Guided Discovery to introduce three types of measurement materials—rulers, yardsticks, and tape measures.

Materials to Introduce Using Guided Discovery

Math manipulatives

- Geoboards
- Pattern blocks
- Base ten blocks
- Color tiles
- Measurement tools (rules, yardsticks, tape measures)

Technology

- Devices (tablets, computers)
- Apps

Creative materials

- Paints
- Clay
- Coloring options (markers, crayons, colored pencils)

Science and social studies

- Scale
- Weights
- Measurement tools
- Globe

Lesson Flow

When structuring the flow of a lesson, consider the length of time you will dedicate to each part of the lesson. Second graders will benefit from a purposeful opening lasting around fifteen minutes, followed by a thirty-to-forty-minute body, and then a closing of about five to ten minutes to bring everyone back together to reflect on the learning. The more time allotted for students to work and explore, the better.

Ideas for Second Grade Lessons		
Opening (15 Minutes)	**Body (30–40 Minutes)**	**Closing (5–10 Minutes)**
Teacher-facilitated conversation/discussion	Choice of academic activities	Self-assessment reflection
Interactive learning structure (partner chat)	Interactive learning structure (four corners)	Interactive learning structure (partner chat/ turn and talk)
Open-ended questions	Planned active or inter-active task	Open-ended questions
Envisioning language	Guided Discovery experience	Reinforcing language

Lesson Considerations for Second Graders

When preparing lesson plans for second graders, consider social and emotional learning opportunities, partnerships, energizers, working with a set curriculum, and be mindful of cultural relevance.

Social and Emotional Learning Opportunities

The academic learning happening throughout the day also lends itself to teaching important social and emotional skills. Second graders will participate in a significant amount of partner work and small-group work. In order to be successful, students will need to learn skills related to cooperation, assertiveness, responsibility, empathy, and self-control (C.A.R.E.S.), so it's important that they have ample opportunities to learn these skills and be able to practice them in a safe and supportive environment.

Elements of each of these C.A.R.E.S. competencies can be woven in and out of academically heavy lessons. For example, consider ways to incorporate lessons around cooperation when teaching a new partner game in math, or discuss responsibility when modeling how to organize a writing workshop folder. Each academic lesson can serve a dual purpose. Teaching social and emotional skills alongside academic content, within a single lesson, will help ensure student success.

Partner and group tasks offer many opportunities for teaching and learning around social and emotional skills. Another strategy to consider is role-play. This strategy can be used as a proactive teaching tool or in response to problem situations.

Social and Emotional Skills for Second Graders

Consider practicing these skills during Morning Meeting or through role-play. This will allow children to practice them before using them in academic situations.

- Resolving conflict
- Persisting through challenging tasks
- Making decisions based on their own needs and interests
- Taking risks
- Managing negative emotions (anger, frustration, disappointment)

Partnerships

Second grade students benefit from teacher-created partnerships as well as partnerships of their choosing, and they appreciate having options for selecting their own partners. Second graders will usually gravitate toward same-gender partnerships, and when given a choice they will most likely choose a peer of the same gender. Consider ways to provide students with opportunities to work with various classmates. One of my favorite ways to partner students is by using matching cards. Each student gets a card, and then they find the classmate whose card matches theirs. It's a fun way for students to find a new partner.

What follows are some other suggestions for partnering students, all of which will result in a few laughs.

Ways to Partner Students			
Partnering Structure	**Number of Students**	**Directions**	**Ideas for Use**
Memory	Two	1. Prepare two matching sets of cards with content-related terms printed on them. 2. Give each student a card. 3. Have students find their match. 4. Collect cards.	• **Math:** Equations, sums, shapes, names, number of sides, number of vertices, coins, total amount • **Reading:** Author's name, book title, genre • **Spelling:** Spelling patterns, fill in the blank, synonyms, antonyms • **Science:** States of matter, name of material • **Social Studies:** Famous person, accomplishment • **Art:** Artwork, artist, primary colors, secondary colors
Humdingers	Two or more	1. Review a list of song options and have students practice humming each tune. 2. Give students a slip of paper with the name of their song. 3. Have each student hum their tune and seek out others humming the same tune.	Humdingers is similar to Memory but uses songs instead of content-related terms. Choose songs that your students know such as "Happy Birthday," a theme song from a popular show, or a song that you've sung together at school.
Barnyard Bedlam	Two or more	1. Give students pictures of popular farm animals that make sounds. 2. Have each student make the sound their animal makes and find classmates making that same sound.	Barnyard Bedlam is similar to Humdingers, but uses animal sounds.

(continued)

Partnering Structure	Number of Students	Directions	Ideas for Use
Dance, Dance	Two or more	1. Prepare cards that have different dance moves depicted on them. 2. Review the dance moves on the cards. 3. Give each student a card with a specific dance move. 4. Have students do their dance move and find classmates doing the same move.	Dance, Dance is a partnering structure where students are assigned a dance move and partner up by locating the other person making the same dance move. Some options include disco, Elvis, The Shopping Cart, The Running Person, The Robot, and other popular dance moves known by students.

Interactive learning structures are another partnering structure that allows for student collaboration and discussion around a learned content.

Energizers

Energizers allow students short physical and mental breaks from learning throughout the day. To be used effectively, energizers should be well thought out and modeled for students. Energizers can be used in multiple ways to support student success:

- **Transitions.** Consider facilitating an energizer as students transition from one place to another (for example, when students enter the classroom after recess or return from a special area class). This allows everyone to come back together and participate in a unified activity before engaging in the next part of the day.

- **Wait times.** Class restroom breaks, setting up an activity, and times when waiting is required are moments when energizers could be used to keep students engaged while also allowing for a brief mental and physical break.

- **Calming.** Despite the name, some types of energizers can provide calm for a group of high-energy students. Consider energizers that bring students together in a way that channels their high energy and promotes calm.

Energizers, Interactive Learning Structures, and Activities			
Practice	**Purpose**	**Time Frame**	**Examples**
Energizer	To allow for a physical and mental break from learning	< 5 Minutes	• Heads or Tails • Spelling Stroll • Double This, Double That • Mind Reader • Switch
Interactive learning structure	To engage students in academic content while allowing for interactions with others	> 5 Minutes	• Maître d' • Four Corners • Inside-Outside Circles • Museum Walk
Activity	To provide students practice with academic content and/or social and emotional skills	> 10 Minutes	• Math game • Word search • Science experiment • Slide deck

Working With a Set Curriculum

For many years I taught at a school that used a specific program to teach phonics and early reading skills. This program went against many of the things I knew and loved about teaching second graders and the planning of engaging lessons to meet the needs of every student. Although disappointed by not being able to teach phonics in a way that would feel authentic and engaging for students, I could not change the fact that this was what our school was doing. What I could control, though, was finding a way to make it work for both me and the students.

I tried teaching the lessons as written in the teacher's manual, but I could see that the students were disengaged, frustrated, and bored. (It was no coincidence that half the class suddenly needed to use the bathroom during this time.) After observing the students' behavior and their lack of interest in a topic so necessary for their learning, I did what teachers do: I tried to find a solution to make this part of our day fun and engaging again. I had to pivot.

The professionals who created this program might have had an idea of what engaging lessons looked like for some students, but I knew the teaching and learning methods that would best support the second graders in front of me and the lessons and work that would reflect the needs of all students. With this in mind, I came up with the following tips to make learning more engaging when working with a set curriculum.

- **Take into account the nonnegotiables.** While it was mandated that I had to teach the content within the program and in the same sequence as noted in the teacher's manual, I did have some control over how this information would be delivered. I began using the teacher's manual and suggested scope and sequence as a guide. I used the learning targets and any important vocabulary or processes that students needed to know as the foundation for the lesson, but I structured each lesson in a way that worked best for the students and their learning.

- **Rework the lesson.** Once you have defined the purpose and taken into account the needs of your students, start thinking about ways to rework the lesson to make it more effective and engaging. The process of reworking a lesson involves considering the purpose of the learning and determining how to help students best learn the content in ways that are accessible and engaging.

- **Employ interactive learning structures.** I consider interactive learning structures to be a resuscitator of lackluster lessons. Whenever I encounter a lesson that needs some life or when I'm planning a lesson that needs a little extra something, I look for an interactive learning structure that can help. This strategy allows for student movement, collaboration, and fun—all important things for second graders.

- **Use Morning Meeting as a way to practice and assess academic skills.** Look for ways to connect academic content to the components of Morning Meeting. Consider taking a short activity outlined in a lesson and using it as a Morning Meeting activity, or use an academic-based check-in for the morning message. I will often use the morning message as an assessment tool to gauge how students are grasping a certain concept. For example, if we've recently learned a new vowel team, I might say, "Write a word with a vowel team that makes the long A sound. Remember to mark it up." This allows me to take a quick glance at the morning message and gain a better understanding of how students are doing with a particular concept as a whole.

(i)

See the appendix, p. 335, for more on Morning Meeting.

- **Start with an energizer.** If I know a lesson requires students to focus for an extended period of time, I'll begin with an energizer. Energizers are not only to give students a break from learning. They can also be used to bring students together for a bit of movement and structured fun before the start of a lesson. Second graders need opportunities for movement throughout the day in addition to recess. The more times we can sprinkle movement opportunities throughout the day, the better able students will be to focus when sustained mental energy is required.

Culturally Responsive Teaching

Our libraries have the potential to allow students to learn about the world around them, something that is of high interest to second graders. Representation matters, and all students need to see themselves in books and stories while at the same time learning about other communities that they may be less familiar with.

One year I had two sisters in my class who were new to our district and of the Muslim faith. Both wore hijabs to school, and they spoke Somali, Arabic, and English. At the start of the school year, I always take an inventory of our classroom library to see how well it represents our class. When the girls joined the class, we had just one book that showed women wearing hijabs and that reflected their culture. It was a book about colors that was written in English.

I began gathering books that represented the sisters' culture from the city's library to bring into the classroom. I sprinkled the books throughout the class library, in different bins based on the genre. Each morning students had the option to trade out the books in their individual book bins for new books. One morning, as I observed students choosing books for their book bins, I noticed that one of the sisters had discovered one of the new books I had placed in the bins. Her face lit up and she had the biggest smile on her face. It can only be described as pure joy: she had found a book with a character that looked like her and that was written in both Somali and English. Holding on to the book, she looked around, smiling, until she found her sister, who ran up to her seconds after. Holding back tears from seeing the elation on her face, I walked up to her and said, "Wow, it looks like you found a really good book!" She told me that she could read the Somali words, and then read the entire book to me. Before long the sisters had read the book to most of the students in class.

This book (and others in our library) led to authentic conversations around culture and deepened the understanding and respect in our classroom community. We learned words in Somali that we incorporated into our daily Morning Meeting and other parts of the day, we learned what their hijabs represented, and we made deeper connections with each other.

The sisters took the book home to share with their mom, who was learning English. I had the pleasure of meeting the girls' mother at a parent-teacher conference, and the first thing she said to me was, "Thank you for the book." I think about those two girls and their family frequently and hope that they will see themselves in every classroom library as they complete their education.

Part of being culturally responsive is recognizing when changes can be made and should be made in your own practice for the betterment of all students. And these adjustments should address all practices, not just choosing literature for language arts or your classroom library. The lessons and activities we do with students should move student learning forward and your own learning about students forward as well. If something like a lesson, an activity, classroom setup, daily structure, or a family communication tool is not working for all students, then it's best to reflect on that practice and adjust accordingly.

The *Responsive Classroom* approach lends itself to culturally responsive teaching and provides the foundation for implementing ways to make classroom and school spaces successful for each and every student while honoring our diverse cultures. One key practice that assists in ensuring culturally relevant classrooms is the art of reflection. Taking time to reflect and think through your own implicit biases may bring about information that you may not otherwise have considered and in turn will help further support the learning and community development in your classroom and school.

As you engage in this important self-reflection, consider the following questions:

- What beliefs do I currently have about socioeconomic status, race, culture, and gender? If you are unsure, consider taking Harvard's Implicit Association Test (IAT), available at https://implicit.harvard .edu/implicit/education.html

- How might those beliefs impact the lessons and activities I plan for students?

- What barriers are evident in the classroom, in lessons, or activities that might prevent all students from succeeding with this task?

- What can I do to remove those barriers?

- What changes am I able to make going forward to ensure success for all students?

- How did students respond to these changes?

Setting High Expectations

At the start of the school year, the hope is that all students will meet the goals they have set for themselves and ones the class has set for the year. A part of helping students reach their goals is for us, as teachers, to maintain a standard of high expectations by constantly improving on our own instruction. The following are ways to ensure high expectations are available for all students, every day.

- **Know your students.** Deepen your own understanding of where students are, where they need to go, and any potential barriers to their successes.

- **Use open-ended questions.** To move student learning forward, use open-ended questions, such as "What went well for you?" "How did it feel to _____?" "What strategies helped you?" and "What might you try differently next time?" These questions will help students think about strategies that can bring success and consider additional strategies for continued success.

- **Provide opportunities for choice.** Providing different activities allows students to think about their needs as learners and the choices they might make to advance their own learning.

- **Scaffold lessons.** As you approach lesson planning, think through the strategies you might use to design lessons and activities that will allow all students to be successful with the content.

- **Differentiate learning based on student needs.** Students come to us with a wide range of skill sets and various areas of potential growth. Consider ways to modify your instruction based on student needs, such as allowing for flexible grouping when using small-group instruction. Flexible grouping provides students with the ability to move in and out of groups depending on their needs.

- **Go for depth in content over quantity.** It's tempting when a student has mastered a skill to move on to the related skill in the next grade level. While this might be appropriate for some students, consider instead providing students with opportunities to go "deeper" within a certain skill.

Observing Students

Even on the busiest days, taking time to observe students throughout the day can offer valuable insight into their relationships with others, their interests, and their learning styles. The information gleaned from those observations can add to the knowledge we have of students and influence all aspects of classroom life.

Homework

Second grade is usually the year when the "H-word"—homework—enters into our conversations about student learning. Sometimes parents ask for it, and sometimes students inquire about it. As education has transitioned from a rote learning model to a more exploratory and critical thinking model, so must our thinking around the purpose of homework at the elementary level. Students work hard during the school day and need time outside of school to explore other interests and interact with their families. Our role as teachers is to instill a love of learning in our students and to help them to see the power of wondering, of seeking out information and learning, and not view the process as a burden or something to be avoided.

As you think about assigning homework at the primary level, consider the following:

- What is the purpose of the assignment?

- How will this work benefit student learning?

- Will all students be able to complete this assignment outside of the school day?

- What will this homework tell me about student learning?

- How will I use what I have learned from this assignment to inform my teaching?

For additional information on homework, see Cathy Vatterott's *Rethinking Homework: Best Practices That Support Diverse Needs*.

Make Observations Intentional

Just as you intentionally plan when to teach writing or what book to read for the day's read-aloud, be intentional about the time you put into observing students. Think about your day and your daily schedule. When might be the best times to observe students? Take a moment to jot down times throughout the day or week when you can observe. For example, you could spend the first five minutes of reading choices to note what books students are interested in before starting guided reading groups, or you could observe peer relationships within the class during recess or lunch.

Think Broadly About What to Observe

Expand your list of what to look for when observing:

- **Peer relationships.** Noticing peer relationships can help you make decisions about appropriate partnerships that will support each student.

- **Energy levels.** Second graders have a wide range of energy levels, and noticing which students have more energy than others can help with scheduling breaks for the students to keep them engaged.

- **Learning styles.** Noticing what learning styles work best for each student can guide you on how to approach lessons.

Be Curious

Approach from a place of curiosity and wonder when observing. You might notice something that makes you think, "Hmmm." Challenge yourself to come from a place of curiosity before jumping to conclusions. Once, during our daily quiet time, I noticed a student had fallen asleep and slept for the duration of quiet time. I made the assumption that he was probably just tired from our busy day. The next day, he again fell asleep for the entire quiet time, and I wondered what else might be going on with him. I met privately with this student and opened by asking him, "I notice you've been falling asleep during quiet time. Tell me about that." He shared with me that he wasn't sleeping well at night due to a recent change in his family structure. It made sense now. He needed that ten to fifteen minutes to close his eyes and recharge for the afternoon. I let him sleep during quiet time for most of the year because that is what he needed to do his best learning in the afternoon.

Reflect and Act

An important part of observing students is taking the time to reflect on what you notice and then put any action steps into play. It's helpful to seek the advice of colleagues for a different perspective when you are unsure of what you have observed or when you're uncertain how to resolve a situation for the betterment of a student. Special area teachers and colleagues who work with students outside of the classroom can be excellent reflection partners.

Chapter 5

Connecting With Parents

● ●

Overview

As a counselor, I have participated in countless parent-teacher conferences over the years. Some were easy, with good news and fun stories to share. Many conferences, though, were not so easy—there were tears, angry words, or disappointment. I had many roles: peacemaker, problem-solver, bearer of bad news, sharer of wisdom, bridge builder, hope instiller. I've done a lot of work—a lot of tough work—with teachers and families. But the toughest seat I've ever sat in at a parent-teacher conference was the one on the other side of the table, the parent's seat.

I was fortunate to be able to bring my daughters with me to my school for their first few primary years. I wanted to be part of their initial experience in school. Their teachers were my colleagues—my friends—and those first years felt easy and comfortable. Then, when each of my daughters reached third grade, we enrolled them in our home district so they could put down roots with neighborhood friends in their neighborhood school. I'll never forget sending my older daughter to school that fall. I was no longer entrusting her to a colleague, a friend. Instead, I was sending her to a stranger, and I realized then that this is how families of first-time kindergartners must feel, giving me a new perspective and appreciation of what they experienced.

I was nervous before the first parent-teacher conference, walking into an unfamiliar school and sitting across the table from a teacher I knew only from the welcome letter she had sent and from what I heard from my daughter when she talked about school. I had the last appointment on a Friday afternoon. The teacher greeted me with a warm but tired smile. I knew that look—running on empty after a morning of teaching and an afternoon of back-to-back conferences. Her voice was hoarse from too much talking, and her eyes were red with fatigue. As I sat down across from her, I was eagerly and anxiously awaiting to hear how my daughter had been adjusting to her new school.

My daughter has a big personality, and her parent-teacher conferences would usually begin with a funny story about what she said or did. Instead, right after hello, I was hit with a sensitive question about my daughter's challenges with her attention and focus. I was caught completely off guard. Not because of the question—I was already aware of the issues, since I live with her, after all—but because of the teacher's approach. We had no relationship at this point. There was no starting with strengths and positives. The door was not gently opened. The question was just fired at me—at least that's how it felt.

Knowing now what a wonderful teacher this individual turned out to be for my daughter, I see this experience now as an unintentional "cut to the chase" after a long afternoon of conferences. The teacher read my face, took a deep breath (as did I), and said, "Tell me about your daughter." I shared about my daughter. Her teacher then offered strategies to address my daughter's challenges. By the midyear conference, my daughter had benefited from these strategies. But more than that, it was the relationship her teacher and I developed that made that year a positive one for my daughter and me.

"Parent"

Students come from homes with a variety of family structures. Students might be raised by grandparents, siblings, aunts and uncles, foster families, and other caregivers. All of these individuals are to be honored for devoting their time, attention, and love to raising children, and we include all of them in our thinking in this chapter. It's difficult to find one word that encompasses all these caregivers and fits the importance of the role they play. In this book, for ease of reading, we use the term "parent" to represent all the caregivers involved in a child's life.

I never looked at communicating with families the same way again after that. The words that once so easily rolled off my tongue were now softened with empathy. Saying the words is one thing, but being on the receiving end as a parent gave me a new perspective.

This chapter brings us full circle. Chapter 1 focused on the importance of knowing our students, and we focus now on the importance of knowing our families. Knowing our students' families and valuing their contributions is as important as knowing the children and the content we teach. Truly knowing our students' families is vital to the work we do because it is the foundation to forming supportive relationships with them and connecting with them. As educators, we know that students do better in school both academically and socially when we have positive relationships with our students' families. And the research backs this up:

- Regardless of family background, social status, or income, students with involved parents have higher grades and test scores, better attendance, and demonstrate stronger social skills than students whose families are less involved. They exhibit fewer behavioral issues and comfortably adapt to the school environment.

- One of the most accurate predictors of school success is the extent to which families create a home environment that encourages learning, communicate high yet reasonable expectations for the child's achievement, and are involved in the child's education at school.

- Increased family involvement doesn't just help that family's child, but supports improved performance for all students (Center for Responsive Schools n.d.).

The Benefits of Knowing Our Families

When partnering with families, we get the chance to learn about and learn from different cultures and see the different ways of the world. Partnering with families not only makes school a more rewarding and more successful experience for the students, but it also makes teaching a more rewarding experience for us as educators. We have the opportunity to help equip and support students' families, and thus the community, to be successful.

One of my most rewarding experiences as a counselor started when I received a call from a mom looking for help for her son, a student at the school. She explained that when she was in second grade her parents had gone through a divorce. She shared that it had been a sad and hard time, but there was a counselor at her school who had created a group lunch for kids whose parents weren't living together, and she recalled how much the counselor helped her. We didn't realize it at first because our names had changed, but as we continued to talk, we realized that I had been the counselor. I later met her son, and his face beamed when I told him that when his mom was in school she had sat at the same table where he and I were now sitting. A seed had been planted all those years ago with his mom that said school is a place to turn to if you need help.

Building Trusting Relationships

We know that building a trusting relationship with families is important. But what strategies can be employed to build that trust?

Lead With Empathy

I teach a college course in basic counseling skills, and understanding empathy is a cornerstone of the course. I teach my college students that empathy is more than walking in someone else's shoes: it's walking around in someone else's world, and when we are let into their world, we have to walk carefully and respectfully in it. We don't go into someone else's world and trample all over it with our words, our judgments, our preconceived notions, and our opinions.

There is nothing more important in a parent's world than their child. When we become a child's teacher, we have entered a parent's world, and we have to walk around in that world with great care. This is not easy work. There will be parents that have worlds we don't understand. Worlds that have a tough protective shell and don't easily let others in. Worlds that have different boundaries, values, and beliefs. When we are a child's teacher, we are part of their family's world, and we must lead with empathy.

Psychologists Daniel Goleman and Paul Ekman identify three types of empathy:

- **Cognitive empathy** is like perspective taking—considering how someone else may think or feel about something.

- **Emotional empathy** is being able to "catch" someone else's feelings—you are feeling right alongside them. You may have been through something similar or can relate in some way.

- **Compassionate empathy** is when you go beyond just understanding how someone might think or feel about something. You are actually moved to want to help, to walk alongside them so they know they are not alone (Goleman 2008).

These insights can be helpful to a teacher when working with families. It can be as simple as asking ourselves, "What would I think if someone said this to me about my child?" This question then helps us to choose our words and tone more carefully. We may sometimes actually experience the emotional drain of feeling the parent's frustration, disappointment, and worry, which can make us a better ally for a family. And sometimes we may go above and beyond the scope of our role as teacher, not just because we can but because we are compelled to make life better for our students and families. Regardless of the level of empathy you bring to a situation, remember it's about how we walk around in someone else's world that can make all the difference.

Cultivate Positive Relationships

Positive relationships have to be cultivated and built—they just don't happen. For some families, school is a wonderful place. It's a place where they themselves excelled as students, where they fit in, and where they hope their child's experience will be as wonderful as their own. But for some families, school was not such a positive experience, which can impact the parent's ability to have a trusting, productive relationship with their child's teacher and school.

A colleague had a powerful experience of bridging such a gap. A student was struggling with both learning and behavior. The teacher tried several different times and several different ways to connect with the student's parent, a single dad who was the primary caretaker. The teacher had a few brief phone conversations with the dad and invited him to have a conference to discuss how best to help his son. The dad was always very nice but was quick to get off the phone and seemed to avoid agreeing to a time to meet.

The teacher sought a school counselor for help. The counselor reached out to the dad and skillfully engaged him in a conversation to understand why he might be reluctant to come in for a meeting. The teacher had assumed it was because this parent didn't want to face hearing about his son's challenges. But the counselor and the teacher were wrong. The dad explained that he had attended that same school and had been a student in the very same classroom his son was in that year. It had been a difficult time for the dad when he had been a student, for various reasons—some related to home, but most related to his experience at school.

He wanted to help his son, but he was uncomfortable returning to the classroom because it brought back difficult memories. The counselor empathized with this dad—he wanted to meet and create a better experience for his son, but the physical room itself was the barrier. The counselor suggested using a conference room in a newer part of the building as a neutral place to meet. The dad agreed, and after their meeting he expressed his appreciation for the counselor helping him to overcome this hurdle. It didn't immediately fix everything that was going on with his son, but it was a first step toward getting things on the right track.

A parent's negative school experience isn't the only challenge when making school a welcoming place for all. Consider those parents who didn't go to school in the United States. They may not feel comfortable partnering with the school or participating in their child's school experience in part because they feel like they don't know or understand the norms of schools in the United States. Another example would be parents whose primary language is not English. They may be proficient readers of English and know enough to hold basic conversations, but there are nuances and colloquialisms of the language that they might not know or understand. This can lead to being uncomfortable and feeling insecure when interacting with English speakers, causing them to shy away from interacting or participating in their children's school experience. Consider also families who are outside of the school's dominant culture. Language differences may play a part here, but families could also be reluctant to participate due to any number of cultural differences. Participating in a school environment where the administration, teachers, and students look, talk, or dress differently from you or your family can be a challenge. In fact, it can feel intimidating.

Trying to view the "world of school" through the eyes of these parents will help us better see the gaps, the turnoffs, and the challenges that can keep families from interacting. Seeing through their eyes will also help us make the necessary additions, changes, or eliminations so that all students and families feel welcome at school.

Build on Common Ground and Common Goals

As teachers, we want our students to be safe and happy and to get the most out of their school experience. Families' goals are not so different. Most parents want their children to succeed in school, but their definition of success and how to achieve it may be different. We have to work to understand how families view success and what goals they have for their child. At the same time, we have to share how the school views success and what its goals are. From there, then, it's about finding common ground.

I had a second grader, Matt, who was struggling in school, and we weren't sure if it was a case of "can't do" or "won't do." I was asked to attend the parent-teacher conference with the dad to help facilitate the next steps. Matt's dad sat and listened attentively through the conference as the teacher explained all the areas in which Matt was struggling and our dilemma in understanding what he was actually capable of doing. Matt's teacher was concerned about sending him on to third grade. He appeared to be far behind his classmates, and there were no formal academic services in place to support him. The teacher and I were feeling the pressure to get Matt to a certain place by the end of the year. When we finally let Matt's dad get a word in, he responded by saying, "Well, we've got time.

We've got twenty-one years to get him off the runway." Those words were powerful and have stayed with me. We were so caught up in the here and now that we had lost sight of the journey of childhood and development. To Matt's dad, we were just one school year in his child's whole school career. Success was getting off the runway of life by the time Matt was twenty-one years old. We needed this reminder to look beyond our 180 school days within the four walls of the classroom. Everything didn't have to be figured out that day. Likewise, Matt's dad needed to know that we have benchmarks and indicators that help us understand where and how a child is progressing, information that tells us if we need to access more help for a student and look at teaching them in a different way. The conversation ultimately allowed us to reach some common ground and to work together to set some reasonable goals as we moved forward.

Positive Relationships Are a Two-Way Street

We have to be open to families' input, knowledge, and ideas. The story I shared about my daughter's parent conference shows the power of valuing the parent voice. When the teacher said, "Tell me about your daughter," I felt that my voice mattered and that what I had to say was valuable and helpful in this partnership. Whether it's during a phone call, a parent conference, or a meeting, simple questions such as these can go a long way:

- "What do you hope for your child this year . . . in this class . . . in this school?"

- "What has worked well in the past?"

- "What do you do at home when . . .?"

- "What would be most helpful for you and your child right now?"

- "What do you wish I knew or understood about your child or your family?"

- "What does your child being successful in school look like?"

Communication Is Key

Communication to families from the school and you, the teacher, can create a positive connection with families. Work closely with your colleagues and school leaders to ensure that families not only feel connected to the school community but welcomed into and informed about it.

There are many ways to communicate with families, from handwritten notes, meeting in person, or phone calls, to text messaging, posts, and virtual meetings. When it comes to working with families, I ask what their preferred method of communication is and let them know the ways they can communicate with me. I hear teachers say, "I don't do voicemail" or "I only use email." While you don't want to be overwhelmed with too many different ways of communicating with families, limiting communication options can be a detriment to connecting with families and establishing good relationships. Keep in mind that we—teachers and parents—share similar hopes and goals for students, even if the ways in which we are comfortable communicating may be different.

Share What You Know

Most parents will welcome and appreciate any information that will help them understand their child. Parents are often interested in what goes on in school when their child is away from home and their parent's eyes.

Share Knowledge of Child Development

As a first-time mom leaving the hospital with my newborn, I felt completely clueless. While on maternity leave, I kept thinking that kids four to eight years old were my wheelhouse, but I had no idea what to expect from a child younger than four. Students' families are often in a similar situation.

As a counselor, I am often asked, "Is this normal?" Parents often don't know the cognitive, social, physical, or language milestones that are common at each age level. And they don't know how those developmental gifts and challenges affect the learning process. Knowing these milestones and their effect on learning can be a tremendous help to families in supporting their children's learning in school.

Here is some useful information to share with families:

- **Common developmental characteristics of children at their child's age.** Be sure to preface this information if what you are sharing is based on certain cultural norms.

- **How to respond to those characteristics.** A developmental characteristic is not an excuse. Just because a particular behavior (or a mis-behavior) is common, it doesn't mean that it's okay: it means we have to lead with empathy and help children work through it.

- **What to expect about rates of development.** Development happens at different rates. Not all children will go through the various developmental stages at the same time or at the same rate, so it's important not to compare. No two children are exactly alike.

- **What to understand about growth.** Developmental growth is uneven. There can be big spurts, quieter periods, and sometimes even what appears to be a step backward.

- **What to expect at the next developmental stage.** Provide a heads-up about what developmental gifts and challenges might be coming next as children move from one stage of development to the next.

Because classrooms have children with a range of chronological ages, there will be an even wider range of developmental spans. It is important, then, to equip yourself with information about a range of developmental ages and to know what stages you are seeing in your classroom in order to best support families. The following table provides examples of how to explain teacher strategies for addressing behaviors associated with these developmental stages.

Model Explanations of Developmental Stages		
Age	**A Common Developmental Characteristic**	**Sample Language**
4	Can't sit still or pay attention very long	"Four-year-olds often need a lot of physical activity and can only sit still for short periods. I mix physical activity with sitting and listening. Several short sitting times work better than one long one."
5	Acts on one thing at a time	"It's common for five-year-olds to be very literal. What they see and hear is what they know. So they can only act on one thing at a time. Teachers therefore also focus on one thing at a time by keeping expectations clear and simple."
6	Highly competitive	"Six-year-olds often love to be first. To temper that, we try to have cooperative rather than competitive activities in the classroom. If we do have a competitive activity, we talk beforehand about what good sportsmanship looks and sounds like."
7	Sensitive and moody	"'Nobody likes me.' A lot of seven-year-olds think that. I try to be extra supportive and reassuring for this age. It helps to validate their feelings first, and then make suggestions. For example, I might say, 'Sounds like you're feeling like no one likes you. Who would you like to sit with at lunch today? I'll help you ask that friend to join you.'"
8	Complains of being bored	"At school we see a lot of eight-year-olds with big ideas but not the organization to carry them out, and that can make them feel incapable. 'I'm bored' can often really mean things are too hard. If this is the case, I help students get organized and break their work into manageable chunks."

Adapted from Carol Davis and Alice Yang, *Parents and Teachers Working Together*, Chapter 3 (Turners Falls, MA: Northeast Foundation for Children 2005).

Share Information About Classroom Practices

The current educational environment and the school experience may be quite different from when many parents went to school. For example, I often hear from parents who are concerned about their child being pulled from the classroom for counseling, because when they went to school no one left the classroom. I explain to them that today kids leave the room all the time for all kinds of things. It no longer carries the stigma that these parents remember—in fact, kids who are not leaving will ask, "When do I get to go?"

Providing families with information about school culture, expectations, and classroom practices will help build families' comfort level and confidence in interacting with the school. Share information about classroom curricula so families can help their children with schoolwork and give you helpful feedback. Informing families about the whats, the hows, and the whys behind our teaching will help build their trust that their child is getting the best education. An informed parent makes for a valuable partner and shows the child that we are all on the same team.

There are certain classroom practices that are especially important to highlight for families. Your approach to discipline can be shared in a letter during the first few weeks of school. This will help families understand your goal in your approach to discipline, how you have established rules and expectations, and how you have proactively taught and modeled for students how to follow the rules. In addition, share how you respond to students when rules are not being followed or are broken (loss of privilege; break it, fix it; positive time-out) and explain what is behind your response. This information can be reviewed with parents at a back to school night and then revisited throughout the year.

Morning Meeting may be a new idea for some families, and their children are likely to come home and talk about the fun greetings they share and activities they do each morning. Letting parents know that this twenty-to-thirty-minute daily meeting provides a defined way to start the school day, builds the class community, allows students to practice social skills, and reinforces academic concepts will help them see that this is time well spent. Instructional practices such as centers, offering choice, and use of technology may be new for families as well. Taking the time to explain these in newsletters, in posts, or in person during a back-to-school night can help paint a picture for families to help frame what their child talks about at home.

Share What's Going On in the Classroom

Often parents will hear a response of "Nothing" when they ask, "What did you do in school today?" The day is long and so much is packed in it that it can be hard for children to answer that question. In their little worlds, what happened five or six hours ago may seem like days.

When parents have a sense of the classroom schedule and routine, it can help them have more meaningful conversations about the school day. For example, if families know that the morning message on Tuesdays will have a joke, they can ask, "What was the joke of the day today?" Or if families know what special area class their child had that day, they can ask about that. In addition, teachers can quickly post notes and pictures of the day's happenings to prompt discussions at home. Be creative! Sharing with families the life of the classroom will build discussion at home, which in turn will build a connection between home and school.

Overcoming Barriers When Building Relationships

There can often be challenges to building a relationship with students' parents, but there are ways to break down any barriers and develop a connection between the classroom and home.

Lack of Empathy

Sometimes there can be a misunderstanding about what empathy truly is. This can come from compassion fatigue and burnout from offering empathy but not having it reciprocated. Regardless of the reason, though, we need to practice good self-care and to always lead with empathy.

Self-Care

When I tell people I commute thirty minutes to school every day, they often respond by asking, "Don't you get tired of that drive?" Yes, sometimes I do. But it also serves as a transition time between the world of school and the world of home, and allows me a few moments to practice self-care.

Self-care is an important aspect of our work as educators. Teaching can be a stressful and taxing profession. Doing things to take care of our physical and mental health will help us better manage the ups and downs of teaching.

As simple as it sounds, drinking water and staying hydrated, and maybe having a healthy snack, can help manage your stress. Remember Jean, my colleague and friend with the houseplants from Chapter 4? We used to squeeze in a quick walk during the day when we could. Sometimes we would talk about school-related topics, but more often than not we just talked about life. The combination of fresh air, sunshine, movement, and good company always rejuvenated me. A little bit of exercise or physical movement during the school day or after school can make a big difference. Mindfulness practices have become common in classrooms as a way to promote social and emotional learning with students. These same practices can be helpful for us as well, keeping us connected to our emotions and allowing us to manage them by de-stressing and giving us a way to feel refreshed.

Time

As is often the case in life, time can set roadblocks, slowing us down and making it a challenge to get everything done. Just as we dedicate time in the first six weeks of school to establish routines and procedures with students that serve as the foundation for a smoothly running classroom, we need to dedicate time in those beginning weeks of school to cultivate positive relationships with families. Doing so will lay a foundation on which we can build relationships with parents and involve them in the classroom experience from the start.

Surface-Level Connections

To have meaningful relationships with families, go beyond welcome letters, open houses, and curriculum nights, and do more than simply disseminate information. Get to know families individually by asking them to help you to get to know their children and find out what goals they have for them. Work to develop relationships with the families in the same way you develop relationships with your students.

One way to approach this is by keeping notes for each student's family. The following table provides an example of notes for a few students in an elementary class.

Family Note Examples for Elementary School Class

Family Member Names (who you contact first, and why; other adult and children family members)	Important Family Information	Notes
Jen and Tom Williams (parents); Beth Williams (grandmother)	Children often go to Grandma's.	
Tiffney Jones (mother)	Mom works nights most weekends; Mondays not good for contacting.	Check in with Mom about how the weekends have been going.
Brett and Eva Johnson (parents)	Sports are really important.	Lots of late nights with sports schedule; watch for overtiredness.
Brett and Eva Johnson (parents)	Recent family changes; Mom has moved out.	Monitor if family needs help with anything.

Access

Often, parents face barriers when attempting to access communication from a student's teacher and the school. Technology can be one such barrier. While some families may have easy access to cell phones and computers, other families may struggle to keep phones active, maintain consistent numbers, or have reliable Wi-Fi access. Although it may be easy for teachers and schools to post information or send emails, some families may have difficulty accessing these communications. Keep this in mind when asking families about their preferred method of communication, and find alternatives for those families whose access may be limited in some way. The important thing is to keep families engaged in a way that works for both the school and family.

Language and literacy can also be barriers to keeping families engaged. Make sure teacher and school communications are available in different languages or can be translated for families. At one time I posted messages to families by creating JPEGs of slide decks and posting them as pictures. I used different fancy fonts and colors, making the messages pleasing to look at and read. But a colleague pointed out that there was no way for parents to translate the messages because they were in an image format. I stopped doing this: the information was more important than the aesthetics.

High-Running Emotions

Emotions can get in the way of good relationships. Families can be sensitive when it comes to their children, and educators can be sensitive when it comes to our work. It can be hard not to take things personally.

A kindergarten boy was referred to me for counseling because he was having trouble being safe with peers. He was bigger than most of the kids in his grade. It was especially tough at recess, when he hurt a few kids by playing too roughly. When I met with him he was one incident away from losing the privilege of recess for an extended period of time. I suggested that we have him make a basket of preferred activities so he could sit at the picnic table and play with them during recess. He could even choose a friend or two to join him. We tried it for a few days, and it worked great. Then I received an angry phone call from his mom. She felt like he was being punished and excluded from recess and the other kids.

Looking back, I should have communicated with the boy's mother so that I could discuss our plan and explain what we were doing, and why. But because I didn't, she thought that her son was having to sit at a picnic table at recess while the other kids were free to play.

Being able to deescalate or defuse situations is an important skill for a teacher. Here's a three-step process that can be an effective approach:

- **Step one: Start with appreciation.** Let the parent or family member know you appreciate the information being shared with you, talked about, or brought to your attention. Even if you don't appreciate the manner in which the information is being expressed, starting with statements of appreciation for the opportunity to have a dialogue is a helpful first step. People are like file cabinets. We have a rational, thinking drawer, and we have an emotional drawer and a physical drawer. When we're upset and the emotional drawer is out too far, the other drawers are locked. When we start with appreciation, it can help to push the parent's emotional drawer in enough that the rational, thinking drawer can open. Here are some ways to start the conversation:

  - "I really appreciate you letting me know . . ."

  - "Thank you for taking time to call me about this . . ."

  - "I'm glad you are bringing this to my attention . . ."

- **Step two: Share what you know.** Give your perspective, share your side, and present the facts as you know them. Keeping your emotions in check as you share what you know is important. A few deep breaths can help you push in your own emotional drawer as you share. These sentence starters are useful in sharing your perspective with parents:

  - "Let me share what I know . . ."

  - "I think I see what may have happened . . ."

  - "It was my understanding that . . ."

  - "I heard things a little differently . . ."

- **Step three: Find common ground.** Many times there are misunderstandings that can be easily cleared up with sharing by both sides. There may be times, though, where the two sides just see things differently. Sometimes the parent, perhaps because of other things that have nothing to do with you or school, may not be able to hear your perspective. Listen for and be ready to share back any kind of common ground you can find:

- ○ "Sounds like we both want . . ."

- ○ "You and I both think . . ."

- ○ "We both hope . . ."

In most cases, we can reach that common ground and use it to determine whatever next steps may be needed. Sometimes, common ground can be hard to find and emotions may run too high to problem-solve. Give it some time and space first, and then circle back around to these steps again.

Actively seeking and building connections between home and school makes school an inviting place for all families, helps build trusting relationships with parents, and ultimately supports student success. In the sections ahead, you will find information that parents of children in your grade level will find helpful. You'll also find practical strategies for you to:

- Build and strengthen connections with families.

- Understand and address families' concerns about children in your grade level.

- Communicate with parents.

- Hold productive parent-teacher meetings.

- Involve parents in events and activities.

- Handle tricky situations.

Grade

Today's parents constantly get messages that lead to feelings of inadequacy and anxiety. They can view flawless holidays on social media, watch commercials showcasing perfectly behaved children, or receive targeted online advertising that highlights parenting solutions and promises of quick fixes if they just "click here." It is not surprising, then, that many parents of kindergartners send their children to school worried that their children are behind and that they as caregivers are not doing enough.

Part of the role of the kindergarten teacher is to be a comforting breath of fresh air. We want to consistently let the parents know, "You are enough, and your children are enough." We want to be that warm welcome into the school system that lets parents know we value their family, their children, and their culture.

Building and Strengthening Connections

In Chapter 4, we talked about leading with love and empathy as we observe and interact with children. This same advice applies to our interactions with families. We can do this throughout the school year by communicating directly and regularly with families, presenting ourselves as approachable professionals who care about—and know about—their children. And we can ensure a productive working relationship by emphasizing the positive in our communications, showing parents that we see the good in these very important children.

What follows are some strategies to ensure that we are leading with love and empathy with our families.

Connecting at the Start of the Year

At the beginning of the school year, there are many different ways to start building a strong foundation with families. What follows should be considered a menu of ways to connect, not a list of have-tos. Decide which ones would work best in your community and in your school while keeping in mind your own availability and comfort level.

- **Home visits.** A short visit to see the child and family in their own space can be helpful for starting to establish those connections and supporting children's big feelings away from home. For example, if you have had a home visit, you might be able to reassure a student on the first day of school by saying, "I remember that superhero blanket you had on your bed at home. Do you like to snuggle that when you feel sad?" For families that feel comfortable welcoming you into their home, a visit can go a long way in creating that connection in a meaningful way.

- **Letter or postcard home.** Consider sending a postcard or short letter to children's homes before school begins. Include a picture of yourself, if you can. Share a little about your background and one or two things about yourself unrelated to teaching. People strive for connection, so knowing more about you gives families more areas in which they can connect with you.

- **Video greeting.** Record a video introduction, telling a little about your teaching experience and about yourself.

- **Phone call.** A call home at the beginning of the year sends a warm message that the student's family is important enough to talk with before the school year starts. I used to block out ten minutes for each phone call and try to do five or six each night over the course of a work week.

See the appendix, p. 348, for a sample questionnaire.

- **Questionnaire.** A short questionnaire sent home at the beginning of the year allows you to gather a little more information than might necessarily be included on the emergency contact form that families fill out for the main office. You can discover skills, hobbies, or talents that family members have that they might be willing to share with your class. It also allows you to learn about more areas of connection.

- **Early conferences.** Consider having one of your parent-teacher conferences early in the school year. This will allow you to learn more about your students from the families and set goals together.

Building Connections Throughout the School Year

Over the years, many families have told me that when their children get home and are asked what they did at school that day, their answer is, "I dunno. We had . . . recess?" Sharing with families about activities in the classroom will give them a sense of what is going on. Here are some ways to help families feel connected during the school year:

- **Short newsletter with photographs.** I created a template called "Our Week in Pictures." It has four photographs with space for a short blurb beneath each one, and a space in the center for a short paragraph summarizing an activity from the week.

Our Week in Pictures

Here we are practicing observational drawing.

We learned a new card game at indoor recess.

Dear Families,

Welcome to the end of our second full week of school. It's important to me that I keep in touch and let you know what we're working on in school. In the classroom, I take many pictures of children working. So, with the idea that a picture is worth a thousand words, I thought a weekly picture round up would both keep you updated on our work, as well as provide you and your child with a jumping off point for conversation.

So, welcome to our first installment of the *Week in Pictures!*

We used numbered blocks as a math tool.

We've been using the play structure at recess and playing some new games.

- **Photo-hosting site.** Some schools may have a subscription service to a photo-hosting website. Each classroom has their own password-protected album online, and images can be uploaded for families to view.

- **Social media account or blog.** Create a private web page for families to allow further connection and insight into the learning their children are doing. (If your social media site is public, be sure to get permission from families for the use of their children's images, or be very careful not to use faces, names, or identifying features.) Explore other social media options for communicating with families and choose one that works best for your students' families. You can also use social media to connect with other teachers in order to share insights or to discuss and be frank about the excitement as well as the very real demands of teaching.

- **Office hours.** Monthly or weekly office hours allow you to set a time to show families that you value their questions and will also allow you to set your own boundaries. Office hours can be conducted via phone or videoconference.

- **Parent coffees and child playdates.** You can also help jumpstart relationships between families. For example, a family might be new to the area or to the school and might appreciate the chance to get to know other families in the class. Consider a playdate at a local playground for families or a weekend coffee date for just the parents. You could have your room parent arrange a few of these over the course of the year. Plan to show up at one or two of these to connect with families and help facilitate other connections.

Role of Room Parents

Many teachers find it helpful to have a room parent or two to help out. Usually this role can include helping to plan class parties, arranging volunteers for class events, and coordinating chaperones for field trips. Room parents are often a point of contact for the school's PTO or PTA, and usually coordinate gifts and other gestures of appreciation for teachers.

Room parents are another point of contact for families and can be a valuable resource for teachers to help families feel connected to the school. Remember that while teachers may have a family for just one school year, many members of your class cohort will see their children go through elementary school together. The room parent can make connections, find commonalities, and help forge friendships that will continue.

Here are three suggestions for where a room parent can assist:

- **Class directory.** Prepare and manage an opt-in list with names, addresses, and phone numbers of each family so people can arrange playdates and other get-togethers.

- **Class playdates.** Arrange playdates at a local park or playground to build connections beyond the classroom.

- **Parents' night out.** Organize a get-together at a local restaurant for parents to attend without their children so they can get to know each other.

Ensuring That All Parents Feel Seen and Welcome

Take the time to regularly consider families you have not connected with recently. Send a note or email to tell them something about their student, ask a question, or just check in. Talk with colleagues to see what strategies they use to involve all families, and adopt some of their strategies.

Be open to changing what you do. Strategies can and should change. Because one student learned something one way, it doesn't mean we will use the same strategy for every student. The same thought process applies to our families: something that worked last year may not work this year. Be open to inventing, learning, and reaching out in new ways.

Be sure as well to display pictures of all the children in your class, and the children's own work, in the classroom environment. Think about what families see when they visit our classrooms. Do they see photographs of their students in multiple places? Is their child's work represented? Can they tell us the valuable contributions of their child by what is displayed in the room? Representing the children this way can also ensure that all families feel seen, welcomed, and valued.

Special Concerns of Kindergarten Families

As a kindergarten student begins elementary school, their family typically has a few questions:

- "Are they behaving?"

- "Are they learning? And what are they learning?"

- "Do they have other kids to play with?"

- "How can I help them at home?"

Keep these questions in mind and address them throughout the year in communications with the families. At our back to school night, I talk about the curriculum and share examples of things the students will learn and how I will communicate with families to let them know what learning is happening. I explain the ways we will be building our class community and how children will be building connections with others and practicing social and emotional learning skills. I will also share key developmental considerations for ages four to six. Once a month, I might highlight a developmental milestone, either through an article or a summary I write, and include it in a weekly newsletter I send to families.

I keep in mind that my students' families are the experts about their child and I am the expert about this age. The more I can proactively share information, the better equipped families will be to know, understand, and parent their child.

I keep in mind, as well, that for some families, kindergarten is the first step in their child's education. Even for children who have attended preschool, kindergarten may be a very different experience.

Kindergarten has undergone changes in the last twenty years. It was originally a half-day program, geared toward a slower, play-based introduction to school. Today, kindergarten is often a full-day program with extensive expectations and standards for students. In many ways, kindergarten now looks like what first grade used to look like.

Most districts have children entering at ages from four to six. This is quite a developmental range. With this in mind, there are a couple of points to consider as we establish and deepen our connections with families.

First, it might be a tricky year. Despite the best and most proactive work, some children will still struggle to get their footing in kindergarten for a number of reasons: they are in school for a long day, they are learning within a large group of kids, or they are developmentally not quite there yet. Some young children may stumble through kindergarten, and then, for whatever reason, they will land feet first and ready in first grade.

Second, it might be the child's first time in school. In some cases, families will be sending you their first or only child, with all of the concerns and emotion that comes with it. I recall talking to my mom when I was a freshman in college, homesick and overwhelmed. She would worry for days, until we spoke again and I sounded better. I think about this as families watch their children entering kindergarten feeling frightened, nervous, or anxious, and I can empathize with the parents in the moment. I have looked many parents in the eye while holding a crying kindergartner and told them kindly, "They will be fine. I promise." Later, I'll send a photo in an email or a text message to show the family their child in a moment of happiness.

Communicating With Parents

The most effective way we can communicate with kindergarten families is through brief, regular, and consistent messages. When we follow a regular format for messages throughout the year, parents can use the information in the way that works best for them. The format I followed included a section for reminders, one for notes about students, and sometimes a more in-depth discussion of something related to learning.

Meaningful connection doesn't need to take up a lot of time. Brief, simple messages tell families that we see evidence of learning every day, and they help deepen our connection. For example, you could send a text message or email with a photo and a quick note about what the child is doing in the photo. When the class has had an interesting piece of learning or a child has had a specific accomplishment, you might affix a label on their shirt to wear home that says, "Ask me about two things scientists do!" or "Ask me about the new word I learned today!"

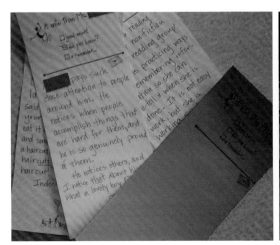

I keep a small bin in my teacher space with pens and brightly colored notes. A few times a week, I take time to write two or three notes to send home with students for their families. I set a goal of one note per month for each student. One student told me, "Those love notes? My mom puts them in my special box so I get to have them when I'm growned [sic] up."

Tailor the communication style and preference to each family. Some parents may prefer a short text exchange or communicating via email because it involves less pressure and less risk. Others prefer a phone conversation or a face-to-face talk (either in person or virtually). I used to set office hours so parents would know when I was available for a call, text, or email. If I'm clear when I'm going to be available, it helps me to be fully present during those times. I ask parents to let me know what they would like to discuss ahead of time. I find it helpful to set boundaries to keep focused and efficient.

Holding Productive Parent-Teacher Meetings

When I was a relatively new teacher, I stepped out of a day of conferences to head to the copy room before a quick lunch break. My principal walked through the copy area, and I beamed at her.

"Kirsten, you are so happy! What's going on?" she asked.

"Conferences! I get to talk to the people that know and love these kids more than I do!"

She laughed and gave me a hug. "Then I know you're having the best day."

One of the guiding principles of the *Responsive Classroom* approach is that partnering with families—knowing them and valuing their contributions—is as important as knowing the children we teach. When we take the time to get to know and value the relationship we have with families, our community strengthens.

To hold productive meetings of any kind, we need to be clear about what our goals and expectations are. Taking the time to plan and set goals up front will make your time with families more efficient and effective. What follows are the types of meetings you will hold during the school year and strategies for ensuring they are productive:

- **Introductory meeting.** This might be a short meet and greet at an open house or a kindergarten orientation. The goal here is to make everyone feel welcome.

- **Class visit.** To introduce the student and their family to kindergarten, most classrooms will offer class visits, usually before the beginning of the school year. These visits can be scheduled so that they have staggered starts, when children come to school for a shorter day in small groups, or they can be organized into ten-to-fifteen-minute blocks, when children come to school with their parents to see the classroom and meet the teacher. The goal here is to make everyone feel welcome and to make a connection. During these visits, I often take a photo to share with the parents later, telling them about something I noticed their child doing or something they were interested in.

- **Check-in.** This is a time to touch base about one quick thing over the phone, in person, or virtually. Be clear about what you want to communicate, and be open to listening. If your time is limited, be sure to start by respectfully letting the parent know how long you expect the conversation to last.

- **Formal parent-teacher conference.** Formal parent-teacher conferences for kindergarten should first and foremost be about celebrating the child. Being this age only happens once, and it is worth taking the time to honor the child's resilience and learning. For these conferences, there may be assessments your school requires you to share. I encourage you to let that be a very small part of the conference. Do some prep work and reflection ahead of time to think about two or three strengths for each student, as well as one to two next steps.

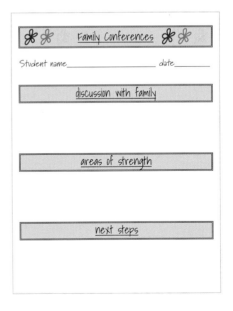

Framing things this way allows for both a growth mindset and a sense of where a child is developmentally (socially, emotionally, and academically). We want to highlight both the child's strengths and the next steps as important to their continued learning.

- **Problem-solving meeting.** A meeting like this may have underlying tension, and families may feel nervous or defensive. Remember to start from areas of strength and communicate your faith in and appreciation of the student. Come to the meeting with solutions, but keep an open mind and listen to the parents as well.

Involving Parents in Events and Activities

When I was in kindergarten, my father was a key player in one of our school events, and I will never forget the joy of having him there. My father, a trained chef, cooked for a pancake breakfast fundraiser. And was he ever in his element! He chatted with everyone, served food, made jokes, and answered questions. I was beside myself with joy, pride, and excitement.

My mother, on the other hand, preferred to do things behind the scenes. She single-handedly set up, organized, and executed a cookie-selling season for my Girl Scout troop that included several thousand boxes of cookies. The idea of being front and center was not her style, but the mental organization, planning, and completion of a daunting task played to her strengths.

These experiences from my childhood have helped me immensely as a teacher. It helped me realize that parents want to be involved, but involvement can look different for different people. The questionnaire that is sent to families at the start of the year could include inquiries about how they would like to be involved.

What follows are some ways that parents can be involved, either in the classroom or behind the scenes.

Visiting the Classroom

Family members can be involved in your classroom regularly or occasionally, depending on their availability and the activities you have planned for your kindergartners, and could include:

- **Fun Friday.** Consider a weekly, bimonthly, or monthly time when families are invited to join the class during a learning time. It could be for a specific subject: for example, families might participate in a math lesson, which will allow them to see their children actively engaged and to learn with them.

- **Morning Meeting.** You could extend an open invitation for family members to join the class Morning Meeting anytime. In the case of a highly active parent body, you can also create a schedule and involve children in writing and extending invitations. One year, our class had two students with siblings who were infants, and they joined us at least once a month. It was amazing to watch the students serve as leaders, caretakers, and delight in the development of our "future classmates," as we called them.

- **Family events.** Does your kindergarten have a language arts event? Perhaps the class does a performance every spring or has an end-of-year school visit to celebrate the learning of the year. These are all events for families to attend that will help them to feel connected to the child's learning and the school.

- **Volunteering.** Families might have a recurring time when they would like to visit the classroom. A family member could be assigned to read individually with children, play a math game, or be a trusted adult stationed in the science area. If you and your students enjoy having a guest reader join your classroom, you could create a sign-up sheet for volunteers who would like to read to the class once a week.

- **Chaperoning.** If your class takes a field trip, even if it's only to a nearby location such as a local library, offer parents the opportunity to be a chaperone.

- **Teaching or sharing a collection or skill.** One year, there was a student in our class whose parent had a collection of vintage flags.

The class had become very interested in flags from all over the world and were avidly reading about and trying to draw flags. The parent volunteered to come in and share some of his collection. The children were mesmerized by his stories and by seeing real, old artifacts.

Behind the Scenes

For those parents who may prefer to work behind the scenes or may not be available during the school day, there are other opportunities to be involved:

- Assisting at a book fair or other school events

- Finding a role on the PTA or PTO

- Helping with classroom prep work such as copying, cutting, stapling, laminating, or mending well-loved books

Advice for Tricky Situations

My husband and I enjoy watching television shows together after our children have gone to bed. But we have a persistent complaint that will make us stop watching a television show: if the problems that drive the plot consistently could be fixed if the characters just talked to each other, we'll give the show three more episodes, and then we move on to a new series.

I keep this in mind when I need to address a tricky situation with students' families. Difficulties in resolving an issue usually stem from misunderstanding or miscommunication and can be readily worked through if we take the initiative to discuss it.

One year, I had a kindergarten class of four- and five-year-olds. We were a full-time extended-day school, so we scheduled a longer rest time than normal. The routine included taking children to the bathroom before rest time. One day, a student told me she didn't have to go. I asked her if she wanted to "try to use the potty," but she insisted she didn't have to go. During rest time, she had an accident, and when she came to let me know,

I commiserated with her and said, "Oh, that's too bad. That probably wasn't a fun way to wake up."

That night, her mother left a frustrated message on the school phone. When I called her back the next day, she was still upset: "Maya told me she had an accident during rest time and when she told you about it, you said, 'Too bad!'"

I responded by telling her, "Oh, I did say that, but let me put it in context for you. When she came to me, what I said was, 'Oh, Maya, that's too bad. That probably wasn't a fun way to wake up.'" After a pause, Maya's mother laughed and said, "Well, that's totally different."

What I really appreciated about this interaction was that Maya's mother came to me with a genuine concern, but she also took the time to listen. When she realized it was a misunderstanding, it became a nonissue. I use this interaction as a lesson to truly try to listen openly when families come to me, and I remind myself of the following:

- Have a sense of humor. Young children are brilliant and hilarious, and sometimes that humor brings a sense of relief to a tense situation.

- **Listen without an agenda.** I read a quote once that said to listen to understand, not to respond. It is such good advice. Every student in my class is someone's baby. I want them to know that their baby is important. If I truly want our relationship to grow, I need to listen to understand their point and perspective.

- **Have a sense of history.** Ask yourself, "What relationship do I already have with this family? What do I know about their previous history at the school? Am I letting internalized biases get in the way of building this relationship? How can this sense of history guide how I approach the situation?" If I know that a family of one of my students has had difficult interactions in the past, I can infer that they might feel defensive, so I want to approach any situation from a supportive place.

- **Be willing to come back to something.** In some situations, you will not have all the answers. It's okay to make a plan for further observation, more information-gathering, and additional reflection, and then come back together at a later time.

- **Be willing to be fallible.** As much as I like to believe I know everything that is going on in the classroom, there are things that happen in what I call "the kid underground" that I just don't know about. It might be at lunchtime, during specialist times, under the play structure at recess, or in any number of times in the classroom. I want families to feel comfortable letting me know what they hear from their students, even if it's something I might be uncomfortable about or might not know about.

No matter what the situation is or the reason for connecting with a family, remember we all want what is best for the child. When we start with that common ground, it feels less daunting.

As teachers, we know that the relationship we have with each student is one of the most important keys to their success. We know that building a strong connection takes effort and that it certainly doesn't happen overnight. The same is true of our relationships with families. When we make that positive relationship a priority, it not only sends the message that the families matter to us, but it also shows students that the adult partnership of their teacher and family is something they can count on. It becomes another layer of security for them.

Grade ❶

When I was a new parent, there were almost no how-to manuals about a child's first couple of years. I remember worrying and thinking, "So we get them to kindergarten, and then we'll know what to do for the next decade or so?" Even though I was an early childhood teacher, I was sure I would need guidance and support. This was before internet search engines and social networks, so my children's first teachers were my lifeline. I approached them with gratitude and an eagerness to learn from them, which was gracefully accepted.

I took a similar stance with my colleagues when I was a new teacher. I was fortunate to be in a school with excellent, seasoned teachers who had a true passion for the education of children and themselves, and I sought to learn from them each day. When I guided my pre-K class down the hall, I would linger and peek inside the other classrooms we passed like a child walking through Cinderella's castle arch for the first time. I wondered what pixie dust allowed these teachers to have such engaged and orderly learning in their classrooms, where children demonstrated prosocial behaviors and a genuine interest in learning, and where mistakes were welcomed and treated as a vehicle for growth. I learned that the pixie dust was not a magic formula but rather a skillful use of the *Responsive Classroom* approach. I discovered that this approach extended far beyond the classroom, to include how families were wrapped into the fabric of the school through teachers' documentation of learning, regular communication between families and teachers, and the involvement of families in their children's education. As one teacher explained to me, "Families are our allies. They know their children best, and we have the gift of knowing children. Together, we can make a powerful impact on the lives of children, families, and ourselves."

Building and Strengthening Connections

Over time, I learned that the best way to start building a connection with a family and their child was an introductory letter to welcome the child and family with respect, enthusiasm, and curiosity. The letter would be addressed to the child and be developmentally appropriate (language, pictures, and simple focus). I would include a picture of myself, so the child had a concrete image of me and saw me smiling in eager anticipation of meeting them. I would also ask them to think about questions for me and to bring a picture of themselves on the first day. In addition, I would include a newsletter for the family that shared a little about myself and first grade.

What to Include in a Newsletter or Parent Primer Before School Starts

- An invitation to begin to think about hopes for the year
- Roles that parent volunteers and helpers could have in the classroom and outside of school
- Plans for field trips and other activities outside of the classroom, and an invitation for ideas and suggestions
- A list of supplies children will need
- Some of the projects and units of study
- The best times and the easiest way to reach the teacher
- An invitation to share any questions or concerns about first grade—from grown-ups or the children
- If you're new to the area, a question about recommendations of places to walk, grab a coffee, or pick up a meal

These seemingly small bits of information can go a long way toward building the relationship. Often, it's the nuts and bolts and logistics of school that can cause so much stress, and by sharing this information ahead of time, you increase the likelihood of a smooth start on the first day.

Some schools offer families short classroom visits before the school year starts. I find these ten-to-fifteen-minute visits very helpful for two reasons. First, they give me an extra incentive to make sure I have my classroom set up, leaving plenty of time to plan and savor the welcoming environment. Without this early deadline, I might often arrange and rearrange my classroom up until the day before the first day of school. Second, and most important, these visits give me the incredible gift of seeing children and their family members one-on-one for just a little bit of time. This has not always been possible during my years of teaching, but when these meetings do happen, they are the perfect way to meet students and lay the foundation for our community and work.

Lead With Empathy and Practice Listening

If we are to walk in someone else's world carefully and respectfully, we need to come into that world with an open mind, free of judgment, and prepared to truly collaborate in the best interest of our students. This is the very essence of a true partnership, where both sides value and care about children, but we may have different ways of supporting and demonstrating our care. As teachers, working with families can be one of the most challenging aspects of our work. When I first started teaching, I found this to involve a steep learning curve, as I was confident in my education and skills around teaching but did not yet fully grasp the nuances of communicating with families. Since then, I've spent many years learning—and continue to learn—ways to lead with empathy and work with families. Here are some things to keep in mind:

- **Engage in self-reflection.** Admit that you know a lot of things about a lot of things, but you don't know everything. We learn from families. We do not know everything.

- **Keep a growth mindset.** While working with other people can sometimes be a challenge, remember that we are wired for connection. Ask a colleague or friend to let you role-play to prepare for a difficult conversation. Improve your listening skills through articles, podcasts, or books to help you develop these skills. Work with your team or colleagues to better understand and communicate a curriculum area you are unsure of.

- **Show gratitude and validate.** Verbalize your appreciation for parents' efforts to support the children and work with you. Let parents know you understand the challenges of parenting and finding the time to meet: "I realize there are many things you could do with your time this afternoon, and I appreciate you making it a priority to talk to me about Lucas." Provide specific feedback about the child's strengths and demonstrate you care.

- **Leverage support.** Talk with colleagues and your school's leadership to get their experiences with families. If you need to share complex information or are uncertain, ask someone to join you in the meeting.

- **Share your love.** Be ready to share observable behaviors and details of your curriculum, but have several examples of what you love about the child or how you've seen them grow. Building trust will help demonstrate empathy.

Importance of First Impressions

No matter how you connect with families before and during school, the most essential piece is to treat everyone in the community with a sense of welcome and respect. The first impression your first graders and their family have of you will be remembered. Many of my first graders are now in college, and they will sometimes share what they remember about our first meeting. One recently said, "The air conditioning didn't work in our car, and apparently it wasn't working in school either because I was just so hot, and I felt like my new teacher would see me all messy. But when we met on the green carpet, you sat with me and asked me questions. You let me walk around the room and look. I calmed down and thought first grade would be fun. Then I yelled, 'Hey, I'm not all drippy wet anymore!'" I don't know that I can take credit for dropping the air temperature in the room, but creating a space that welcomes children and families helps to establish a sense of community and conveys empathy for the changes that come with the transition to the start of school.

At these before-the-start-of-school visits, ask students and their families to share their expertise by asking questions such as:

- "What do I need to know about this school?"

- "What's something you love about this school?"

- "What are you and your child looking forward to?"

Building on Connections

Building and strengthening connections with students and their families should continue over the course of the school year. Here are some strategies to consider:

- **Connect early and often.** Many of us are conditioned to only connect with teachers or families when there is a problem. The surest way to build a positive relationship is to call early with some good news and to make it a habit to share good news on a regular basis. My school asked teachers to contact each family within the first ten days of school with good news. This was an opportunity to offer a warm welcome to the family and to share something positive we had observed in their child. It was also a good time to reiterate any essential information, such as forms or supplies still needed, logistics, and how to contact us. Throughout the school year, I'd plan a week to repeat this process in between more formal outreaches such as conferences, interim reports, or final reports. The cadence of communication became a predictable path to sharing the good news, goals, and concerns. Because some parents might have had a visceral reaction to the school calling, I learned to quickly add a comment such as "I'm calling to share good news!" or "Janine is fine today—I'm calling today just to check in" after I introduced myself.

- **Maintain a regular, consistent, and clear communication cadence to the class community.** This includes any family members authorized to receive information in newsletters or blogs, not just the primary parent. Parents are often busy and can't always read communications from the school right away, but most parents are always deeply appreciative of big-picture examples and details of our learning. And as we've become more digitally connected, it's easier to share these updates through blogs, platforms, or social media. As you get to know each family and student, you will learn what works best for them. Some may prefer printed newsletters, while others may find social media the best way to connect. Strive to meet families where they are while telling the story of your class's learning and preserving the privacy of your students.

- **Make learning visible.** Documenting student learning remains essential for students, educators, and visitors. Allowing students to play a part in creating panels and displays is a valuable part of learning. Ensuring that the hallways and classroom walls include work created by all students helps us make learning visible when families are visiting the school.

- **Make yourself available.** I try to keep office hours available for quick questions. Here are some things to consider when setting office hours:

  - Decide what times best fit your schedule.

  - Determine a frequency that works. For example, I usually offer two thirty-minute windows.

  - Set parameters for the calls. I tell families that we can use these calls for quick questions or points needing clarification that can be addressed in ten minutes or less.

  - Determine the best format for the call (phone or video call).

  - Decide whether to have scheduled appointments. Some teachers prefer to work during this time and await phone calls, while others like to plan ahead and schedule calls so they know whom to expect.

- **Don't be afraid to share.** When you see families informally, share something positive you've observed or experienced with their child ("Hey! Lucy drew a picture of that lizard she found on your porch. She was very excited and proud of her illustration!"). These can be comments made when families are at school or when you bump into them in town. I have made it my commitment to always tell families (and their children) something positive and affirming when I see them outside of school, and I know it conveys that I see the good in their child and their family.

Ensuring That Parents Feel Seen and Welcome

Making families feel seen and welcome can start in the most literal and fundamental way—looking them in the eye and saying, "Hi," "Hola," "Ciao"! We're modeling and teaching children how to greet and talk with each other, so it's even more important to take the opportunity to authentically greet and welcome their families.

The sixth guiding principle of the *Responsive Classroom* approach states that "partnering with families—knowing them and valuing their contributions—is as important as knowing the children we teach." We need to truly seek to understand the demographics and culture of our students and their communities. This can be done in many ways—querying colleagues, reading community news, engaging in community events, and asking families to share what's important to them. It means we need to embrace a growth mindset and be open to new learning and understanding. Along with that openness comes the vulnerability to take risks, make mistakes, and then apologize sincerely when we make a mistake of omission, ignorance, or oversight.

Greeting parents and getting to know the cultures of students' families are critical. The building blocks of our relationships with students of all cultures are critical as well, and include offering clearly written communications, sharing information about community services, and offering a flexible schedule that allows families to attend school events and meetings.

One school I taught in had students of the Jewish faith, many of whom attended the same temple. I got to know many of these families through teaching some of their children and by attending community events at the temple. I was by no means an authority, but I thought I understood the most significant aspects of their culture concerning school and interacting with families. There were also a few families that attended an Orthodox temple, and I didn't know them as well. The first time I met the father of one of these families, I offered my hand as a greeting. He politely and silently shook his head. I noticed his wife looked down as we proceeded with our conversation, while he maintained a solemn composure. I was puzzled.

I later shared this exchange with a colleague. She explained the nuances for Orthodox Jewish men of shaking hands and that it was widely known that this father did not physically touch women. My colleague apologized for not mentioning this to me. I thanked her for the honesty and agreed that this was a fruitful learning experience for me.

Several years later, while presenting a *Responsive Classroom* workshop, I had a participant I suspected observed Orthodox traditions. After seeing that he had brought his own meal, I inquired about his thoughts on the workshop and if he needed anything from me. He asked if we could provide kosher meals in the future, and I agreed to follow up on this. More importantly, I understood this to likely mean he would not be comfortable touching the women in our group. With this in mind, I offered energizers and other activities that would not require participants to shake hands, tap toes, or other forms of contact.

Here are some suggestions for building connections with families of all cultures and backgrounds:

- **Provide translations of newsletters.** Learn the languages spoken and understood by your families so that you and your students' families do not need to rely on your first graders as translators. Online translators can allow you to offer your newsletter in multiple languages, as can some e-newsletter services.

- **Enlist the support of community helpers.** Learn about available local community help in your school and district that will support the linguistic, transportation, or economic needs of students' families. For example, during the 2020 pandemic, a group of local restaurants in my town teamed up with the school resources department at two local elementary schools to increase food pantry offerings. This group of restaurants leveraged its resources and built a network through social media to provide food and personal items at the schools. Teachers at the schools shared information about these resources on virtual learning platforms and also coordinated deliveries to those unable to get to the school for pickup.

- **Be flexible and think ahead.** Offer conferences, meetings, and gatherings at various times. (As a working parent and teacher, I missed many events my kids had at school—and we attended the same school!) It can be difficult for some parents to attend meetings or events due to work, health issues, lack of childcare, transportation, or a conflicting priority. Acknowledge that times you set may not work for every parent, and convey information in a way that will help assuage any guilt or bad feelings parents may have for not attending. And, of course, virtual meetings are an option and perhaps more convenient for some parents.

It's essential that we let students know that when we invite families we also understand if they cannot make it. The last thing we want is for our six-year-olds to be feeling unhappy that a parent couldn't attend a meeting. I once had a busy working father ask me at our fall conference to identify the most important events of the year that he should plan to attend. He went on to explain the nature and rhythm of his job and that by planning ahead he could make sure he had the time off. I had an aha moment there—letting parents know a week ahead of time in a newsletter about an event for families to participate in was probably not enough notice for all families. After this, I made sure that I had the significant dates listed in our newsletter at the start of the year.

Special Concerns of First Grade Families

Having weathered kindergarten and sometimes pre-K, parents come with a bit of experience in schools that can assure them they know what they are doing, but they may also be concerned that they don't know what they and their children are in for in first grade. Having taught kindergarten and first grade for many years, I respect these concerns, because I know that while these years are sequential, they are also markedly different.

Temperament, Energy, and Attitude

At around five and a half years old, children tend to get sensitive and willful. This marks a change in cognitive development that comes with tantrums, tears, and social conflicts. By the age of six, temperament seems to smooth out, and enthusiasm and energy are the name of the game.

It takes a lot of energy to be six years old and to keep up with a six-year-old. Many parents find it a bit of a relief when their child reaches this age, only to find that they are being peppered with questions as their six-year-old tests the world and takes on more than they can handle. This is an age when it is essential to offer children choice and a wide berth with clear boundaries. Your six-year-old will be content exploring and taking ownership of work but then might crash hard from exhaustion. It's our job as adults to give them space and then ensure that they rest and refuel for the next adventure.

Slowing Things Down

As a parent of six-year-olds, I always had snacks and a quiet activity such as a book, audiobook, or gaming device ready for those times when we were out and my children needed to slow down.

It's also important to remember that six-year-olds are talkers—even the shy ones. They will talk to each other, to themselves, and to their imaginary friends and cuddle friends. And they will talk over each other and during play. They may even talk in their sleep. Accept chatter and conversation to be a steady backdrop, and keep a sense of humor about it.

One way to have your students practice talking and stopping is using energizers such as Laughing Scarf or interactive learning structures such as One-Minute Walk and Talk. These activities will help first graders learn to quickly share and quickly stop.

Reading

American culture has perpetuated the ideal that all first graders should be reading, often fluently. The truth, though, is that many are not reading fluently, but are still okay. Reading to and with first graders is essential—to answer their questions, expand their imagination, and help develop literacy skills.

First graders are often curious way beyond their reading abilities and eager to be read to. My son's first grade teacher read Greek myths to the class, which at first glance I thought was odd. But then she explained that they were deep into reading aloud the Harry Potter series and enjoying the mystical nature of imagination in those books. She understood that first graders could not yet read the Harry Potter books, and many families had lamented that they couldn't read aloud a hundred pages. Reading shorter myths, however, allowed for rich conversations about stories based in fantasy and in life lessons.

Reassuring Parents

I still keep in touch with the parents of a first grader who contacted me one day with an urgent meeting request. Both parents were well educated—one was a former teacher and writer, and the other had a PhD in biomedical research. They deeply valued education and had many age-appropriate books available for their child. The parents had a few concerns that we danced around before uncovering the real issue: their nearly seven-year-old child was not reading fluently. I empathized, remembering how hard it is with your firstborn, having read all the books that map out development, only to find your child is forging their own path. I confirmed with them that what they were doing at home was fantastic—library and bookstore trips, modeling reading at home, reading aloud, asking questions, and finding books on topics their child enjoyed. They seemed a bit relieved, but not fully on board. I had assessment data on hand and shared where their child was and the typical continuum for children his age, and emphatically let them know that I was certain he was on the right track and that he would be a reader when these pieces came together.

I had the same child in third grade. When I met with the parents for our before-the-school-year-starts visit, they exclaimed, "He's a reader!" That year, he grew to be an even more avid and skilled reader.

Social Struggles

Along with the energy, enthusiasm, and loquaciousness of first graders, there will inevitably be social conflict among them. Proactively teaching social skills will go a long way in building relationships and the skills to navigate conflicts, but first graders will need support from adults.

I advise parents to take what their child shares as a portion of the truth, especially around social conflicts. (Or, as one parent once told me, whatever their daughter reported when she was six years old was likely to be about 50 percent accurate.) We know from neuropsychology that when we are jazzed up and involved in a conflict, we are often not listening and may be highly reactive. This is especially true for six-year-olds, who don't yet have a fully developed brain and are enthusiastic about their own point of view and needs. Adults who can listen and validate feelings (and even offer names for them) can help calm children and see that social conflict both teaches us lessons and allows us to strengthen relationships. It's important that we prepare families for the potential of conflict and give them tools to help manage these at home and at school.

Communicating With Parents

Parents of first graders are likely to be juggling many hats, and reading long or complex notes from school may not be a priority. I've had many smart, well-meaning, and otherwise fantastic parents chuckle as they tell me, "Oh, I never read those emails" or "I have a stack of newsletters I have never read!" Nobody wants to write something that goes unread into the trash or recycling bin. With this in mind, what follows are a few tips to keep your communication efficient, readable, and accessible:

- **Find a system that works for you and stick to it.** Choose a template and use it consistently. Don't waste time recreating the format, font, or design each week. Simply open the last document, create a copy, and add new content. Save information you might later need to reuse—dismissal routines, homework reminders, how to reach you—as a separate document so you can copy and paste as needed.

- **Block time to write (and proofread).** As you plan your week, block time in your schedule to work on the newsletter. I find it easier to chunk portions of the newsletter into small pockets of time. For example, during special classes on Tuesdays, I'll update the calendar portion of the newsletter in five minutes or less. To write about an upcoming project or field trip, I'll block out twenty minutes or so after school or from my home, when it is quieter.

- **Buddy up with a colleague.** Ask a colleague to read your newsletter and offer to do the same. This can help eliminate any pesky typos and help strengthen connections with colleagues.

- **Involve students.** Have your students be a part of the newsletter. For example:

  - Include photos of them working or of their work.

  - Add their quotes.

  - Talk to them about your writing and communication—you're an ideal role model.

  - Tell them when communications go out to their families. They just might ask to read it at home.

○ Display a print copy of your newsletter in the classroom or hall-way, and make hanging it one of the class jobs.

Keep in mind that families won't necessarily have the same communication style as you or your school. They are busy and might miss emails or never find the printed communication in the bottom of their child's backpack. Be clear on your communication schedule, and lead with empathy and flexibility without compromising your time and energy.

Holding Productive Parent-Teacher Meetings

When preparing to meet with parents, be clear on the date and time of the meeting. When possible, use technology to help everyone remember the time and place. There are also free scheduling apps that will send a reminder the day before or hours before the meeting.

Be clear in your mind what the purpose of the meeting will be. If the parent has initiated the meeting, ask what the nature of the discussion will be. Take the time to plan what you need to share, what questions you have, and how you will document the important parts of the meeting. If you have data assessments or observable behavior, make sure that information is easily accessible for the meeting to avoid needing to dig in folders or track it down during the conference. This is true for observational notes as well. Having detailed notes that describe rather than judge behaviors will illustrate how much care and observation you are putting into getting to know and support a student more effectively than simply trying to recall anecdotes from memory.

If you're taking notes, be sure to review them soon after the meeting so you can add anything you might have missed or take the first action step while the discussion is still fresh in your mind. If you or the parents have prepared questions ahead of time, online forms offer an efficient way to quickly record answers to these questions during the meeting, and will save time in documenting what was covered.

The table that follows provides some tips on various types of meetings with parents.

Tips for Parent-Teacher Meetings		
Type of Meeting	**Timing**	**Tips**
Welcome letter Invitation to meet	Two to three weeks before start of school	• Send age-appropriate note to child. • Include welcoming newsletter for families, share logistics and supplies. • Invite to sign up for Let's Meet! meeting.
Let's Meet!	One to two weeks before start of school	• Hold face-to-face meeting with student and family in the classroom. • Plan for each meeting to last ten minutes.
Office hours	One to four times a month	• Set a time that works for you to take phone or video calls. • Consider possible topics to cover (for example development, behavior, updates about home and school). • Be clear on appointment time and length. • Consider having families sign up ahead and respond to an online questionnaire so everyone is prepared and focused.
Parent conferences: "well visit"	Week before school if not doing Let's Meet! and as schedule permits; then quarterly or as school deter-mines	• Communicate what will be covered ahead of time (for example brief curriculum updates on specific, observable behaviors and on skills you have documented). • Consider using online forms to outline what you will share and have parents submit questions ahead.

(continued)

Type of Meeting	Timing	Tips
Time-sensitive, family-initiated meeting: "urgent care visit"	Ad hoc, as requested by family	• At the start of school, determine and share how you will handle those urgent "five-alarm-fire" concerns families may experience. • Be clear about how families can reach you with an urgent issue and in what time frame you will accommodate urgent appointment requests.
Time-sensitive, school-initiated meeting: "results are in and we need to problem-solve"	As needed, often in conjunction with other staff	• Consider how and when you will meet with families when an incident, behavior, or concern arises. • Be mindful that often all parties may benefit from time to regain a sense of calm to look at all sides and develop possible solutions for a path forward that honors the dignity of all.

Virtual Connections

With all of the readily available ways to meet online, we don't necessarily need to be in physical proximity to partner with others. Consider offering different virtual platforms for meeting with parents. Be prepared for any technology issues by providing a phone number as a backup.

Some of the benefits of virtual meetings include the following:

• They can be easier to schedule for some families.

• They can be conducted from any location.

• There are no concerns about unavailable transportation, lack of childcare, or health issues that may prevent travel.

• They may be more accessible and feel less stressful than coming in person to school.

Offering virtual meetings as an option lets parents exercise choices that will be more convenient and accessible to them. Be sure to explore the options you and your school can provide for those who may be hearing or visually impaired or who will need a translator.

Involving Parents in Events and Activities

Keep in mind the following when inviting families into your classroom:

- **Think developmentally and about your class community.** Many first graders bask in the independence of being away from home and being a part of the "kid underground" at school they don't always want families to know about. Giving first graders a few weeks to settle in as a community will help establish a rhythm before you invite visitors.

- **Consider the space.** Look at the physical space of your classroom and imagine how the addition of more adults would impact work and play. If your room is small, look at working outdoors or in a larger shared space when adults visit.

- **Think about how helpers can add value, while respecting their time.** Always have a plan in place and a task ready so that helpers feel comfortable and useful. If your library time feels rushed because so many first graders need assistance selecting books, maybe family members can help. Or maybe there's a messy art project where an extra set of hands would be helpful.

- **Ask what families can offer.** As I shared in Chapter 1, I would have never thought to ask parent photographers to help with a photojournalism unit. Connecting and inquiring about what families can offer not only builds your relationship with them, but it may open your eyes to ways to bring family members into the classroom that you could never imagine—and enrich learning!

Connecting with parents is an essential part of the work we do as educators. We simply cannot do this work without them, and to the extent we can see them, listen to them, and include them, the better we can serve our students: "The most accurate predictors of student achievement in school are not family income or social status, but the extent to which the family creates a home environment that encourages learning, communicates high yet reasonable expectations for the child's achievement, and becomes involved in the child's education at school" (Center for Responsive Schools n.d.).

Regardless of their educational or economic status, some parents will need support to create a home environment that encourages learning. When we are clear and confident in our work and take the time to communicate about our work, we help parents understand what happens in first grade. Without this understanding, it will be a challenge to create a learning environment at home. Regular communication in newsletters or social media will help parents see and understand how learning evolves. When families have regular insights about their child, they are more likely to have reasonable expectations, as well as see and support their child. Individual conversations, reports, and conferences will help families appreciate not just how much we know about first grade and pedagogy but also the value we place on their child's unique strengths, their path, and their challenges. Finding meaningful and authentic ways to involve families will make the learning experience more complete.

Connecting Digitally

As we become more comfortable with technology, there may be more ways to connect with parents digitally. For example, I offer "Welcome Wednesdays," when up to three adults join us for Morning Meeting. When COVID-19 protocols made that impossible, we improvised: we set up a livestream for Morning Meetings once a week. This didn't allow for viewers to interact with us, but it gave them a literal window into our mornings and was deeply appreciated.

Advice for Tricky Situations

Working with first graders provides endless opportunities to learn and laugh. It is often hard for parents and family to appreciate this side of six- and seven-year-olds. By leading with empathy and a true desire to be partners, we can include families in first grade life and create pathways for their role in school life. I always try to work from a presumption of good intent, knowing that families want what is best for children, even when they may struggle with the demands of life.

Despite this, it's easy to assume we understand what is happening at home or for families to assume they know what is happening in school. We once had an event with a family that could have easily escalated if we had not had an open and positive relationship. And it always reminds me that it takes effort to understand what a six-year-old is thinking.

During a conversation a couple of months into the year, a parent casually mentioned that "something curious" came up over dinner. Later that week, she mentioned it again to my teaching partner, and my partner suggested a quick call with one of us. During that call, she did in fact implicate another child who had presumably taught her child "the f-word."

It was clear the parent was flustered and felt her child was innocent. In our classroom during the days that followed, we sat closer, listened, and observed, and we also asked colleagues to listen for any inappropriate language.

A couple of days later, I was sitting with some children who were working with clay. One child rolled several tiny balls of clay, then picked them up and waved them around, winking at her peers. I asked what story she was telling herself in her head, and the children burst into laughter. This caught the attention of my partner, who joined us and, once the laughter died down, asked the child privately what she was making. She responded, "It's nothing." Play continued, and it was my turn to approach the child, so I whispered, "So what's up?" My little friend said, "I can't. It's bad." So I suggested she whisper it to me. "It's what a fart looks like!" she said, and then she and the child next to her fell off their chairs laughing.

"That's clever . . . Everyone farts, but we can't really see it, right?" I asked. More laughter, which brought kids from the block corner and easel over to the clay table. Everyone was laughing now. At the closing circle I asked, "What was a fun part of your day?" My friends from the clay table agreed: "Making the f-word was the funniest thing ever!"

When deciding how to share this with the family, we wanted to balance the seriousness the parent brought to the initial discussion while helping her see that things are not always as dire as they may first appear. (Using this f-word is a developmentally appropriate way for first graders to explore cause and effect.)

We opted to meet face-to-face with the parent for a few minutes after school to reinforce our personal relationship and so we could read any nonverbals that might be masking additional concerns. We briefly explained what we had witnessed and what her child had shared, and were able to get a chuckle in real time with her. We let her know we valued her concerns and that using bathroom language like this is something we were accustomed to hearing in first grade. She was appreciative and relieved that it wasn't a different f-word, and thanked us for explaining to her child that these things happen. We walked away feeling proud of our efforts and laughing about the kind of language that often feels normal to teachers who work with many young children but so out of the ordinary to parents who know just a handful of children.

Grade

Educators have the extraordinary privilege of spending each day with the tiny humans who are the center of somebody's world. When students start school, they bring with them a history of experiences, interests, likes, and dislikes, all of which are known and understood by their families. The families of students also bring with them a history of experiences, positive and negative, related to school. In order to build strong and supportive relationships with students, it is also important to focus on connecting with and building a partnership with each student's family in a way that feels welcoming for all.

Building and Strengthening Connections

Building a family connection can begin prior to the start of the school year. Once families are notified that you will be their child's teacher, they will often begin looking for information about you. They might search for you on the school's website or on social media, or connect with the families of their child's friends from the previous school year to see who has the same teacher. Families are curious about you and are eager to get to know you.

Prior to the start of a new year, consider updating any social media platforms that you might use for family communication (for example, websites, class portals, social media) to include a picture of yourself and maybe one with you and your family, a welcome message, and a little bit of information about you. Families searching for information can then easily find out more about you and get to know a little bit about you before meeting in person. One year I posted a welcome video for families. I walked down the hallway, into the classroom, and gave a tour. I highlighted a few spots in the classroom and encouraged families to join us at an open house in the next few days. The video was a big hit with families and students.

This first contact with families sets the stage for the type of partnership you want to develop for the school year. Prior to the start of the year, consider sending an email, personalized postcard, or handwritten note to introduce yourself and to welcome everyone to second grade. Invite families to a beginning-of-the-year event, such as an open house or back-to-school night. A simple note, regardless of the form, sends a message that you are interested in connecting with them to create a positive school experience for them and their child.

Making Open House Accessible for Everyone

Open house, or family night, offers a time when families and their children can tour the school, visit the classroom, and meet their teachers. When planning an open house prior to the school year, consider any barriers that might prevent families from being able to attend, and then consider possible options so that each family will have an opportunity to visit the school and classroom before the year begins. Here are some tips on making open house accessible for everyone:

- **The more the merrier!** Encourage families to attend with any members who are interested in visiting the school. Open house is a time for you to meet the child and their family, and for the families to meet you. Remind parents that if they are unable to attend it is perfectly fine to have a relative or neighbor bring the child to the open house. You might not be able to meet the parents, but you will get to meet another person who is a part of the child's "village."

- **Offer multiple times.** Scheduling only one time on one day for an open house can be limiting. Consider setting a couple of different days and times that might make attending the open house easier for all families (for example, one during the day and one in the evening).

- **Make it an event.** Consider scheduling your open house along with another community event such as a pancake breakfast or summer book fair. A school I once worked with as a consultant hosted their open house at the same time as a back-to-school carnival. Scheduling both events at the same time allowed families not only to tour the school and meet their child's teachers but also provided an opportunity to visit the gym and participate in games, sign up for the school's PTO, check on their child's bus number and lunch account, get a library card, and meet the school counselor and school nurse. Open house was both an event and one-stop shopping for families to prepare for the upcoming year.

- **Make it fun.** Families visiting the classroom may feel a bit nervous or even overwhelmed. To help break the ice, plan a fun activity for families to do together, such as a family scavenger hunt or a "Welcome to Second Grade" photo booth.

- **Create alternatives to an in-person open house.** In addition to an in-person open house, consider offering a virtual open house option or posting a short video of the classroom with your own open house tour and welcome message.

A good start to keeping an open line of communication between the school and families is a class information packet for families. This packet, which can be provided digitally or as a hard copy, could contain any information specific to the classroom, such as the daily schedule, how and when to send in snacks, how to sign up to volunteer, and how to best contact you. Also consider sending each family home with a contact magnet or contact card with your picture, name, direct extension, and email address. You could also include the school's main phone number and attendance line. This will keep your phone number or email within easy reach of the families.

Strengthening Connections

Use the first weeks of the school year to focus on learning more about each family. Make a point to connect with each family one-on-one in a positive way. This could be a positive email exchange, an encouraging note home, or a video call. Your first one-on-one conversation should be a positive experience for both you and the family, and focused on getting to know each family a little bit more. Be sure to come from a place of curiosity and wonder.

A few years ago, I started what I call a "beginning-of-the-year teacher talk." I would make time available to talk over the phone, via video, or in person with families to learn about them, their child, and their thoughts concerning school. I let families know that I had no agenda, and that I simply wanted to get to know them a little bit more. Each teacher talk would last about twenty minutes. I would spend most of the time listening and taking notes, and ask questions like "What can you tell me about your family?" "What is important to know about your child?" and "What hopes do you have for your child this school year?" What I learned from those questions guided any additional questions, and by the end of our talk I had learned a great deal about each student and their family, much more than I might have otherwise learned. During one of those calls, I learned that a student had lost his father in a tragic event over the summer, which was likely the cause of some behavior struggles I had noticed at the start of the year. Another student had just welcomed a puppy to their family, and since at the time I had a one-year-old puppy at home, I empathized with them about shoes ruined by sharp puppy teeth. And in one conversation, the parents shared that they were divorcing but hadn't told the kids yet, and wanted me to be aware of this in case their child seemed out of sorts in the coming weeks. The information in each of these instances was important to my full understanding of the student and only enhanced the relationships I had with those families and students.

Family Hopes and Dreams

It is important to offer families an opportunity to share their hopes and dreams for their child for the year. This helps you learn what is significant for each family, and you can reference their hopes and dreams throughout the school year during more formal parent-teacher conferences.

Wait to gather families' hopes and dreams until during or after a beginning-of-the-year phone call or video call. Similar to students, families need some context as to what students will be learning in second grade. I find it helpful to gather a family's hopes and dreams using an online form, which allows me to have every family's hopes and dreams in one place where they can be easily referenced during the year.

It is important to keep up communication and continue to connect with individual families as the year continues, as well as to convey information that is important for the entire class. The following table provides some options for staying connected to individual families and the whole class.

Communication Options		
Individual Communication Options	**Whole-Class Communication Options**	**Individual and Whole-Class Digital Communication Tools**
• Notes (written or emailed) • Phone calls • Video conferences	• Newsletters (Smore, hard-copy templates) • Social media (Twitter, Instagram, Facebook)	• ClassTag • Remind • TalkingPoints

Welcoming All Families

A part of building relationships with families is finding ways to involve them in what's happening at school. Parents want to be involved in their child's education—they just need to know how to go about doing that in their child's classroom.

Volunteering is one way to bring families into the classroom to support the learning happening at school. To prepare potential family volunteers, consider offering a training session to discuss procedures and responsibilities. This will ensure these family members are on the same page and know exactly what to do and expect when they volunteer in the classroom for the first time. It's also important to remind volunteers that any information learned during their time in the classroom is to be kept private. If you believe this may be an issue for some individuals, have those volunteers support the classroom in other ways to protect each student's privacy. If you have an especially eager volunteer, consider offering them the role of room parent or volunteer coordinator, which will allow them to involve themselves in the classroom a bit more but in a way that also supports you.

Just as students have areas of expertise, families also do. Consider asking families about their areas of expertise related to what will be studied in second grade and find ways to involve them in helping students learn more about those areas. An online form link sent in an electronic newsletter is an easy way to collect information about areas of expertise and families' willingness to contribute to the learning happening around specific content areas.

At the start of the school year I send a form to each family listing the topics we will be studying and asking if they would like to help in supporting our learning of any of the topics. Families can then check the topics they would be willing to help support. The next question offers the ways they are willing to contribute to our learning, including in person, virtually, via video, or as part of Morning Meeting. Once I have this information I am able to reach out to those interested in contributing to our learning and then set up the activity.

I have learned a lot from the experts who have been willing to partner with the class and contribute to our learning. But the most important lesson that I have learned is that bringing families into the fold of school not only strengthens the teacher's relationship with those families but also further enhances the teacher's relationship with students.

Here are some additional ways to involve families in events and activities:

- Family nights
- Guest readers
- Book fairs
- Concerts
- Carnivals
- Presentations

Making Space for All Families

One day one of my students, Avi, came skipping into the classroom holding up her arms. The Indian festival of Diwali had just begun, and she was eager to share the beautiful Mehndi artwork that covered her hands and forearms. Noticing her excitement, the class couldn't wait for the Morning Meeting to ask questions.

She explained the process of designing and applying the Mehndi and noted that her mom had done the design on her hands. I had met Avi's family a few times that year and communicated with them using an app that autotranslated what I was saying into their native language. Avi's family had not offered to volunteer to help in an area of study, but I wondered if her family might be willing to share information with the class about Diwali and the significance of the Mehndi designs. I sent their family a message, and later that day her mother replied with a yes.

Her mother was not able to physically come to the classroom. Knowing that Avi was tech savvy, though, I sent home an iPad with her so she could record her mother. A few days later, Avi brought in the recording. We played the video of her mother explaining Diwali traditions as she created these beautiful Mehndi designs on Avi, while Avi translated what her mother was saying. All of us were in awe as we watched, and we learned so much. I saw this experience as being less about the actual content of the video and more about honoring the cultures and traditions of all students in the classroom and providing opportunities for all families to contribute to the learning happening at school.

Connecting Families to Each Other

A new school year often means new friendships for students. One way to support building peer-to-peer relationships is offering ways for families to connect with each other outside of school. Providing a class directory with up-to-date contact information for each student can help facilitate connections outside of the classroom.

Before distributing a class directory, explain the purpose (to set up playdates or invite classmates to birthday parties, for example) and give families the option of whether they would like their information included in the directory.

Special Concerns of Second Grade Families

Each year brings about new expectations for learning and developmental milestones. Families coming into second grade often have questions and concerns around two topics: friendships and academics. More specifically, they wonder, "Does my child have friends?" and "How are they doing (academically) in school?"

Friendships

In the previous school year, families might have described their child as social, which is typical for first graders, who tend to hop easily from friend group to friend group. Second graders, though, typically gravitate toward one preferred friend rather than socializing with various groups.

Lo was a student I had in first grade and second grade. As a first grader, she was often seen laughing and smiling with different groups of students. She attended many birthday parties and was involved in several after-school activities. She was incredibly sweet and kind to everyone and well-liked. About a month into second grade, her mom emailed me. She was concerned about Lo's lack of friendships. She noted that Lo only talked about one other student, and she wanted to know what was going on and if she should seek out a counselor. I read the email and smiled, thinking to myself, "Ah, she's becoming a second grader." Lo hadn't regressed socially; she was doing exactly what was expected as a second grader. Her mom and I had a positive conversation about this change, and I reassured her that it was typical of students at this age.

Academics

"Is my child being challenged enough?" is a common concern of families of second graders. This concern often comes from the observation that their child chooses easier tasks. Second graders will show a risk-averse nature, which could be interpreted as a student showing less growth when compared to previous years.

Second graders will often shy away from challenging tasks and will require a lot of support when taking risks. They are making academic progress and growth; it just looks different than it did in previous years. Second grade is the year that students take the big ideas they've learned up to this point and begin to consolidate their learning. For example, as students learn to read in first grade, they might advance through eight reading levels in a school year. Second grade students, though, will shift to focus more on reading comprehension, which means they might move through three reading levels. Growth is still happening in all areas, but it is just less substantial than in previous years.

If you find that a family would benefit from additional understanding around developmental, social, and academic expectations for second graders, they may want to consult Chip Wood's *Yardsticks: Child and Adolescent Development Ages 4–14* (Center for Responsive Schools 2017).

Communicating With Parents

The key to any successful relationship is communication, and the key to a successful family-teacher relationship is consistent two-way communication. Start by deciding which form of communication works best for you and for each student's family and determine how you can manage this in a way that is consistent and useful. Consider surveying families in an effort to gather information on their preferred communication format, frequency of contact, and what they hope to gain from the chosen communication tool.

I once had an administrator who sent the staff a weekly email update every Sunday morning. Staff members always knew when to expect this email, and for many of us, reading this email became a part of our Sunday morning routines. What made this a positive experience—and one many of us looked forward to—was knowing when it would arrive in our in-boxes each week, the predictable format of the email (a brief note, reminders, upcoming events, inspirational quotes or videos), and the fact that the information was relevant and informative.

Newsletters are an efficient way to share whole-class information with families. This type of communication keeps families informed of the learning taking place in the classroom and could include pertinent reminders for the entire class.

Emails, Texts, Reminders . . . Oh My!

Many of us are inundated with emails, text messages, and calendar reminders all day long, and receiving additional notifications can sometimes feel overwhelming to a family, especially one that has more than one child in school. Here are some tips to make sure your communication with families is streamlined, manageable, and sustainable:

- **Choose just one or two methods of communication.** There are many wonderful communication tools available, and it might be tempting to use them all. Take the time to focus on your purpose for each communication method and decide on the best one or two. This will help keep communication manageable for everyone.

- **Collaborate with colleagues.** Discuss options with your colleagues to decide on the best tool to use, so that communication to families will be consistent. Collaborating can also allow you and your colleagues to share the workload. For example, you might work together to create a monthly grade-level newsletter.

- **Share your communication plan.** Clearly articulate your communication plan so families know when to expect any newsletters, emails, or messages, and how to go about communicating with you.

- **Help families sign up and understand various features.** Some digital communication formats might be new to families. To ensure everyone is able to access and effectively use your chosen communication method, consider providing how-to videos of the important features. You can also discuss and demonstrate your communication method during an open house or offer a check-in during your beginning-of-the-year one-on-one conversations.

Two-way communication tools are an effective way to connect with families quickly and in real time. Being able to exchange messages with families through apps only further strengthens the developing partnership between families and teachers.

Social media platforms are popular modes you can use to share classroom learning with families and followers such as colleagues, principals, and district administrators.

As you consider a potential communication tool or social media platform to use to connect with families, be sure to check your school's communication guidelines and social media policies. Knowing your school's expectations and what tools are approved—or not approved—will only support you in choosing an appropriate communication tool.

Holding Productive Parent-Teacher Meetings

When planning meetings with families, consider your relationship with them. The more time and effort you put into creating a positive relationship, the more productive those meetings will be, and the more smoothly they will go. Knowing a little bit about each other beforehand will ensure a productive conference. Here are some strategies for productive family-teacher meetings:

- **Gather input from families.** Before your planned conference, reach out to the family and ask that they send you any questions, concerns, or topics they would like to discuss. Consider using an online form or sending a hard-copy questionnaire or letter to their home a couple of weeks before conference time.

- **Have a plan, but be flexible.** To make the most of your time together and ensure that the conference goes smoothly, it is important to have a plan so you can discuss topics the family has submitted beforehand but also have time to talk about and respond to any questions and concerns raised during the conference.

- **Start by making a connection.** Consider what you know about each family and begin your time together with a simple connection. I use the walk from the door to the table or the few opening seconds on a virtual call, when everyone is getting situated, to say something like, "I heard the puppy learned a few new tricks! I'm impressed that he's picked them up so soon. It took our dogs months to learn how to shake!" or "Gemma shared that you're coaching her soccer team. My daughter plays soccer too." Starting this way can bring some laughter and calm to start your time together.

- **Lead with a positive student observation.** This is the moment to show the family just how well you know their child and the significance they hold in your classroom. Families want to know that you see their children for who they are beyond their academic accomplishments. Share a story that highlights the student's personality or an observation of a social and emotional strength. The more genuine your story or observation, the better. At a recent family-teacher conference, I shared a story that highlighted the student's sense of humor and outgoing nature. The family laughed and said, "Yup, that sounds just like him." As we wrapped up our conference, they noted how well I knew their son and commented that he usually reserved his silly side for home, adding that our class was a special place if it allowed their son to feel comfortable enough to be himself. That was one of the best compliments I've gotten as a teacher.

- **Highlight areas of strength, growth, and needed development.** To avoid overwhelming families, focus on just a few of these areas. Consider a 3-2-1 system, where you share three areas of strength, two areas where you've noticed growth, and one area that the student can further develop. Of course, you may have students with more than one area of needed development that will be important to discuss with families during a conference. In this situation, lead with empathy as you communicate the additional areas of needed development.

- **Offer a follow-up call or email.** As the end of the conference approaches, offer a time to follow up within the next month. You might say, "I know we talked about a lot today. Let's touch base in a couple of weeks to see how things are going. Would that work for you?" Conferences are brief and, depending on the information shared, might feel a bit overwhelming for families. Families may need time to process and digest the information discussed, and offering a time to follow up and check in is one way to offer support.

> ## Past School Experiences
>
> Each family comes to us with their own history of experiences with school that can affect the way they think about family-teacher conferences. Some may view this time in a negative light, as burdensome or anxiety-provoking. It is important to remind each family about the purpose of the conference—your partnership. Also, providing an agenda before the conference will let them know what to expect from your time together.

Advice for Tricky Situations

Tough situations are challenging for everyone—families want the best for their children, and we want the best for their children too. Sometimes, though, in the middle of a heated conversation, it can feel like you are on opposite teams. Some of the toughest conversations with families are often because of a miscommunication, a misunderstanding, or the sensitivity of the topic.

I once had a situation that encompassed all three. A student's family had a history of attention challenges. As a child, the father had struggled with attention issues and hyperactivity and did not have a good experience at school because of this. The family noted in a survey I sent home before school started that their child had a lot of energy. This was apparent when I met the child at our open house, when he ran laps around the classroom and then cannonballed into a pile of stuffed animals in the corner of the classroom library. I thought to myself, "Lots of energy—plan many opportunities for movement, modeling, and practice."

I met with his parents several times as the year progressed to discuss how their son was doing in class, and we had many great conversations about how we were supporting him at school and how they could support him at home. Later in the year, it was recommended by a team of educators and counselors at my school that the family meet with their pediatrician to discuss the potential that the student might fall into the category of attention deficit hyperactivity disorder (ADHD) and it might be necessary to explore additional support for him. The student struggled to keep up academically—this had been true for the three years he had been in the district—and as he grew into a second grader he was becoming more aware of his struggles when compared with his peers and would comment on his perceived faults.

When we brought this up to the family, the father's body language completely changed: he crossed his arms and frowned. The mother became quite explosive. She stood and slammed her hands on the table and became very defensive. I was taken aback because I did not expect such a strong reaction, and I thought that there was more to this than met the eye. The father then spoke and shared more about his experience in school. He had been diagnosed with ADHD at a young age and remembered how school was for him—it was challenging, and he was often sent out of the classroom and punished for behaviors he could not control. They did not want that same experience for their child. For the next hour empathy came first. We listened to their concerns with open minds, reinforced our partnership, and were able to make a plan that everyone agreed to in order to support their son at school and at home.

Here are some key guidelines to keep in mind when dealing with tricky or sensitive situations:

- **Lead with empathy.** Put yourself in their shoes. How might it feel to be on the receiving end of this information? What might be behind a family's reaction? Try not to take negative reactions personally. Let their reactions be their reactions, but keep in mind that your goal is to partner with families for the betterment of the student. Very rarely is a reaction ever directed at you. More often than not, something else is driving it. Try saying, "I can tell this is really important to you" to convey empathy, and then reflect on what you hear the family say.

- **Listen and pursue understanding.** It can be easy to go on the defensive, especially when confronted with misinformation about a situation. Remind yourself to really listen to what the other person is saying and ask questions to probe for more information. "I would like to understand this a bit better, so can you share more?" or "Tell me more about that" are two ways to pursue additional understanding.

- **Reinforce partnerships.** No matter the conversation, take time to remind families that you and they are on the same team and are working toward a common goal—to make the year a success for your student. Using words like "together" and "we" helps remind families that you and they are a partnership and can achieve more when working together.

It's Okay Not to Know

One of the best pieces of advice given to me during my teaching career is "It's okay not to know the answer to everything." Teachers are used to being "knowers of everything," and I was no different. When a parent asked a question, I thought I had to have an answer right then and there, and if I didn't have an answer, I felt it reflected poorly on me. But this is not the case at all. If you are confronted with a question and unsure of the answer or need additional time to think about a response, say, "I'm not quite sure. I'll get back to you about that in a couple of days." Or you might say, "Let me think about that a little bit more. I'll touch base with you within the next week with an answer." Families will appreciate your honesty and the thoughtfulness you put into seeking the appropriate information.

Chapter 6

Healthy Teachers, Healthy Classrooms

● ●

Overview

In the first five chapters of this book, we discussed significant topics in the field of education: how to respond to students' developmental needs, manage classrooms effectively, build positive communities, engage students in meaningful academics, and connect with families to support students' success. We know from experience and from research that these five areas are crucial for teaching and learning, and taken together, they create classrooms where all students feel safety, significance, and a sense of belonging—just what they need to make academic, social, and emotional progress and find success in the classroom and beyond. But there is one element of education that we haven't mentioned yet, and while it's by far one of the most impactful areas of any educational setting, it's often given the least amount of time (if any time at all) in teacher preparation programs, professional development, school schedules, and more: teacher health and well-being.

Everyone should take steps to support their own health and well-being, but it's a particularly important habit for people in high-stress professions. In a Gallup poll on occupational stress, teachers and nurses tied for the highest reported levels of daily stress (Gallup 2014)—and that was before the toll of the COVID-19 pandemic in 2020 and 2021. While the pandemic changed and complicated teachers' experiences in many stressful ways, it's important to remember that the teaching profession has always had its challenges. According to a 2017 survey from the American Federation of

Teachers and the Badass Teachers Association, 61 percent of teachers described their daily work as often or always stressful.

What Is Stress?

Lisa Dewey Wells

Stress is the body's way of responding to anything that requires our attention or action, including physical, psychological, or emotional strain. The human body has a two-part nervous system, the sympathetic and parasympathetic systems, that help us respond to stress.

The sympathetic system's job is to help us respond quickly to danger, such as an approaching lion or a child who darts across the street to get a ball as we're driving. This system allows our bodies to rev up, gather energy, and respond quickly, and it also makes us sweat, breathe quickly, and then sometimes have that shaky feeling when the threat dissipates. The parasympathetic system helps our body rest and digest. It calms our breathing, heart rate, and mind. It lets us process information and emotions and restores a sense of calm.

Stress itself has benefits as well as drawbacks. Good stress, called eustress, can help us be more creative and productive and even boost our mood. Bad stress can be overwhelming and often makes it hard to handle the situation at hand. It's important to have time to reflect on stressors and how you handle them. Take a moment to jot down a few of your current stressors. Naming our stressors can help us begin to identify if they create good stress or bad stress and then choose how we want to respond and manage these stressors.

So what is it that makes teaching so stressful? While there are different factors at play for everyone, common themes for many educators include the amount of time and effort they dedicate to their work—far more than forty hours a week (Diliberti, Schwartz, and Grant 2021)—and how effective they feel they are able to be within their classrooms, schools, and districts. Educators are deeply invested in their work and in seeing their students succeed, and feeling ineffective is a significant source of stress and worry among teachers.

Stressing Student Success

Teachers' remarkable dedication to their work and their deep desire to make a difference in students' lives are two of the causes of educator stress. It's a vicious cycle: teachers work so hard to support their students that they can become burned out, which in turn makes them less effective in the classroom, so they need to work even harder! According to Jones and Bouffard (2012), teachers who have strong social and emotional competence themselves are better able to build positive relationships with students, manage their classrooms successfully, and teach social and emotional learning skills effectively. That means that educators dedicated to meeting their students' needs and helping them succeed may find the most success by starting with themselves. In order to be an effective educator, you need to find ways to support your own social and emotional needs. Healthy teachers make healthy classrooms!

In addition to educators' own social and emotional learning skills, there's another powerful, teacher-focused element that contributes to student success. Collective teacher efficacy, or teachers' mutual belief that they are successful in their shared work in their school, is the most significant factor influencing student achievement. Collective efficacy has more than three times the impact and ability to predict student success than socio-economic status, home environment, or student motivation (Hattie 2016). That's remarkable to think about: a group of educators who share a strong belief in the collective work they do in their school can make more of a difference in student success than even the students' own motivation or home life! There is real power in shared teacher beliefs and in the community that teachers find with their colleagues.

These studies about the impact teachers have on students may come as no surprise to you. Anyone who has seen the progress that students make over the course of a school year, the way that educators collaborate to create meaningful learning experiences, and the challenges that both students and teachers can overcome together won't bat an eye at these findings. The powerful impact teachers make doesn't happen magically; it comes from deep commitment, tireless effort, and ceaseless collaboration.

This work takes a toll, and so it's worth restating two important points: healthy teachers make healthy classrooms, and no one can do it alone.

In this chapter, we'll delve into:

- What it means to be a socially and emotionally healthy educator.

- How you can become a strong leader in your classroom and beyond.

- Why it's important to understand your implicit beliefs.

- How you can keep growing and learning as a teacher, colleague, and leader.

- How to take care of yourself so you can take care of your students.

• • • • • • • • • •

Adult Social and Emotional Learning

In Chapter 1, we discussed developmentally responsive teaching and the four principles of child development. Social and emotional development adheres to those same principles, following a reasonably predictable pattern that individuals progress through at their own pace and at a varying rate over the course of their lives. Social and emotional growth, like all human development, is uneven. There are periods of intense growth and change followed by relatively quiet periods, a spiraling pattern that continues throughout our lifetimes.

That last part is the key, and it's a fact that is often forgotten: human development continues throughout adulthood! Social and emotional growth, in particular, lasts for a lifetime, with readiness to demonstrate social and emotional skills influenced by a variety of circumstances, including sociocultural and economic factors as well as individual personality and experiences.

Lifelong Social and Emotional Learning

These truths about social and emotional development mean that it's possible, and important, for adults to continue learning and demonstrating new social and emotional skills. How many times have you used the phrase "lifelong learner" as an educator? Effective teachers are often the most committed learners, deeply curious about the subjects they teach and the best ways to reach their students. You've probably been focused on your own social and emotional growth throughout your life without even realizing it. Have you ever intentionally focused on being effective while working with others, standing up for yourself, taking responsibility for something in your community, listening and caring for others, or persevering through a difficult time? You've been honing your social and emotional competence throughout all of those actions and more.

Everyone relies on social and emotional skills to be successful in life. Teaching is a deeply social and emotional profession, so it requires educators to call on those skills every minute of every day. The emphasis on these two types of skills is another reason why professions like teaching can be so exhausting and stressful at times; it takes a toll not only on your physical and cognitive energy but also on your social and emotional energy. When you understand more about your social and emotional strengths and tendencies, you are better able to develop the skills you need to be calm, focused, successful, and happy.

Social Competence and Emotional Competence

Social and emotional learning is often talked about as if it's one idea, but there are two crucial parts: social competence and emotional competence. *Social competence* is the ability to make positive contributions to the community and society and to cooperate well with others; it encompasses interpersonal skills like relating to others. *Emotional competence* is the ability to understand your emotions and how those emotions impact the way you feel, think, and act; it encompasses intrapersonal skills like managing your emotions.

Developing Social and Emotional Learning Skills

While that goal may sound lofty, it's possible for anyone to achieve. Like any skill, social and emotional skills can be explicitly taught and intentionally learned. It takes time, practice, and patience to improve your skills, but it makes a difference, not just in your own life, but in the lives of the people around you, from your family to your colleagues to your students. If we don't model, live by, and believe what we say, nothing will change for our students. We know that social and emotional skills are crucial for our students, and they are just as important for us.

Just as we would do with our students' learning, when we focus on our own learning, it's helpful to start with a sense of the skills and competencies we aim to develop. Over time, there have been many different definitions and terms applied to these skills and competencies. Two organizations that have been committed for decades to bringing social and emotional learning to the forefront of education are Center for Responsive Schools, founded in 1981, and the Collaborative for Academic, Social, and Emotional Learning (CASEL), founded in 1994. Both organizations have identified five core social and emotional learning competencies, and while the two organizations use different terms to describe these competencies, the terms correspond closely to each other.

The chart that follows provides definitions of each of the terms and shows how the Center for Responsive Schools competencies (in the left-hand column) and the CASEL competencies (in the right-hand column) connect to each other. In the center column are anchor standards that connect to each one of the Center for Responsive Schools competencies. These standards encompass the abilities an individual needs to exhibit to successfully demonstrate social and emotional competence. They provide a solid grounding for considering learning goals for your students as well as yourself.

C.A.R.E.S.
Competencies

CASEL
Competencies

C.A.R.E.S. Competencies	Anchor Standards	CASEL Competencies
Cooperation The ability to establish new relationships, to maintain positive relationships and friendships, to avoid social isolation, to resolve conflicts, to accept differences, and to be a contributing member of the classroom and community in which one lives, works, learns, and plays	• Able to make and keep friends • Works with others toward a common goal • Resolves differences quickly • Cooperates as a group leader or a member of the group • Exhibits helpfulness	**Relationship Skills** The abilities to establish and maintain healthy and supportive relationships and to effectively navigate settings with diverse individuals and groups
Assertiveness The ability to take initiative, to stand up for one's ideas without hurting or negating others, to seek help, to persevere with a challenging task, and to recognize one's individual self as separate from the environment, circumstances, or conditions one is in	• Expresses strong emotions and opinions effectively • Able to seek help • Shows openness and honesty • Persists through challenging events • Takes the initiative to do what is right, fair, and just • Makes choices one feels good about later	**Self-Awareness** The abilities to understand one's own emotions, thoughts, and values and how they influence behavior across contexts
Responsibility The ability to motivate oneself to act and follow through on expectations; to define a problem, consider the consequences, and choose a positive solution	• Selects the best option among choices for a suitable outcome • Holds oneself accountable • Demonstrates social, civic, and digital responsibility • Takes care of property	**Responsible Decision-Making** The abilities to make caring and constructive choices about personal behavior and social interactions across diverse situations
Empathy The ability to recognize, appreciate, or understand another's state of mind or emotions; to be receptive to new ideas and perspectives; and to see, appreciate, and value differences and diversity in others	• Recognizes and manages one's own emotions and recognizes the emotions of others • Respects and values diversity in others • Respects differing cultural norms • Aware of the impact of one's actions on others	**Social Awareness** The abilities to understand the perspectives of and empathize with others, including those from diverse backgrounds, cultures, and contexts
Self-Control The ability to recognize and regulate one's thoughts, emotions, and behaviors in order to be successful in the moment and remain on a successful trajectory	• Adheres to social, behavioral, and moral standards • Manages overwhelming thoughts or emotions • Controls impulses and delays gratification • Shows hope and perseverance	**Self-Management** The abilities to manage one's emotions, thoughts, and behaviors effectively in different situations and to achieve goals and aspirations

Demonstrating Readiness

As you read the anchor standards listed in the chart you might have found yourself pausing on certain skills and thinking, "I do this most of the time, but not all the time." For instance, you might usually work well with others toward a common goal, but if your strong feeling about how to achieve that goal clashes with someone else's, you might choose to stand your ground. Maybe you make choices you feel good about most of the time, but every so often, there's something you regret in hindsight. That just means you're human! This back and forth is all part of social and emotional learning.

There is no such thing as complete mastery of social and emotional skills. No one can make the right choice all the time, or resolve every single difference quickly, or show hope and perseverance every minute of every day. But we can strive for readiness to demonstrate these skills most of the time, and we can learn more about ourselves and deepen our skills when we encounter moments that challenge us.

Learning About Yourself

It's also important to emphasize that developing social and emotional competence means coming to understand yourself and the ways you tend to feel, think, and behave. There is no one right way to demonstrate the five core social and emotional competencies of cooperation, assertiveness, responsibility, empathy, and self-control. There are many possible ways to be assertive, for instance; some ways work for certain people or in certain situations, but not in others. Understanding your social and emotional tendencies—the way you usually approach situations involving these competencies—can help you manage your emotions, thoughts, and behaviors.

One way to think about your tendencies is to consider your own range of possible reactions within the competencies. Each of the five social and emotional learning competencies encompasses a spectrum of behaviors. At the end of each spectrum are two dichotomous sets of behavioral tendencies for demonstrating social and emotional competence. Within each spectrum, there are many variations and possibilities. For example, under the social and emotional competency of cooperation, at one end of the spectrum we have the Synergist, whose tendency is to be highly collaborative, and at the other end we have the Insulator, who will engage in group work if invited but whose tendency is to view people's roles separately rather than collectively. Each of the dichotomies, and the variations in between, can represent a meaningful and valid way to behave and to react in academic and social settings. The key for us as teachers is to understand where our tendencies lie within this spectrum.

Understanding Your Social and Emotional Type

The dichotomies for each of the five social and emotional learning competencies were developed through research done at Center for Responsive Schools as part of the development of Fly Five, a social and emotional learning curriculum for kindergarten through eighth grade. Part of the Fly Five program includes the Social and Emotional Type Inventory, a typological assessment for adults to help educators better understand their own social and emotional competence as they teach social and emotional learning skills to their students. Scan this QR code for more information about Fly Five.

As your social and emotional skills grow and change over the course of your life, where you fall along each continuum can and will shift. Take a look at the traits for each dichotomy in the five social and emotional learning competencies to get a sense of your tendencies.

C.A.R.E.S. Competency Traits

Cooperation	
Synergists:	**Insulators:**
• Are highly collaborative and want to hear all ideas and suggestions. • Are quick to help resolve conflicts. • Develop long and lasting friendships. • Are highly collaborative no matter the situation.	• Engage meaningfully in group work when there is a clear benefit to it. • Consider everyone's role separately rather than collectively. • Are not interested in conflicts, either resolving them or starting them. • Develop shorter, intense friendships.

Assertiveness	
Expectors:	**Hypothesizers:**
• Express their ideas, feelings, and emotions clearly while acknowledging those of others. • Are usually open to receiving help or feedback. • Are confident in their ability to succeed at new or challenging tasks.	• Carefully analyze situations. • Can sometimes hesitate to express their own ideas, feelings, and emotions for fear of hurting others. • Are quick to think for others, but tend to doubt themselves. • Don't always trust others to do things, so they take on extra responsibility themselves.

Responsibility	
Navigators:	**Traversers:**
• Are intrinsically motivated as they want to be seen as trustworthy and dependable. • Work hard to manage their emotions in order to modify their behavior and consider the consequences of their actions in order to best align with expectations. • Tend to be careful and consistent.	• Rely on extrinsic cues, prompts, and reminders to help them make good choices. • Often make decisions by choosing a preferred option, which can sometimes lead to unforeseen consequences. • Tend to be spontaneous and impulsive.

Empathy	
Associates:	Limiters:
• Can read and understand the emotions and behaviors of others. • Value the diverse perspectives they gain from connecting with others. • Consistently act on their feelings of empathy to care for others.	• Make decisions based on their own feelings and emotions. • Do not always consider the impact of their actions on others. • Show compassion and caring for those similar to themselves but do not always extend that empathy to those who are significantly different.

Self-Control	
Regulators:	Adventurers:
• Like to be in control. • Hold themselves to high standards. • Are motivated to see their goals through to the end. • Use their willpower and confidence to stay hopeful and persevere through difficulties.	• Do things differently and think outside the box. • Live in the moment without thinking about the consequences of their actions. • Seek strategies, resources, and help outside of themselves to solve problems.

Cooperation, assertiveness, responsibility, empathy, and self-control are vital skills for everyone, especially those in professions like education that require strong social and emotional skills. As teachers, we connect with a wide range of colleagues, families, and students all day every day, and inevitably, we find ourselves in situations with people who react differently than we do. Recognizing our own social and emotional tendencies and those of the people around us can help us better understand ourselves and others.

Imagine, for instance, that you tend toward the Regulator end of the self-control spectrum and like to plan in advance and stay in control of a situation, and you work with a grade-level partner who tends to be more of an Adventurer, someone who spontaneously changes direction and is guided by what's happening in the moment. How would you approach that partnership compared to one with another Regulator? What challenges would that pairing present, and what strengths would it bring forward? Now imagine that you tend to be more of an Expector in the realm of assertiveness; you are eager to try new approaches and thrive on immediate feedback. Your supervisor is more of a Hypothesizer, someone who meticulously reviews a situation before responding and is tentative about delegating. How would your awareness of your own approach and your supervisor's approach change how you might assert yourself in this situation?

Growing Pains

Linda Berger, coauthor of *Empowering Educators*, grades 6, 7, 8

Recently, I led a four-day workshop at a middle school with a primarily Black student population and a primarily white teaching staff. The workshop took place at the end of the school year, at a time when the educators were exhausted from a demanding year yet deeply committed to returning in the fall with a renewed passion for equity and relationships.

Our discussions often revolved around how to foster authentic connections with students who desperately need and want to be seen. How can we reach students with academic challenges that reflect not only the reality our students live in but also their aspirations for the future? Where can we find meaningful, culturally responsive materials to teach the required curriculum? Does our teaching truly come from a place of empathy and understanding?

As we questioned our beliefs, our practices, and our resources together, we recognized that we all have room to grow. That knowledge can be uncomfortable. But when growth comes from a place of true compassion, the results elevate us all and help create a better world for our students.

As you consider your own social and emotional competence and grow more aware of the skills and tendencies you recognize in the people around you, it's important to keep in mind that there are no right or wrong reactions to emotions. There is no one way that you, or the people you encounter, should feel. Developing your skills in and understanding of the C.A.R.E.S. competencies allows you to gain insight into how you feel, how others might be feeling, and how you can respond to those emotions so that you stay on a successful path.

Awareness of your social and emotional strengths and areas of growth is the first step in developing skills in social and emotional competence. As you become more aware of your emotions, thoughts, and behaviors, you can embark on your own natural learning cycle and learn more, set goals, practice skills, and continue your social and emotional development.

Teacher Leadership

Teachers wear many hats: instructor, coach, cheerleader, referee, entertainer, mentor, and so much more. A particularly important role is that of leader. You might think of yourself as a leader in your classroom, but it's important to remember the leadership role you occupy in other areas as well. As educators, we usually think of ourselves in relation to our students, but we are also part of a crucial community of adults within our school. How we work together as adults to create a safe, joyful, and inclusive environment is as important as our individual contributions or competence. No matter how effective an educator you are within the walls of your classroom, the environment outside your classroom is just as important for your students. It's vital that we work together with other adults in our school, in our students' families, and in our community to support student success. You are not just a leader among your students; you are a leader for your students.

Understanding yourself as a leader starts with thinking about your leadership style. Your teacher leadership style impacts the community you build in your classroom, how you manage your classroom, and how you relate to others, including your students, their families, and your colleagues. Think back to the C.A.R.E.S. competencies and dichotomies we were just discussing. The way you firmly yet fairly understand, manage, and balance your classroom community connects with every one of the five social and emotional competencies. The professional way you conduct yourself with your students, their families, and your colleagues sends an important message about who you are as a leader and your implicit beliefs about students and their potential.

What we say and how we say it are also part of who we are as leaders. Our words reveal what we believe. We all have implicit beliefs and biases that we have to learn to recognize, and the words we choose can give light to those implicit beliefs. We've talked a lot in this book about teacher language and how powerful our words are. Your leadership style is reflected in what you say and also in how you act, two crucial aspects of effective classroom management and behavior management. Your approach to discipline comes out of your leadership style. (See Chapter 2 for more information about these topics.) Your words and actions are impactful outside the classroom, too, and they send important messages to the adults in your community about who you are and what you believe. Thinking about your current leadership style and how to grow to become the type of teacher leader you want to be can also help you clarify your beliefs and approach to teaching and learning.

Leading In and Out of the Classroom

Amanda Stessen-Blevins, coauthor of *Empowering Educators*, grades 3, 4, 5

Recently, I was in an adult meeting in which people were talking over each other, making it difficult to hear the ideas of those trying to share. Frequently, the loudest person kept interrupting and bulldozing over everyone else's ideas until they were the only one speaking. We've all probably been in a meeting like this at one point or another; it's unproductive and incredibly frustrating.

In this particular meeting, it suddenly occurred to me that had this behavior occurred in a classroom setting where I was the teacher, it would have played out very differently:

- I would have stepped in to make the space safer for all voices to be heard. I would have authoritatively supported students to take turns talking if students were not yet able to do that themselves.

- I would have supported students who were learning to be more assertive by asking, "Could you say more about that, _____? It didn't sound like you were finished sharing your idea."

- For students having difficulty leaving space for others' ideas, I would encourage their developing skills in self-control, empathy, and cooperation by reminding them of our classroom norms, incorporating visual cues to activate their listening skills, and using redirecting language to guide their behavior.

- In my role as the teacher, I would have scanned the space and challenged my implicit biases, asking myself, "Are there voices that have been heard more than others? Do I observe anyone who looks like they want to say something but hasn't yet?"

As I was processing my realization of how differently I would have managed the situation with children compared to adults, I had to ask myself some challenging questions: "Why do I feel more comfortable supporting students with this common conflict? Why don't I feel comfortable to assert myself in the same way when I'm in a meeting with adults?" I realized that the same skills I teach my students and strive to model in the classroom are also strategies I can apply outside of the classroom with family, friends, and yes, even with colleagues in a professional meeting. Just as we support students with curiosity and compassion, we must give the same grace to ourselves and our own learning.

The following leadership styles represent broad categories of what teacher leaders can look like in a classroom. While the styles are described from a classroom perspective, imagine how it might feel to work with someone who models each of these styles. What type of colleague would you prefer to work with?

Teacher Leadership Styles

	Autocratic	Permissive	Flip-Flop	Authoritative
Sounds like . . .	"Because I said so."	"Can you please cooperate now?"	"I said no. Okay, one more chance. This time I mean it! Actually . . ."	"Let me show you . . ."
Looks like . . .	The teacher tends to rely on external means—punishments and rewards—to get students to behave.	The teacher tends to rely on ignoring and bargaining to keep students happy.	The teacher bounces back and forth between autocratic and permissive approaches.	The teacher uses strategies like Interactive Modeling, teacher language, and logical consequences to shape positive behaviors.
Sends the message that . . .	Children are naturally unruly and impulsive, requiring strict rules to keep them quiet and obedient.	The most important thing is to be liked, which is achieved by being nice, offering praise, and ignoring undesirable actions.	The teacher's reactions are inconsistent, and it's not clear to students what the expectations are.	The teacher believes students want to do what's right and supports that goal with clear guidance and expectations.
Leads to students feeling . . .	Anxious, angry, and resentful.	Tense, unsure, and emotionally unsafe.	Confused, frustrated, and anxious.	Empowered, confident, and successful.

You may recognize the authoritative leadership style as the one we have described throughout this book: firm, fair, professional, respectful, kind, and empathetic. Just as social and emotional growth takes time, so does growing as a leader. Being aware of the message your words and actions send is the first step to becoming an authoritative leader. The second is coaching yourself when you make a mistake and rehearsing alternative choices. Your leadership style is an important tool for your work with students and adults alike. As you become aware of your current leadership approach and set goals for developing your authoritative approach, you will have opportunities to consider what you believe about education and how your words and actions can support those beliefs.

● ● ● ● ● ● ● ● ● ●

Power of Teacher Beliefs

Our individual and collective beliefs have a huge impact on our work in schools and our effectiveness as educators. When our beliefs are conscious and healthy, like the collective belief in teacher efficacy described in the overview of this chapter, then the results are often positive and productive ones, such as improved academic outcomes for students and high morale for teachers. But we all have implicit biases, attitudes, or stereotypes we hold outside of our conscious awareness. Those implicit biases can get in the way of our conscious dedication to equity in education and impact our words, emotions, and actions.

Extensive research, particularly in K–12 school settings, has shown that implicit bias has a significant impact on discipline in schools, perceptions of behavior, and even teaching practices and leadership styles (Kirwan Institute for the Study of Race and Ethnicity 2018). It's crucial for educators to recognize their individual beliefs and biases, but the work doesn't stop there. The next step is to consciously let go of biases and of the beliefs that do not serve educators or students well, and cultivate or hold on to beliefs that are beneficial.

Identifying Implicit Biases

A first step is bringing awareness to implicit biases by intentionally pausing and asking yourself questions to get below the surface of your actions and words (Kirwan Institute for the Study of Race and Ethnicity 2018). Three simple questions, recommended by the National Education Association (n.d.), that you can ask yourself are:

1. What is true for you? Consider what past experiences you've had that you may carry with you.

2. What do you value? Think about what's most important to you and identify what your priorities are.

3. What's your privilege? Bring your awareness to the advantages you have had in your experience that others have not.

Another step in growing your awareness of implicit or unconscious biases is to explore an implicit association test, or IAT, like the ones developed by psychologists at Harvard University, the University of Virginia, and the University of Washington at Project Implicit (Project Implicit 2011). These IATs examine the link between hidden biases and observable behavior. There are several IATs available through Project Implicit that measure implicit associations about a wide range of topics. The IATs are available for free and may be taken easily online. These tests may not provide all of the nuanced data that an individualized, in-person assessment might offer, but they do give useful initial insights into biases you may not have been aware of. As you explore your own beliefs and biases, you can increase your awareness and work on changing your beliefs by building empathy for those with different perspectives and building connections with people who are different from you (Kirwan Institute for the Study of Race and Ethnicity 2018).

As you bring your focus to your implicit beliefs, you can also think about your explicit beliefs and ensure that they serve you and your students well. Some beliefs contribute to our collective efficacy and to students' growing social and emotional learning skills. Those are beliefs we want to embrace, develop, and share with others. Shared teacher beliefs don't develop overnight, but they improve through strong instructional leadership and consistent opportunities for teacher collaboration, like structured professional learning and opportunities to observe colleagues. In turn, these shared beliefs can lead to improved student achievement (Goddard et al. 2015).

Putting Student Behavior Into Perspective

Brian Smith, coauthor of *Empowering Educators*, grades 6, 7, 8

Often, teachers are the first adults that students see each day besides their family members. Sometimes, they may see their teachers even more than certain family members! Young people will often lash out at the ones closest to them, and so we often find ourselves at the center of a young person's life when they need to vent. This behavior can be hurtful and feel personal, but it's important to remind yourself that student behavior usually has very little to do with your classroom or your teaching. Most of the time, in fact, students are often not even aware of the impact their behavior has on their teachers or others around them.

The sooner we realize that we are not the target of student behavior, even if it appears that way, the sooner we are able to get students the help and support they need. Keep these tips in mind:

- **Stay calm.** We must maintain a professional and kind front no matter how a student behaves.

- **Remind them you care.** When the student is ready, take a quiet moment one-on-one to talk and determine how you can help them.

- **Use your resources.** If you feel overwhelmed by the situation, take the student to another adult who can offer a fresh perspective.

- **Be firm yet kind.** Our students rely on us for a stable and consistent environment. Once a student has calmed down, they should be able to rejoin the class and maintain their sense of belonging in the classroom community.

Teacher Beliefs That Promote Social and Emotional Learning

Teacher beliefs are a set of principles, assumptions, values, and convictions that educators hold true regarding students, the classroom, education and educational concepts, curriculum, pedagogy, and discipline. This belief system guides and informs their thoughts, actions, and classroom behaviors, forms the basis for decision-making, and helps to sort, organize, and prioritize information. Center for Responsive Schools has identified eight teacher belief domains that are critical to teachers' approach to education. These eight domains lie at the heart of social and emotional learning in the classroom and the school.

Conditions for Learning	Belief that students learn best in environments of high expectations that are student centered, developmentally responsive, academically challenging, and safe to make learning mistakes.
Conditions for Effective Teaching	Belief that teaching is most effective when lessons are planned and designed with knowledge of students, including evidence-based practices and strategies, and offer learning goals and instructional activities that are directly related to expectations for what a student should know and be able to do at the end of the instructional chunk.
Goal of Discipline	Belief that the goal of discipline is to teach students to be in control of themselves and to choose socially and morally responsible behavior because it is the right thing to do, not because of fear of punishment or hope of reward. Belief that teaching students self-discipline and self-control develops goal-setting, problem-solving, and critical thinking skills and helps them to become good citizens who exhibit prosocial behaviors and demonstrate respect for self, others, and property.
Goodness of Student Intentions	Belief that educators should hold and communicate positive beliefs and expectations for all students, including those who may have different values than they do; are culturally, racially, or socioeconomically different from them; who appear disengaged and unmotivated; or who struggle and misbehave. Belief that problem behaviors result from unmet needs or lack of skills rather than the student's character, family background, or intention to do harm.

Nature of Learning	Belief that learning is cognitively constructed and relies on social, emotional, and cooperative processes. Belief that learning builds on prior knowledge, is facilitated through choice and through understanding of students' context and interests, and becomes transferrable to a new context when there is an emphasis on process as well as outcome. Belief that changes in the learner happen because of the learning experience.
Purpose of Education	Belief that the purpose of education is to build in students a social consciousness and a strong sense of self, to cultivate the attitudes and dispositions of good citizenship, and to teach students to participate in the democratic process. Belief that education should provide new experiences and open windows for students to see and pursue a bright future for themselves, their families, and their local and global communities. Belief that the purpose of education is to enable students to read, speak, write, and listen well; to work well with numbers and technology; to think, reason, wonder, and be curious; to appreciate and value music, art, culture, movement, and athletics; and to manage themselves and know how to cooperate well with others.
Role of Social and Emotional Skills in Learning	Belief that the social and emotional curriculum has equal weight as the core academic curriculum and that social and emotional learning includes (a) school and classroom environments that support the development of social and emotional learning skills and (b) time and resources given for explicit instruction in social and emotional skill development.
Role of School and Classroom Environment	Belief that the school and classroom are a community in which all students belong, can operate autonomously and responsibly, and feel represented, welcome, and accepted as members of the school and academic community.

Imagine the power of a school community in which all educators consciously share these eight powerful beliefs and strive to ensure that their words and actions align with those beliefs. That kind of community would need to commit to continued exploration, collaboration, and reflection—an ongoing learning cycle that supports these shared beliefs and the teachers who hold them.

Building Shared Beliefs

Collective efficacy doesn't happen overnight. It's something school communities have to work toward and constantly fine-tune. You might find yourself in a school community where you have a different mindset or belief system from those around you. Feeling alone or different from your colleagues can be frustrating and discouraging. How do you create a community of colleagues from the ground up? Start by making a connection with one person from your school. See the next section, "Professional Growth," for ideas that can help build these bonds.

Exploring your own implicit biases and beliefs is deeply personal work, and it can have powerful results for you and your students. It's not easy, and it is a particular challenge to address in isolation. Finding colleagues or, even better, a whole school community committed to embracing this work will make it even more engaging and effective. Remember to have empathy for yourself as you go through this reflective process. You will be learning new ways of thinking about the world and your place in it, and there will be moments of discomfort and disquiet. That's an important part of the learning process, and going through it allows us to make stronger, more meaningful connections on the other side. Give yourself the same grace and patience you offer your students. Just like them, you are learning, growing, and changing through this work.

Professional Growth

Whether it's learning more about your students and their families, discovering new books and resources to bring into the classroom, honing instructional approaches, exploring new information in a content area, or finding the answer to a student question, there is always more to learn when it comes to teaching. The most effective teachers are those who are eager to delve more deeply into the art and practice of teaching, and who are always ready to try something new or consider an idea from a new perspective.

In the same way that we encourage our students to take the initiative to ask questions and seek answers, it's important to support our own continued growth and learning. Professional growth feeds your curiosity, challenges your brain, and makes you a better teacher. It's also a great opportunity to model your own learning for your students. Learning more about new approaches can ultimately help you work smarter, not harder! However, with school schedules only getting busier and busier, professional learning is often something many educators put off until another time. So how can you make time to dive more deeply into a topic when your daily schedule barely has time for lunch?

The Gift of Time

Kirsten Lee Howard

Years ago, my partner and I were brand-new parents to a tiny baby. We were overwhelmed navigating our new life as parents. We'd already figured out how to be full-time working adults, but we suddenly had a tiny person we wanted to spend time with, so staying an hour or two late at work or going out of town for a workshop were no longer attractive options.

One night, as I was trying to get work done at 10:30 p.m. after an evening of family time and rocking the baby to sleep, I lamented, "I just need five full hours to get stuff done!" At first, that seemed like an impossible wish, but the more we talked about it, the more realistic it became. It turned out that if we took time to plan for it, each of us could have one monthly catch-up night.

That night became a gift of time. I worked it out with the administration and the custodial staff at my school so they knew to expect me. Once a month, I'd either order dinner or pack one, say goodbye to my students at dismissal, shut my classroom door, and have several uninterrupted hours to accomplish what I needed to do. Some nights, that meant organizing the space and rotating stations, while other nights, it was deeper learning and planning for the future.

Because I would schedule the time in advance, I could keep a running list of tasks for my catch-up night, which also helped me prioritize valuable time during the school day for planning lessons and making adjustments to the learning my students were doing. It was so freeing to keep a small bin in the classroom for catch-up night and give myself permission to focus on other tasks until then. By the end of the night, I would be exhausted but exhilarated. Walking into the classroom the next morning and seeing all I had accomplished the night before gave me such satisfaction.

In the grand scheme of things, I don't always advocate for teachers spending long nights at school—we often do too much of that—but for me, planning for one long night every four to five weeks gave me a sense of balance. When I was at home, I could focus on my family, and when I was at school, I could use my time fully and well.

When we think about professional growth and development, we often think of formal opportunities like doing graduate work, taking a course or workshop, or participating in schoolwide learning. These options are valid, useful, and interesting, but they also require an investment of time and money that means they are not choices we can make every day. Luckily, there are many other, informal ways to incorporate professional learning and growth into your busy schedule.

You don't need to wait for scheduled professional development days to begin exploring the options available to you for learning and growth. Informal opportunities for professional growth are all around us, from free webinars to meaningful reading material to insightful colleagues. The following are some easily accessible and often free ways to support your own growth as an educator that can work with your schedule and that you can tailor to your particular needs and interests:

- **Find a mentor.** Perhaps, as a new teacher, you were lucky enough to be assigned a mentor teacher—someone to guide you, answer questions, offer advice and insights, bounce ideas off of, and more. If not, don't let that stop you! A professional mentor can be a colleague you have worked with, a match through your college alumni network, a connection you make at a workshop or conference, or even someone you've never met but find through mutual friends, shared interests or experiences, or social media. Wherever they come from, mentors are an invaluable resource for building confidence, offering guidance, and supporting your growth.

- **Observe other classrooms—and welcome observers into your own.** Watching other teachers in action is one of the best ways to learn. You might choose to observe your own students with a special subject teacher, visit the classrooms of colleagues who teach in the grades above and below you, seek out grade-level colleagues, or even observe someone who teaches content completely different from yours. Classroom observations don't have to be long—just ten or fifteen minutes can often be enough. If peer observations aren't already part of your school's routine, you can suggest this practice to your administrator as a free and effective way for colleagues to learn from one another. If you have breaks during your teaching schedule, you might be able to work in an observation or two each term on your own. Most colleagues will be flattered that you are interested in observing them, and they may want the chance to see you in action, as well. It's a great opportunity to discuss your practice with a trusted colleague and learn from their insights.

- **Read, listen, and watch.** There are more amazing books, podcasts, videos, and webinars available to educators now than ever before. Many are free, but many of those that aren't are affordable and worth the investment. Whether it's social and emotional learning, culturally responsive teaching, brain-based strategies, approaches for different content areas, or something else, the resources are robust and readily available. You can read, listen, and watch independently, or find a colleague or two to start an informal book group or discussion to further build on your learning.

- **Think outside the box.** Learning a new skill, delving more deeply into a hobby, or reading about something completely outside of education can inform your teaching in unexpected ways. When you take on the role of the learner rather than the teacher, you have the chance to experience your own natural learning cycle, understand your cognitive approach in different ways, and develop empathy for what your students experience on a daily basis in your classroom. Plus, it's fun to learn something new and to make connections to your prior knowledge and experience.

- **Intentionally seek others' perspectives.** Whether it's on social media or in real life, we can easily find ourselves in a bubble with people who share our viewpoints and backgrounds. Consciously reaching out to people outside that bubble can be an eye-opening experience. A first step toward this goal could be diversifying the media you consume—those you follow on social media, what you watch and listen to—to include new voices and perspectives that could add to your learning.

- **Look at your curriculum through a new lens.** At some point in your planning for the next school year, term, or unit, you will likely take some time to review the lesson plans and student-facing resources that you use in your classroom. That's the perfect moment to look at your lessons and curriculum through a new lens. You might ask yourself:

- ○ "How can I link this content to current events to make real-life connections?"

- ○ "What perspectives are missing from this lesson? Whose stories aren't being told?"

- ○ "Where can I add opportunities for students to engage with each other and learn both actively and interactively?"

- **Create your own professional learning community.** Many schools build professional learning communities, or PLCs, into their annual professional development work. PLCs can be a wonderful way to connect with colleagues and explore resources relevant to your school or district. You can also build your own PLC with colleagues who share interests, goals, and questions that are similar to yours. With so many online resources and connections available, your PLC can be local or global, in person or virtual, and short or long term. Learning alongside other practitioners can be an effective way to add to your teacher toolbox.

- **Set and track professional goals for yourself.** There are so many opportunities for professional learning out there that it's easy to become daunted. Identifying one or two professional goals to focus on each year, and then breaking those goals up into actionable steps, is one way to approach your professional learning. Sharing these goals with a mentor or a PLC can also be an effective way to collaborate on, and stay on top of, achieving these goals.

No matter how many years you have been teaching, there is always more to learn. Sometimes it seems like the more you learn, the more you realize there is to learn! Professional learning is also a wonderful way to expand your interests, connect with colleagues all over the globe, and of course, better meet the needs of your students. In addition, the knowledge and resources that come with that learning can go a long way to helping you feel confident, effective, and hopeful in your teaching practice, even when facing a challenge.

Taking Care of Yourself

Teaching is one of the most challenging and rewarding professions out there. Educators take on and deal with so much each and every day. We stay up late thinking of ways to help struggling students, stay after school planning engaging activities, and spend our free time reading books like this one—all in an effort to be the best teachers we can be for our students.

This work can take a physical and emotional toll, and summer break is simply not enough time to recharge batteries that are fully drained after an intense school year. You know yourself and what you need to be at your best. Think about what you already do to take care of yourself. Are you someone who needs a solid eight hours of sleep every night? Do you need to take a walk every day? A quiet cup of coffee in the morning? A few minutes to unwind with a favorite podcast? Everyone rejuvenates in different ways; what's important is that you find a way that works for you.

What Is Self-Care?

Lisa Dewey Wells

Self-care tends to get a pretty shiny, exciting, and enticing reputation. But it doesn't have to be about a spa day, massage, or weekend with your best friends (unless that's what works for you!). A simple, practical, and nourishing way to think about self-care revolves around two key elements: it's something you do just for yourself, and it's intentional.

I know a parent who uses dinner prep time to put on headphones and listen to a favorite podcast. For her, that's self-care. I know countless people who get up early to run or swim, and that's their self-care. It doesn't matter what you do to refill your cup and nourish yourself, but devoting just a few minutes each day to intentionally doing something just for you can help strengthen you for the heavy lifting of teaching and caring for others. Self-care can be as simple as:

- Moving (walk, swim, yoga, tennis, dancing)
- Resting (a quick nap in the afternoon or cutting back on binge-watching or social media scrolling to get just a few more minutes of sleep)
- Laughing (alone, with friends, with your students)
- Creating (knitting, building, painting, preparing a meal)
- Breathing (slowly and deeply on your own, with an app, or in a class)
- Connecting (being truly present with just yourself or with someone you care about)

If you're looking for more ideas for self-care routines, the following are some tips we've compiled for practices you can embed in your daily life so that self-care is something you do every day:

- **Take care of your physical body.** Simple things like replacing soda with water, choosing healthy snacks, decreasing your sugar intake, adding more water to your diet, or getting enough sleep can make a huge difference in how you feel physically. When your body feels energized, it has a positive impact on your thoughts and feelings.

- **Talk about it.** It's important and healthy to talk about your thoughts, feelings, and experiences. Think of it like a balloon; if we don't let air out of our balloons by talking about things, eventually we pop. Make and take time to talk to someone (family member, friend, colleague) about your work. Sometimes a colleague who doesn't teach what you teach can be the best sounding board. When you have a trusted relationship, it provides the ability to brainstorm, discuss, and confide, supporting your own emotional well-being. There is also an active and enthusiastic online community of educators on social media platforms that offers valuable connection, support, and ideas no matter where you are. Now more than ever, we're recognizing the part mental health plays in overall wellness. If you're feeling overwhelmed, distressed, or anxious, consider consulting a healthcare professional. Many schools offer employee assistance programs with counseling, and your insurance provider or local community will also have resources. You don't have to go it alone.

- **Look for ways to bring joy to your day.** Even in a job you love, there will be days that are less exciting and happy than others. When those days happen, it is important to have a few strategies to call on to boost yourself up. You might need to step outside to get some fresh air on days that are particularly stressful or run to the local coffee shop during lunch. Maybe you need to set aside a few minutes to do a quick mindfulness exercise. On days that are hard, ask yourself, "What can I do today to take care of myself? What will bring me joy today?"

- **Use energizers.** Consider incorporating a fun energizer into your teaching when things feel tense. These activities only take a short time, but often those few minutes of fun and activity are all it takes to bring a smile back to your face. Using this strategy can also be a teachable moment for your students. On a demanding day, for instance, you might say, "I'm noticing that my mind is wandering. I think I need a quick break to refocus and recharge. Let's play Double This, Double That together."

Finding a Healthy Balance

Andy Moral, coauthor of Empowering Educators, grades 3, 4, 5

A few school years ago, I struggled with maintaining a healthy balance between my professional life and personal life. Many days, I would come home after a long day feeling exhausted, emotionally drained, and irritable. These feelings, coupled with what seemed like a never-ending to-do list, had me questioning whether I was nearing the point of teacher burnout.

I spent the following summer identifying ways to recalibrate my mental health. With time to recharge and reenergize, I felt great heading into the next school year, but I worried about supporting my well-being as the year progressed. I knew I couldn't wait until summer break to rejuvenate; I needed to dedicate time to taking care of myself throughout the school year and even during the school day. That year, I set a few goals for myself. I tried to:

- **Focus on the five senses.** When you set up your classroom space, be sure to incorporate homey touches that make your workspace a welcoming, comfortable environment. A favorite water bottle, a beautiful plant, or a funny family photo will bring a sense of calm or a smile to your face during the day.

- **Support the need for social interaction.** Teachers share the same needs for social interaction their students have! Connect with teammates and colleagues in your building—have lunch together, join a committee together, or work together on planning a student project.

- **Practice being grateful**. At the end of the school day, maybe before you leave your classroom or during your commute home, identify something you are happy about from that day with students. You could even jot a note about it in your plan book to keep a record of these important moments.

- **Create healthy boundaries.** Be cognizant of the amount of time spent outside the school day working on school tasks. Taking steps like setting a time at night when you no longer check email until the following morning will preserve a healthy separation between home and work.

Incorporating these strategies into my days has helped me stay better calibrated in my professional and personal life. Find out what works best for you to support your well-being, avoid teacher burnout, and be the best teacher that you can be.

- **Put quiet time on the schedule.** Quiet time is an after-lunch practice that allows students to make a quiet, independent choice. Teachers look forward to those five to ten minutes to take deep breaths, relax, and prepare for the afternoon possibly more than the students! Try allowing for quiet time after lunch or lunch recess if you feel a small break might benefit you in taking care of yourself during the school day.

- **If you need a break, take a break.** With some preliminary arrangement, you can lean on your colleagues for support and let them lean on you. If you need a break, you can let your colleagues know, and they can step in for you for a moment while you grab a drink of water, make a cup of coffee, or go outside for a few seconds.

- **Notice the positives.** We often focus on the negatives—what didn't go well, what we shouldn't have said—and skip over the positives. There's great benefit to dwelling on those positive moments and reminding ourselves of all the good and growth we witness in our daily work. You can build this practice into your weekly schedule with a routine like jotting down your "wins of the week" (WOW) in your planner to help develop the habit of identifying and reflecting on the positives. Another positive practice is creating a smile file, a place to stash those one-of-a-kind, tug-at-your-heart notes, artwork, and messages from students, families, or even administrators and colleagues. On difficult days, you can pull out your smile file and remember why you do this, that you can do this, and that there are always better days ahead.

- **Step away.** In the evenings and on the weekends, it's easy to be tempted to keep working. There are always lessons to prepare, emails to respond to, and assignments to review. Remember, though, that taking care of yourself so you can be there for your students is what's most important during those off-duty times. Take time to step away so that you can return with renewed strength and perspective.

Focus on Ta-Das, Not To-Dos

Kirsten Lee Howard

I have a former colleague and good friend with whom I have a lot in common. We're both wildly energetic, very positive, and truly love teaching. We also both used to have way too much stuff, and packing up our classrooms at the end of the school year was quite a process. It took us both longer than we would have liked.

It was difficult, too, being around others that were quite efficient and quick at packing up. Well-meaning colleagues would stop by to say goodbye for the summer and might comment, "Oh, you still have quite a lot to do."

After one of those experiences, I appeared in my friend's doorway in tears. I knew I still had a lot to do. Being reminded of it had shaken me out of my can-do mindset, and I was overwhelmed.

She empathized because she'd been in that situation, too. We walked back to my classroom and looked around. She pointed out everything she could see that I had already done. It helped a lot to be able to focus on what I had done: my ta-das rather than my to-dos. We went back to her classroom and pointed out all of the things that she had done, as well. We both jumped back into packing up with a better mindset and a lighter heart.

It became an end-of-the-year tradition for us to stop by each other's rooms and say, "Wow! Look how much you have done already!" We don't even live in the same state anymore, but to this day, more than fifteen years later, one of us always texts the other sometime in June to say: "Your classroom looks great! You're almost finished!"

Communication Self-Care

Becky Wanless

It was around 10:00 p.m. and I was getting ready to call it a night when I heard my phone ding. It was an email from a parent, who was clearly very upset over a situation that had happened at school that day. She gave few details about the situation and demanded I call her immediately. I was left wondering what she was talking about as I reread her email countless times. Needless to say, I couldn't sleep at all that night.

I arrived at school the next day bright and early, an extra-large coffee in hand, having had little sleep and feeling nervous. I took a deep breath, reminded myself to be curious, and made a call to the parent. There had been a situation at lunch that involved another student in a different class. The situation had ultimately been resolved by a lunch teacher, but it hadn't been shared with me. The parent had been taken aback when her child shared what had happened and was upset that she had not been contacted. I listened to her concerns and reassured her that I would gather more information and call her back later that day so we would both have the full story. We ended the conversation on a positive note, and later that day I was able to provide more details about what had happened.

While this situation was ultimately straightforward to resolve, I literally lost sleep over it. I'd spent ten hours in a panic, and I wasn't going to let that happen again. That was the moment I set up some healthy communication boundaries. I immediately removed my school email from my cell phone.

While it is tempting to check or respond to emails at night or make a quick parent phone call, you also need to unplug from the school day and allow yourself time and permission to recharge and take care of yourself. You spend the day giving your all to families, students, and colleagues. Whatever emails are in your inbox after the school day is done can wait.

Removing your school email from personal devices and setting clear communication boundaries with families (and colleagues) about availability can be two of the best things for your mental well-being. Here are some tips for communication self-care:

- **Communicate your hours of availability.** "I will respond to emails from 9:30 to 10:00 a.m. and from 3:30 to 4:00 p.m. I am busy teaching during other hours of the day. If you have an emergency, please call the office at . . ."

- **Let families know that you are unable to respond to emails during the evening.** "I am unable to respond to emails after 4:00 p.m. as I am spending time with my family" or "I am unable to respond to emails after 5:00 p.m., as I am likely resting and rejuvenating from a day full of joy and learning."

- **Give families a time frame in which to expect a response.** "While I try to respond to all emails in a timely manner, it might take twenty-four hours for you to receive a response."

In the same way that we work so hard each and every day to make sure our students have what they need to be successful academically, socially, and emotionally, we also need to make sure we have the same support in place for ourselves. To best help our students, we need to take care of ourselves first. When educators are empowered to create healthy classrooms that are developmentally responsive and effectively managed, with positive communities and engaging academics, all students can succeed.

Appendix

Guided Discovery

Guided Discovery is an inviting way to introduce students to materials, classroom or school areas, or activities. A teacher might use Guided Discovery to introduce a learning center, such as the library or computer area; a specific material, such as crayons or a compass; or an activity, such as journal writing or quiet time.

A Guided Discovery consists of five steps:

1. **Introduction**—The teacher names the material, area, or activity in a way that piques students' curiosity.

2. **Generating and modeling ideas**—The teacher asks for children's thoughts on how they might use a material or area or do an activity, and then models a few of their ideas.

3. **Exploration**—Children actively explore and try out various ideas while the teacher observes, reinforces, and redirects if necessary.

4. **Sharing**—Children share their explorations and observations in response to a focused question from the teacher.

5. **Cleanup and care of materials**—When the Guided Discovery is complete, the teacher asks children for ideas on how to put away materials and clean up work areas.

Working with the whole class, small groups, or individuals, teachers can use Guided Discovery both to introduce new materials, activities, and areas, and to help children explore new ways to work with those that are familiar. Offering a Guided Discovery for every material or activity is unnecessary; instead, teachers use it selectively in situations where they want to encourage creative exploration and elicit a wide variety of ideas from students about how to use a material or area or do an activity.

Interactive Modeling

Interactive Modeling provides children with a clear visual model of positive behaviors. They see and hear what to do, they notice and explain what's happening, and then they get the opportunity to practice with teacher support. In Interactive Modeling, children learn exactly what is expected in a situation. Interactive Modeling is best used when there are specific actions you want students to practice.

The steps of Interactive Modeling are as follows:

1. Say what you will model and why.

2. Model the behavior.

3. Ask students what they noticed.

4. Invite one or more students to model the same behavior.

5. Again, ask students what they noticed.

6. Have all students practice.

7. Provide reinforcing feedback about what you saw.

For more information, see *Interactive Modeling: A Powerful Technique for Teaching Children* by Margaret Berry Wilson (2012).

Logical Consequences vs. Punishment

When students need support to help get their behavior back on track, teachers might choose to use a logical consequence. Logical consequences are a way of helping children see the connection between their behavior and the effect it has on others. It helps children understand that we are all responsible for the consequences of our actions.

Unlike punishments, logical consequences are respectful of students, realistic to carry out, and relevant to the misbehavior. Understanding the differences between logical consequences and punishment is important. The two approaches to discipline differ in both intent and application.

	Punishment	Logical Consequences
Intention	To ensure compliance by using external controls that make the student feel ashamed or bad in other ways	To help students recognize the effects of their actions and develop internal controls
Underlying belief	Students will do better only because they fear punishment and will seek to avoid it	Students will want to do better and can do better with reflection and practice
Teacher's approach and tone	Reacts automatically with little thought; voice is angry and punitive	Gathers more information before reacting; voice is calm and matter-of-fact
Nature of the consequence	Not related to the behavior or the damage done; not reasonable for the student to do	Related to the behavior; reasonable for the student to do
Message to the student	The student is the problem	The damage done, not the student, is the problem

Morning Meeting

Morning Meeting is a twenty- to thirty-minute whole-class gathering at the beginning of each day. The purpose of these meetings is to set a tone for engaged learning in a climate of trust, to build and enhance connections among class members through meaningful interactions and lively activities, and to give students practice in academic and social-emotional skills. Morning Meeting addresses students' basic needs to feel a sense of belonging and significance and warms them up for the day of learning ahead.

The four sequential components of Morning Meetings are:

1. **Greeting.** Each child is greeted by name, the most basic way of providing a sense of belonging.

2. **Sharing.** Children share news or information about themselves, which helps them get to know one another and strengthen communication skills.

3. **Group activity.** A whole-group activity reinforces learning and encourages cooperation and inclusion.

4. **Morning message.** A brief note from the teacher to the class further reinforces skills and sparks children's excitement about what they'll be learning that day.

Although the Morning Meeting format is intentionally predictable, there's plenty of room for variation within this format. Meetings vary from class to class, with each meeting reflecting the different styles and goals of individual teachers and classes.

Ideas for the Sharing Component of Morning Meeting

- **Around the Circle:** This structure allows for all students to share their response to a question. Consider modeling a connection sign (for example, thumbs up) to allow for students to indicate they too share the same response and make connections with one another.

- **Partner or Small-Group Share:** This structure allows for students to share their response to a question with a partner or small group of peers.

- **Individual Share:** This structure allows for one student to share their community or group news with the class. Consider offering a sharing schedule for the group so students can plan for their sharing day.

Community News Versus Private News

There may be times when a student brings news to the group that may feel uncomfortable for some in the class. To ensure the news shared with the group is appropriate for all, consider a lesson that covers the following:

- Share with students that community news is information that helps us learn more about you or information that the class might be interested in hearing more about.

- As a class, create a community news anchor chart with a list of acceptable topics, including hobbies, favorites, something you are good at, after-school activities, a book you are reading, a special piece of art or writing, life event, pets, and family celebrations.

- Discuss private news. Share with students that private news is something that might make you sad or feel uncomfortable and will most likely make others sad or uncomfortable, too. Think about letting students know that if they have private news to share, you would love to hear it first, one-on-one, and if they are unsure if their news is community or private news, they can check in with you before Morning Meeting.

- Let families know about the sharing component of Morning Meeting and that you have discussed community versus private news with the class. If you have a class sharing schedule, send it to the family. This will allow families to help their child identify appropriate news to share with the class.

For more information, see *The Morning Meeting Book,* 3rd ed., by Roxann Kriete and Carol Davis (2014).

Role-Play

Role-play is a tool for teaching skills in situations where there are likely many different behaviors that can work or that are more nuanced. This is a collaborative process that can be used with individuals, small groups, or the whole class.

Here are the steps of role-play:

1. Describe a specific situation. (Bring it to life.)

2. Name the positive goal. (Connect it to classroom rules.)

3. Invite and record children's ideas for solutions. (Frame them positively.)

4. Act out one idea, with the teacher in the lead role.

5. Ask students what they notice, including tone of voice, body language, specific language.

6. Act out another idea.

7. Again, ask students what they notice.

8. Continue acting out other ideas.

9. Sum up lessons learned.

10. Follow up. (Follow-up continues regularly through the days and weeks ahead.)

Rules

Classroom rules are connected to students' and teachers' goals for academic, social, and emotional learning. Often, students and teachers create the rules collaboratively during the first few weeks of school. Here are steps for co-creating classroom rules:

1. Envision with the students things that you'll be learning throughout the year. Use artifacts such as work examples and photos of student's work, and photographs from previous years if you have them.

2. Students envision their own hopes and dreams for the school year and choose one. Then, they illustrate and share that hope and dream with the class.

3. Lead a discussion: "If we want everyone to be able to reach their hopes and dreams this year, what rules do we need in place to help that happen?" Record their responses.

4. Group their responses together in categories; for example, care for each other, care for classroom materials, etc. Continue until all suggestions have been grouped.

5. Use language that will encompass all of the suggestions in one category (for example, "Take care of our materials" for suggestions related to toys, books, and other materials) to create a shorter list of 3 to 5 positively worded rules.

6. Write or type up these rules on a sheet of paper and have everyone sign below to show their agreement and ownership.

7. Post the rules where they can be seen and referred to quickly.

8. Reference the rules frequently.

The Birthday Cluster Exercise

(from *Yardsticks: Child and Adolescent Development Ages 4–14* by Chip Wood, Center for Responsive Schools 2017)

You can use the Birthday Cluster exercise to get an idea of the overall developmental abilities and behaviors you're likely to see in a class. While chronological age does not always correlate directly to developmental age, this exercise is a good place to start in understanding the needs of your students.

Step 1: Create a chronological listing by listing students in the class from youngest to oldest using a "year, month" format (for example: 9 years, 2 months). This will help you easily see the range of ages you will be teaching.

Step 2: Calculate the age of each student on September 1 (beginning of the year) and six months later on March 1 (middle of the year) and add this age to your chart. To make this step a bit easier, consider using an online age calculator tool such as My Age Calculator (www.myagecalculator.com) or the DATEDIF function in a spreadsheet program.

Step 3: Once you have a completed chronological age chart, take time to see where the birthday clusters lie. Once you've noted birthday clusters and unique scenarios (that is, students who are particularly young or old), begin to ask questions such as the following:

- "What impact might this age cluster have on the classroom?"

- "What do I need to be aware of as we go through the school year?"

- "How might the classroom dynamic change as students get older?"

Step 4: The final step is to use what you've learned to create an optimal learning space for all students. Here are a few tips to consider:

- Reference the birthday cluster document after winter break and in the spring to note any changes you might want to take into consideration. Ask yourself questions such as these:

- ○ "How might my class change?"

- ○ "What do I need to be aware of as we move into the next part of the school year?"

- ○ "Do I need to rethink our classroom space or the way students are partnered?"

- Use the birthday cluster document when problem-solving student behavior or struggles with learning. Consider these questions:

  - ○ "Are the academic expectations I've set developmentally appropriate?"

  - ○ "Is this behavior indicative of a seven-year-old or of an eight-year-old?"

  - ○ "Is this student a young seven-year-old or an older eight-year-old?"

Think about sharing your birthday cluster document with other teachers who work with that group of students (aides, lunch teachers, special area teachers, school counselors).

Sample Schedules

Kindergarten	
Sample Schedule A	**Sample Schedule B**
8:30–8:45 Arrival and morning routine	8:30–8:45 Arrival and morning routine
8:45–9:15 Morning Meeting	8:45–9:15 Morning Meeting
9:15–10:15 Math play and workshop	9:15–10:15 Reading play and workshop
10:15–10:30 Snack and movement break	10:15–10:45 Special
10:30–11:15 Science or social studies play and workshop	10:45–11:30 Recess
	11:30–12:00 Lunch
11:15–11:45 Recess	12:00–12:15 Quiet time
11:45–12:15 Lunch	12:15–1:00 Writing workshop
12:15–12:30 Quiet time	1:00–2:00 Math play and workshop
12:30–1:30 Reading play and workshop	2:00–2:30 Recess
1:30–2:00 Recess	2:30–2:45 Snack and read aloud
2:00–2:30 Special	2:45–3:10 Science or social studies play and workshop
2:30–3:10 Writing workshop	
3:10–3:30 Pack up, closing circle, dismissal	3:10–3:30 Pack up, closing circle, dismissal

Grade 1

Sample Schedule A		Sample Schedule B	
8:00–8:20	Arrival routine	8:00–8:20	Arrival routine
8:20–8:40	Morning Meeting	8:20–8:40	Morning Meeting
8:40–8:45	Transition	8:40–8:45	Transition
8:45–9:45	ELA mini-lesson, Academic Choice, and reading groups	8:45–9:30	Writing workshop
		9:30–9:45	Read aloud
9:45–10:05	Snack and read-aloud	9:45–10:05	Word study
10:05–10:25	Recess	10:05–10:15	Snack
10:25–11:20	Math	10:15–11:00	Reading workshop
11:20–11:50	Rotation: special or word study	11:00–12:00	Math
		12:00–12:30	Lunch
11:50–12:00	Clean up and read aloud	12:30–1:00	Recess
12:00–12:30	Recess	1:00–1:15	Quiet time
12:30–1:00	Lunch	1:15–2:00	Science or social studies
1:00–1:15	Quiet time	2:00–2:15	Energizer and snack
1:15–1:55	Writing	2:15–2:45	Special
1:55–2:05	Energizer	2:45–2:55	Pack up
2:05–2:35	Science or social studies	2:55–3:00	Closing circle
2:35–2:45	Pack up	3:00	Dismissal
2:45–3:15	Special		
3:15–3:25	Closing circle		
3:30	Dismissal		

Grade 2

Sample Schedule A		Sample Schedule B	
8:00–8:15	Arrival and morning choices	8:00–8:30	Arrival and recess 1
8:15–8:45	Morning Meeting	8:30–9:00	Morning Meeting
8:45–9:45	Learning block 1	9:00–10:00	Learning block 1
9:45–10:15	Recess 1	10:00–10:10	Energizer
10:15–11:15	Learning block 2	10:10–11:10	Learning block 2
11:15–11:25	Restroom and handwashing	11:10–11:50	Special
11:25–12:10	Lunch and recess	11:50–12:00	Energizer
12:10–12:25	Quiet time	12:00–12:15	Read aloud and snack
12:25–12:40	Read aloud	12:15–12:50	Learning block 3
12:40–1:25	Learning block 3	12:50–1:00	Restroom and handwashing
1:25–2:05	Special	1:00–1:45	Lunch and recess 2
2:05–2:25	Recess 2 and snack	1:45–2:00	Quiet time
2:25–3:15	Learning block 4	2:00–2:45	Learning block 4
3:15–3:30	Cleanup and closing circle	3:45–3:15	Recess
3:30	Dismissal	3:15–3:30	Closing circle
		3:30	Dismissal

Preparing for a Guest Teacher

Few teachers make it through an entire year without missing a day. Having plans and routines in place can help students feel prepared for a change and set them, and the guest teacher, up for success. Here are some tips:

Reassure students that the routines they are used to will remain the same.

- Use role-play to act out different guest teacher scenarios. Some examples include: What should students do if the guest teacher doesn't know the routine for reading choices? What if some students are having a hard time following the class guidelines?

- Involve the class in a conversation about their time with the guest teacher. Ask questions such as "What kind of day do we want to have with the guest teacher?" and "What worries you about having a different teacher?"

- Create lessons that are familiar, and follow existing routines and procedures. For example, provide the guest teacher with guidelines for Morning Meeting, science centers, and closing circle.

- Create a schedule of the day's events to be reviewed prior to the guest teacher's arrival. Make a note to have the guest teacher reference the daily schedule throughout the day.

- Record a short video of yourself with a message to the class that can be played on days when you are unexpectedly absent. Your video might include a reminder of the class guidelines and encouraging words for the day.

- Invite a teacher, special area teacher, or administrator whom the class is familiar with to stop by the classroom when a guest teacher is there to read a book or facilitate an energizer with the class. Seeing a familiar face can sometimes bring a sense of comfort to the group.

Classroom Organization

Goals of Classroom Organization	Consider this . . .
Welcome all children	Do the students see themselves when they walk in the room? Do they primarily see their own work or premade posters? Do the books in the class library reflect what the students look like, what they are interested in, and what they celebrate? Does the classroom reflect more of you (the teacher) or your students? Can all students say, "I belong here"? Is there anyone in your class who might not be able to say this because they are different in some way from the majority?
Value everyone's ideas and work	What are you displaying? Are you displaying works in progress that demonstrate strong effort or only A+ work? Are you displaying only academic work or other things that reflect students' interests? Are displays of student work frequently changed? Do you use clothespins or clipboards so that work can be changed over quickly and easily by the students themselves, allowing them to build their independence and responsibility?
Support active, engaged learning	Are you making space for movement opportunities? Do you have a whole-group meeting area that allows for circling up for energizers and interactive learning structures? Does your space allow for students to mix and match with different classmates often? Does your classroom have space for individual, partner, and group work? Do all students have equal access to learning materials, technology, and home support?
Supportive of diverse developmental levels and learning styles	Are you using what you know about the developmental needs of your students to design your space? (Many five-year-olds like to stand; seven-year-olds like little nooks and crannies to escape into.) Have you done an inventory of your own biases and how they may affect how you view your students' abilities?

Goals of Classroom Organization	Consider this . . .
Foster independence, responsibility, and cooperation	How are you helping students be independent and responsible through your room setup? Do you use visual cues and anchor charts? When and how are you teaching cooperation?
Cultivate care of materials and equipment	Are materials easy for students to access independently and responsibly? Are bins clearly labeled and at the right height for students to reach?

Questions to Consider Before Setting Up a Classroom

- "How do I want the classroom to feel this school year?"

- "What worked well in this space last year?"

- "What were the challenges with this space last year?"

- "What special considerations do I need to think more about?"

Questions to Consider During the Classroom Set-Up Process

- "What does this space say about the learning that will take place this year?"

- "How does this space represent our diverse classroom community?"

- "How does this space meet the developmental needs of this grade-level of students?"

Questions to Consider Throughout the School Year

- "What is working well?"

- "What needs to be changed or modified?"

- "How can I make this space work better for us?"

Whole-Class Problem-Solving Meetings

A whole-class problem-solving meeting is an appropriate strategy to use when a problem behavior extends beyond just one student or a few students, goes against the agreed-on classroom rules, and is affecting the entire class. What follows are some tips to support whole-class problem-solving meetings.

- **Ask, "Does this affect the whole group?"** If the problem only affects a small group of students, consider facilitating a problem-solving meeting with just those students.

- **Choose an appropriate meeting time.** Pick a thirty-minute block of time for the meeting that does not coincide with recess or Morning Meeting (both of which serve important purposes that are necessary for the development of the classroom community). Whole-class problem-solving conferences are meant to be a positive problem-solving experience with encouraged discussions focused on improvement.

- **Name the purpose of the meeting and connect the problem to the class rules.** Be brief, direct, and genuine in opening the meeting. For example, say, "Today we are going to meet about some things I have noticed during our reading choice time. Our class rules say 'Take care of our learning' and I am seeing a lot of us doing things that make it tricky for all of us to follow that rule."

- **Use open-ended questions to gain input and allow for equal voice in problem-solving.** Bring students into the conversation by asking what they have noticed in relation to this classroom issue. You might say, "What have you noticed about this during reading choice time?" Regardless of the method, remember to offer the option to pass for students who may not be comfortable sharing.

- **Gather potential solutions.** As in the previous step, allow time for students to offer solutions. Once everyone's ideas have been heard and noted in some way, pull together group ideas that are similar or the same and then paraphrase these solutions.

- **Try a solution.** Lead the class in a discussion about which choice they could try first. Students can show consensus using a thumbs up

("Yes, let's try it!"), thumbs to the side ("Maybe, I can live with this") and thumbs down ("No, I can't live with this").

- **Confirm the plan and use tools to reinforce the plan.** Once a solution has been agreed to, restate the solution and how the class will go about making this solution viable. Later in the day or even the next day, consider using Interactive Modeling or role-play to allow students an opportunity to better understand the solution they have identified. Use reminding language and reinforcing language.

- **Follow up.** A couple of days after reaching a solution, you may want to facilitate a brief 10- to 15-minute follow-up meeting. This is a time when students can share their successes or any additional concerns related to the initial problem and an opportunity for the group to work together to fine-tune the solution if needed.

Sample Questionnaire for Families

Surveying families at the beginning of the school year is a helpful way to gather information about students. Consider including questions like these on your questionnaire:

- The first three words I think of when I think of my child are . . .

- Three things that interest my child are . . .

- A current challenge for my child is . . .

- A hope I have for my child is . . .

- What do you feel will be most important for your child in school this year?

- In what ways would you like to see your child grow socially?

- In what ways would you like to see your child grow academically?

- Is there anything else I should know about your child?

Resources for a Diverse Classroom Library

To grow your classroom library, talk with other teachers, librarians, parents, and students to discover additional books and authors and to build your community of readers. Utilize social media and search the hashtags #classroombookaday and #WeNeedDiverseBooks for titles. The following websites are also a great resource for expanding any library:

- African American Literature Book Club
  https://aalbc.com/

- Association for Library Service to Children (ALSC)
  https://www.ala.org/alsc/

- Caldecott Medal Books
  https://www.ala.org/alsc/awardsgrants/bookmedia/caldecott

- Colorín Colorado: A bilingual site for educators
  and families of English language learners
  https://www.colorincolorado.org

- Coretta Scott King Medal Books
  https://www.ala.org/rt/emiert/cskbookawards

- Lee and Low: Diverse book publisher for young readers
  https://www.leeandlow.com/

- Pura Belpré Medal Books
  https://www.ala.org/alsc/awardsgrants/bookmedia/belpre

- Robert F. Sibert Informational Book Medal
  https://www.ala.org/alsc/awardsgrants/bookmedia/sibert

- Bates College Diverse BookFinder
  https://www.diversebookfinder.org

- We Need Diverse Books
  https://www.diversebooks.org

- Social Justice Books: A Teaching for Change Project
  https://www.socialjusticebooks.org/booklists

Recommended Books for Grades K–2

First Day of School/First Week of School

School's First Day of School by Adam Rex, illustrated by Christian Robinson

A Letter From Your Teacher: On the First Day of School by Shannon Olsen, illustrated by Sandie Sonke

Our Class is a Family by Shannon Olsen, illustrated by Sandie Sonke

How to Get Your Teacher Ready by Jean Reagan, illustrated by Lee Wildish

We Don't Eat Our Classmates by Ryan T. Higgins

Hopes and Dreams Books

The Magical Yet by Angela DiTerlizzi, illustrated by Lorena Alvarez

This School Year Will Be the BEST! by Kay Winters, illustrated by Renée Andriani

Emmanuel's Dream: The True Story of Emmanuel Ofosu Yeboah by Laurie Ann Thompson, illustrated by Sean Qualls

Grace for President by Kelly DiPucchio, illustrated by LeUyen Pham

Jeremiah Learns to Read by JoEllen Bogart, illustrated by Laura Fernandez and Rick Jacobson

Salt in His Shoes: Michael Jordan in Pursuit of a Dream by Deloris Jordan with Roslyn M. Jordan, illustrated by Kadir Nelson

Ruby's Wish by Shirin Yim Bridges, illustrated by Sophie Blackall

Children Taking Care of Each Other

The Big Umbrella by Amy June Bates with Juniper Bates

Be Kind by Pat Zietlow Miller, illustrated by Jen Hill

Come With Me by Holly M. McGhee, illustrated by Pascal Lemaître

Excluding and Including

Two Speckled Eggs by Jennifer K. Mann

All Are Welcome by Alexandra Penfold, illustrated by Suzanne Kaufman

Strictly No Elephants by Lisa Mantchev, illustrated by Taeeun Yoo

Respecting and Appreciating Differences

I'm New Here by Anne Sibley O'Brien

Someone New by Anne Sibley O'Brien

Lovely by Jess Hong

The Sandwich Swap by Queen Rania of Jordan Al Abdullah and Kelly DiPucchio, illustrated by Tricia Tusa

The Day You Begin by Jacqueline Woodson, illustrated by Rafael López

Dear Girl: A Celebration of Wonderful, Smart, Beautiful You! by Amy Krouse Rosenthal and Paris Rosenthal, illustrated by Holly Hatam

Dear Boy: A Celebration of Cool, Clever, Compassionate You! by Paris Rosenthal and Jason Rosenthal, illustrated by Holly Hatam

Here We Are: Notes for Living on Planet Earth by Oliver Jeffers

Standing Up for Others

Hooway for Wodney Wat by Helen Lester, illustrated by Lynn Munsinger

The Recess Queen by Alexis O'Neill, illustrated by Laura Huliska-Beith

Enemy Pie by Derek Munson, illustrated by Tara Calahan King

We're All Wonders by R. J. Palacio

References

American Federation of Teachers and Badass Teachers Association. 2017. *2017 Educator Quality of Work Life Survey*. Washington, DC: American Federation of Teachers. https://www.aft.org/sites/default/files/2017_eqwl_survey_web.pdf.

Center for Responsive Schools. n.d. "What Research Says About Parent Involvement." Responsive Classroom. https://www.responsiveclassroom.org/what-research-says-about-parent-involvement/.

Center for Development of Human Services, SUNY Buffalo State. 2015. *Child Development Guide*. New York State Office of Children and Family Services.

Diliberti, Melissa Kay, Heather L. Schwartz, and David Grant. 2021. *Stress Topped the Reasons Why Public School Teachers Quit, Even Before COVID-19*. Santa Monica, CA: RAND Corporation. https://www.rand.org/pubs/research_reports/RRA1121-2.html.

Gallup. 2014. State of America's Schools: *The Path to Winning Again in Education*. Washington, DC: Gallup. http://www.gallup.com/services/178709/state-america-schools-report.aspx.

Goddard, Roger, Yvonne Goddard, Eun Sook Kim, and Robert Miller. 2015. "A Theoretical and Empirical Analysis of the Roles of Instructional Leadership, Teacher Collaboration, and Collective Efficacy Beliefs in Support of Student Learning." *American Journal of Education* 121, no. 4: 501–530.

Goleman, Daniel. March 1, 2008. "Hot to Help." *Greater Good Magazine*. https://greatergood.berkeley.edu/article/item/hot_to_help.

Greene, Ross. 2014. *The Explosive Child: A New Approach for Understanding and Parenting Easily Frustrated, Chronically Inflexible Children*, 5th ed. New York: HarperCollins.

Hammond, Zaretta. 2014. *Culturally Responsive Teaching and The Brain: Promoting Authentic Engagement and Rigor Among Culturally and Linguistically Diverse Students*. Thousand Oaks, CA: Corwin.

Hattie, John. 2016. "Keynote Speech." Third Annual Visible Learning Conference: Mindframes and Maximizers, Washington, DC, filmed October 31, 2016. Video of lecture, Parts 1 & 2: https://www.youtube.com/watch?v=kPlJh5Yp-1Y and https://www.youtube.com/watch?v=hXMQ7jYqohg.

Jones, Stephanie M., and Suzanne M. Bouffard. 2012. "Social and Emotional Learning in Schools: From Programs to Strategies and Commentaries." *Social Policy Report* 26, no. 4 (Winter): 1–33.

Kirwan Institute for the Study of Race and Ethnicity. 2018. "Implicit Bias Module Series." Videos. The Ohio State University, the Center for the Study of Social Policy, and the Schott Foundation for Public Education. https://kirwaninstitute.osu.edu/implicit-bias-training.

National Education Association. n.d. "Racial Justice." EdJustice. Accessed May 17, 2021. https://neaedjustice.org/social-justice-issues/racial-justice.

Project Implicit. 2011. "Implicit Association Test." Harvard University. https://implicit.harvard.edu/implicit/takeatest.html.

Vygotsky, Lev S. 1978. *Mind in Society: The Development of Higher Psychological Processes*. Cambridge, MA: Harvard University Press.

Wood, Chip. 2017. *Yardsticks: Child and Adolescent Development Ages 4–14*. 4th ed. Turners Falls, MA: Center for Responsive Schools.

Further Resources

All of the recommended practices in this book come from or are consistent with the *Responsive Classroom* approach to teaching—an evidence-based education approach associated with greater teacher effectiveness, higher student achievement, and improved school climate. *Responsive Classroom* practices help educators build competencies in four interrelated domains: engaging academics, positive community, effective management, and developmentally responsive teaching. To learn more, see the following resources published by Center for Responsive Schools and available at www.responsiveclassroom.org.

Classroom Management: Set up and run a classroom in ways that enable the best possible teaching and learning.

Interactive Modeling: A Powerful Technique for Teaching Children by Margaret Berry Wilson. 2012.

Teaching Children to Care: Classroom Management for Ethical and Academic Growth K–8, revised ed., by Ruth Sidney Charney. 2002.

Morning Meeting: Gather as a whole class each morning to greet each other, share news, and warm up for the day of learning ahead.

The Morning Meeting Book, 3rd ed., by Roxann Kriete and Carol Davis. 2014.

80 Morning Meeting Ideas for Grades K–2 by Susan Lattanzi Roser. 2012.

80 Morning Meeting Ideas for Grades 3–6 by Carol Davis. 2012.

Doing Math in Morning Meeting: 150 Quick Activities That Connect to Your Curriculum by Andy Dousis and Margaret Berry Wilson. 2010. (Includes a Common Core State Standards correlation guide.)

Doing Science in Morning Meeting: 150 Quick Activities That Connect to Your Curriculum by Lara Webb and Margaret Berry Wilson. 2013.

(Includes correlation guides to the Next Generation Science Standards and A Framework for K–12 Science Education, the basis for the standards.)

Doing Language Arts in Morning Meeting: 150 Quick Activities That Connect to Your Curriculum by Jodie Luongo, Joan Riordan, and Kate Umstatter. 2015. (Includes a Common Core State Standards correlation guide.)

Doing Social Studies in Morning Meeting: 150 Quick Activities That Connect to Your Curriculum by Leah Carson and Jane Cofie. 2017. (Includes correlation guides to the National Curriculum Standards for Social Studies—*The Themes of Social Studies, the College, Career, & Civic Life C3 Framework for Social Studies State Standards*, and the Common Core State Standards for English Language Arts.)

Positive Teacher Language: Use words and tone as a tool to promote students' active learning, sense of community, and self-discipline.

The Power of Our Words: Teacher Language That Helps Children Learn, 2nd ed., by Paula Denton, EdD. 2014.

Teacher Language for Engaged Learning: 4 Video Study Sessions. 2013.

Engaging Academics: Learn tools for effective teaching and making lessons lively, appropriately challenging, and purposeful to help students develop higher levels of motivation, persistence, and mastery of skills and content.

The Joyful Classroom: Practical Ways to Engage and Challenge Elementary Students. From *Responsive Classroom* with Lynn Bechtel and Kristen Vincent. 2016.

The Language of Learning: Teaching Students Core Thinking, Speaking, and Listening Skills by Margaret Berry Wilson. 2014.

Make Learning Meaningful: How to Leverage the Brain's Natural Learning Cycle in K–8 Classrooms by Kristen Vincent. 2021.

Teaching Discipline: Use practical strategies, such as rule creation and positive responses to misbehavior, to promote self-discipline in students and build a safe, calm, and respectful school climate.

Teasing, Tattling, Defiance and More: Positive Approaches to 10 Common Classroom Behaviors by Margaret Berry Wilson. 2013.

Teaching Self-Discipline: The Responsive Classroom Guide to Helping Students Dream, Behave, and Achieve in Elementary School. From *Responsive Classroom* with Laurie Badge, Suzy Ghosh, Earl Hunter II, Caitie Meehan, and Cory Wade. 2018.

Responsive School Discipline: Essentials for Elementary School Leaders by Chip Wood and Babs Freeman-Loftis. 2011.

Foundation-Setting During the First Weeks of School: Take time in the critical first weeks of school to establish expectations, routines, a sense of community, and a positive classroom tone.

The First Six Weeks of School, 2nd ed. From *Responsive Classroom*. 2015.

Movement, Games, Songs, and Chants: Sprinkle quick, lively activities throughout the school day to keep students energized, engaged, and alert.

Closing Circles: 50 Activities for Ending the Day in a Positive Way by Dana Januszka and Kristen Vincent. 2012.

Energizers! 88 Quick Movement Activities That Refresh and Refocus by Susan Lattanzi Roser. 2009.

99 Activities and Greetings: Great for Morning Meeting . . . and Other Meetings, Too! by Melissa Correa-Connolly. 2004.

Preventing Bullying at School: Use practical strategies throughout the day to create a safe, kind environment in which bullying is far less likely to take root.

How to Bullyproof Your Classroom by Caltha Crowe. 2012. (Includes bullying prevention lessons.)

Solving Behavior Problems With Children: Engage students in solving their behavior problems so they feel safe, challenged, and invested in changing.

Sammy and His Behavior Problems: Stories and Strategies from a Teacher's Year by Caltha Crowe. 2010.

Solving Thorny Behavior Problems: How Teachers and Students Can Work Together by Caltha Crowe. 2009.

Child Development: Understand children's common physical, social-emotional, cognitive, and language characteristics at each age, and adapt teaching to respond to children's developmental needs.

Yardsticks: Child and Adolescent Development Ages 4–14, 4th ed., by Chip Wood. 2017.

Yardsticks Guide Series: Common Developmental Characteristics in the Classroom and at Home, Grades K–8 (based on *Yardsticks* by Chip Wood). From *Responsive Classroom*. 2018.

School-Home Connection: Learn a variety of resources and strategies to build effective and positive school-home relationships and collaborate confidently with students' families.

Strengthening the Parent-Teacher Partnership by Jane Cofie. 2021.

Special Area Educators: Explore key *Responsive Classroom* practices adapted for a wide variety of special areas.

Responsive Classroom for Music, Art, PE, and Other Special Areas. From *Responsive Classroom*. 2016.

Professional Development/Staff Meetings: Learn easy-to-use structures for getting the most out of your work with colleagues.

Energize Your Meetings! 35 Interactive Learning Structures for Educators. From *Responsive Classroom*. 2014.

Index

About the Publisher

Center for Responsive Schools, Inc., a not-for-profit educational organization, offers professional development, curriculum, and books and resources to support academic, social, and emotional learning.

Center for Responsive Schools (CRS) is the developer of *Responsive Classroom*®, a research-based education approach associated with greater teacher effectiveness, higher student achievement, and improved school climate, and of Fly Five, a comprehensive social-emotional learning curriculum for kindergarten through eighth grade.

CRS Publishing, the independent publishing arm of Center for Responsive Schools, creates inspiring yet practical books for educators and students to support growth, learning, and success in and out of school.

Center for Responsive Schools' vision is to influence and inspire a world-class education for every student in every school, every day, and to bring hope and joy to educators and students alike. Visit us at crslearn.org to learn more: